Mickey Rooney

Mickey Rooney

*His Films, Television Appearances,
Radio Work, Stage Shows,
and Recordings*

Alvin H. Marill

McFarland & Company, Inc., Publishers
Jefferson, North Carolina, and London

LIBRARY OF CONGRESS CATALOGUING-IN-PUBLICATION DATA

Marill, Alvin H.
    Mickey Rooney : his films, television appearances, radio work,
stage shows, and recordings / Alvin H. Marill.
        p.   cm.
    Includes bibliographical references and index.

    ISBN-13: 978-0-7864-2015-5
    softcover : 50# alkaline paper ∞

    1. Rooney, Mickey.   I. Title.
    PN2287.R75M36   2005
    791.4302'8'092 — dc22   2004021869

British Library cataloguing data are available

Cover image: Mickey Rooney in the early 1930s and on stage in the 1979
production of *Sugar Babies*. Background image: ©2005 Brand X Pictures

Manufactured in the United States of America

McFarland & Company, Inc., Publishers
  Box 611, Jefferson, North Carolina 28640
    www.mcfarlandpub.com

Table of Contents

Acknowledgments   vi

Preface   1

Sonny Days and "Himself": The First Decade   5

Puck, Huck, Andy H. and Louis B.: The Second Decade   13

"Babes in Arms" and on His Arms, Then Uncle Sam:
    The Third Decade   30

"I Do!" "I Do!" "I Do!" "I Do … Not!" — and the Boob Tube:
    The Fourth Decade   42

Down and Out — and Up: The Fifth Decade   50

W.C., Jan C., "Sugar Babies" and Rebirth: The Sixth Decade   62

The Kid's Still Trouping: The Seventh Decade   66

Still "Girl Crazy" After All These Years: The Eighth Decade   68

One Man, One Wife: The Ninth Decade   70

Filmography   75

Television Appearances   165

Radio Work   175

Stage Performances   177

Discography   186

Index   189

Acknowledgments

Many thanks to those who helped make this book possible. A special nod to Jane Klain of the Museum of Television and Radio, John Cocchi, James Robert Parish, Gary Hamann (Filming Today Press), Guy Giampapa, Vincent Terrace, and the staff of the Billy Rose Theatre Collection of the New York Public Library at Lincoln Center. Thanks also to show business colleagues who shared Mickey Rooney memories with the author through the years: screen mom Spring Byington, screen girlfriend Ann Rutherford, boyhood pals Jackie Cooper, Freddie Bartholomew, Sidney Miller, Billy Barty, and actor-turned-director Richard Quine, dinner theater chums Donald O'Connor and Eddie Bracken, and latter-day costar Ann Miller. Most of these entertainment chums, unfortunately, have passed on. R.I.P. The Mick, though, continues forever.

Preface

In the *Playbill* for the musical *Sugar Babies* in 1979, which, incredibly, marked his Broadway debut after only 58 years in show biz, the mini-biography of the leading man ran an economical 12 words: "Mickey Rooney ... formerly Andy Hardy ... formerly Mickey McGuire ... formerly Joe Yule, Jr." Obviously a few details were omitted about one of the most remarkable, never-a-dull-moment theatrical careers in memory. As this book was being written, Rooney at 84 had been trouping for 83 years—eclipsing the career of any other living performer. Well into 2004, he remained unique on the American entertainment scene. Like a roller coaster, there were the exhilarating rises—topped, perhaps by his seven-year run of *Sugar Babies* on Broadway and around the country (and later on London's West End), which made him a star all over again — and heart-stopping dips.

Indefatigable Mick, as he's been called in the biz for decades, was born in a trunk and raised on the screen. A man of boundless energy, a legendary collection of ex-wives, several dissipated fortunes, a hip pocket full of unrealized projects, a head full of creative ideas. Rooney never stops talking—about this and that, about any topic in a stream of consciousness, and any interviewer had better be prepared with a dynamite first question because there may never be an opening for a second one. One such interviewer labeled Mickey "a bouncer. He bounces into the room, bounces around the room, bounces onto a chair, bounces off again, and all the while his voice is bouncing off the wall, since a casual conversation with him makes one feel as though he were sitting front row center during a particularly strenuous stage performance at Radio City Music Hall."

This book chronicling his remarkable career has represented a challenge of sorts; the effervescent guy's done *too* much in life. There have been more than 200 films ranging from his Mickey "Himself" McGuire shorts as a youngster spanning the silent and sound eras to his status as

America's most famous screen teenager — Andy Hardy of the fictional Anytown USA locale of Carvel — to his Huck Finn and Thomas Edison; cinematic backyard musicals with Judy Garland; and countless good — and bad — screen performances in the succeeding "adult" years, earning four Oscar nominations along the way. And in the last 50 years there has been nearly as much television, with Emmy nominations peppered throughout. For each of Mickey's films, I list the cast and director and writer credits and quote some reviews, and similarly for his TV and stage work through the decades. All are covered comprehensively in this book about "The Mick."

Aside from promotional appearances for the famed MGM movies of Rooney's youth, there have been dozens of theatrical performances, beginning in the early 1950s and highlighted by his overnight stage success at age 59 when he opened on Broadway in *Sugar Babies*. In addition to a parade of infectiously funny sex farces which he performed in regional and dinner theaters, he starred in vehicles ranging from Shakespeare to Sondheim to Simon: *A Midsummer Night's Dream* (at two vastly different times in his career); two tours of *A Funny Thing Happened on the Way to the Forum* — one in the '60s, the other in the '80s; several sailings as Cap'n Andy in *Show Boat*; tours of Neil Simon's *The Odd Couple* and *The Sunshine Boys*; and, during the '90s, Ken Ludwig's *Lend Me a Tenor* and *Crazy for You*, and a couple of cross-country stints as *The Wizard of Oz*.

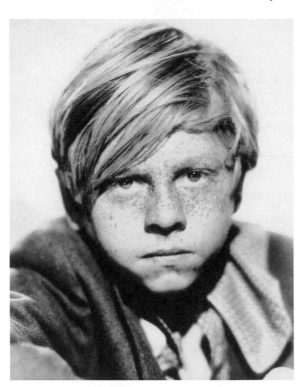

The freckled-faced Mickey (UPI).

And now he's a many-decades-old elder statesman — but never inactive — of show business, assuming the "when I go, I'm taking show biz with me" mantle of late centenarians George Burns and Bob Hope.

This book about the big (in prodigious talent) little (in physical stature) guy also covers his World War II Army days with the Jeep Theatre, for which he received — somewhat belatedly (spring 2004) — a special award at the National D-Day Memorial Sunday in Virginia. Additionally delved into, of course, is his extraordinary private life with his fabled parade of wives, his somewhat public personal journey through casino gambling, pony-playing, tippling, and purported recreational drug experimentation, along with bankruptcy through the decades — *all* the bits and pieces which continue to be fodder for his touring act as himself. All make up the life of this eternal, always-on-the-move-or-I'll die *enfant terrible*, octogenarian though he now may be.

Many of his childhood pals and show biz colleagues from the early days are also quoted in this book. They graciously shared their thoughts about him in personal interviews with the author during the past 30 years. (As of this writing, only chums and fellow players Jackie Cooper, Ann Rutherford, and Gloria De Haven are still with us.) And there was an evocative face-to-face interview with Rooney — actually a rambling hours-long monologue by him about everything show business — for this author's own *Films in Review* piece in the early 1980s and other assorted articles on him.

And so, as the saying goes, "It's showtime!" Mickey Rooney doubtless would concur.

Sonny Days and "Himself"
The First Decade

Rooney put in his first appearance in a theatrical boarding house at 57 Willoughby Avenue in Brooklyn on September 23, 1920. "Sonny" is how he said he was known during his pre-pubescent days ... Sonny Yule. His dad, vaudevillian Joe Yule, Sr. (born Joseph Ninian Yule in Edinburgh, Scotland), was playing a date in town. His mom, Nell Carter — not, of course, the decades-later black entertainer — was a farm girl from the Ozarks who ran away to join the burlesque troupe as a "pony," which was show biz jargon for the dancer on the end. Rooney later recalled that the show was "Jack Reid's Record-Breakers," and it was in playing in Niagara Falls when the two were wed.

Two weeks after baby Joe was born, Nell was back at work with her husband as Yule and Carter on the Irons and Clamidge circuit as part of "Pat White's Gaiety Girls," Joe being a baggy pants comic. Sonny went with them on the road, sauntered on stage with them at the age of 16 months, and has been performing ever since. Actually the manager of the theater where Joe and Nell were playing convinced them to keep the kid in the act, and gave them an extra five bucks a week for the youngster.

The story (now show biz legend) goes that his dad had let a fellow performer, top banana Sid Gold, give tot Sonny — at age five and in a specially-made tux — a spot following his (Gold's) act with Babe LaTour after Sid had heard the kid belting out a top tune of the day, "Pal of My Cradle Days." ("Pal" was a 1925 song written by the notable team of Marshall Montgomery and Al Piantadosi.) Sonny Yule, as entertainment writer George Frazier related in an October 1948 issue of *Coronet* magazine, held his nose after Gold's rendition of it in the act and made a wry face, and the audience was convulsed.

Mickey as a star tot.

"I suppose *you* can sing it better," said Gold haughtily. When the kid agreed, Gold told him, "I'll bet you a dollar you can't." Rooney leaned down into the pit and borrowed a dollar from the orchestra leader. Then he proceeded to sing [the number] without deviation from lyric or melody. As he accepted Gold's dollar, he tore it in half and handed one piece, together with the borrowed bill, to the leader. The improvised role resulted in the kid becoming a regular part of the act. In the vernacular of show biz, he's "been on" ever since.

Among an already glib and surprisingly resourceful young Joe Yule's contributions to the Gold-LaTour act was a bit that reportedly called for him to impersonate the entire recording of "Two Black Crows" by Moran and Mack, blackface stars of the day. At stage right, Sonny would imitate Moran, and then, dashing to stage left, he would reply in Mack's voice. One night, it has been said, he suddenly found himself unable to remember the next line. For a moment, panic threatened, but he took command of the situation almost immediately. "The record," he announced nonchalantly, "got stuck."

But back to Yule and Carter: The act and the marriage were over before Sonny had turned five, with Joe Sr. going off to work in a stock company in Chicago. By 1925, Nell (who was to remarry—first to an L.A. used car salesman, Wynn Brown, several years later and then to an accountant, Fred Pankey, in the mid–1930s) had taken Sonny to Kansas City to live with her parents while she looked for work. Then she decided to try Hollywood with him. With busted hopes of breaking into films, she returned to K.C., and finally went back to L.A. She ultimately found a job in a chorus line at $25 a week—alongside new but years from being stars pals, Joan Blondell and Glenda Farrell (and later managed a tourist bungalow). At six, Sonny found his first movie role—as a midget with a painted-on mustache and a huge rubber stogie in a Fox two-reeler, *Not to Be Trusted* (1926). At the time, she and Sonny were living in a house on Burns Street in L.A. and she was working as a telephone operator. Young Joe Yule had been spotted by a scout from Fox performing in a small musical revue-cum-vaudeville act at Will Morrissey's Orange Grove Theater on Hope Square in downtown L.A. *The Los Angeles Times'* Edwin Schallert also helped out by singling out the kid—still crooning "Pal of My Cradle Days"—for special mention in his review of the show. (Nell Carter reportedly had turned down $15 a week for him to play in "Our Gang" movies comedies before his Orange Grove gig.)

Rooney recalled, "I was a midget and a con man, working with a crack burglar played by Bud Jamison. I would pretend to be a kid, an orphan up for adoption to a rich couple. Once I got established in their mansion, I'd help Jamison steal their diamonds and sapphires and rubies. I had some

Early Mickey, early 1930s.

good scenes with Jamison, going into a tirade with him, complaining that I was already sick of being pawed over by these doting foster parents."

Shortly thereafter, he landed the part of a midget masher in *Orchids and Ermine* (1927) with Colleen Moore as a busy hotel telephone operator. This led to his being cast by producer Larry Darmour in a series of popular two-reel shorts for F.B.O. (later for Radio Pictures and finally for Columbia). Reportedly his mother answered an ad of Fontaine Fox, seeking a child actor to play his comic strip character Mickey "Himself" McGuire in a series of silent comedies based on the popular *Toonerville Trolley* newspaper strip of the day. Young Joe Yule's mom, realizing that dark-haired youngsters were specified in the ad, showed up with her son, whose corn-colored hair she dyed brunet by liberal use of burnt cork. Legend says that the cork was beginning to run onto his freckled cheeks by the time he was interviewed — but he got the part, which paid $50 a day.

"As I played him," Rooney later remembered, "Mickey (Himself) McGuire came to mean 'brash, wise beyond his years, smart-alecky and stubborn.'" The very low-budget Mickey McGuire shorts, nearly 65 of them, shot on the average of one two-reeler every three days, were in answer to the slightly bigger-budgeted series of "Our Gang" comedies that Hal Roach was producing. The first 21 were silents, the rest talkies. In a brief overview of the Mickey McGuires in his book *The Great Movie Shorts*, Leonard Maltin summed up: "The gimmick in these comedies was to have a young McGuire act like an adult, taking charge of everything from making a movie to running a race. Following the tradition established by Our Gang, he had one black cohort, named Hambone Johnson, along with sundry other kids in his 'gang' [including Teeth McDuff, Stinky Davis, Katink', a girl named Tomboy Tailor and midget Billy Barty]. The silent comedies were often quite funny, and despite the economies, boasted some impressive sight gags." Maltin added, "When talkies came in, however, costs went up, and the cheapness of the series was more evident."

Billy Barty (*né* William John Bertanzetti) was one of Hollywood's most prominent and endearing midget actors — he stood 3'9". He played Mickey McGuire's little brother in the later shorts of the series, and through the years acted as a comic foil for longtime pal and "much taller" Rooney. They both were in *A Midsummer Night's Dream* in the 1930s, and he was a hammy comic hood in Rooney's *The Godmothers* in the 1970s and a scummy, gravelly-voiced desert rat who stood up to Rooney in the latter's Western, *The Legend of O.B. Taggart*, in the 1990s. "Mickey was someone I always looked up to. Besides literally, I, like most in the business, always were bowled over by the awesome talent that just was part of him. He just

Above and opposite: With Walter Huston as his dad in *Beast of the City* (1932) and again in *Summer Holiday* (1948), along with Selena Royle (MGM).

never stopped. We were kids together and then we found ourselves old men together. And even when we were old men, we were kids." Barty, in 1957, founded the Little People of America, Inc., and almost until his death in 2000 was its spokesman.

"Making the transition to talkies in the McGuire shorts was not a problem for me," The Mick wrote in autobiography number two. "My

voice — like Mickey Mouse's — was a little squeaky, but that was okay. After all, I was going to play kid parts for the next twenty years."

After the 1927 Colleen Moore flick, Rooney didn't make another feature for five years. But he sure wasn't idle. There were several dozen more Mickey McGuire shorts, and his mom found bookings for him in vaudeville shows in the Southern California area. As always, "Pal of My Cradle Days" was in the act.

Rooney managed more or less to have a school education at Dayton Heights and Vine Street elementary schools; and later at Fairfax High in Hollywood; at Pacific Military Academy in Culver City; at Ma Lawlor's Professional School; and at the MGM Studio School, with classmates Judy Garland, Deanna Durbin (Rooney referred to her in his autobiography as "a winsome little stuck-up songbird"), Bonita Granville, Lana Turner ("nicest knockers I had ever seen!"), Jackie Cooper, Gloria De Haven, future director Richard Quine and others. Mickey used to describe the heady feeling of dating Lana when they were in their teens and driving his first car with the top down and having a dish like her seated beside him. In her 1982 autobiography, though, Lana said, "I never dated Mickey, that adorable nut." The Lana connection, however, continued in various ways through the years. She was in one of the Andy Hardy flicks, she turned out to be one of Ava Gardner's best friends—and Mickey's youthfully red-blooded goal was to get it on separately with each of them. And she and Ava ended up marrying the same guy: Artie Shaw (at various times, of course).

As a kid star, Rooney was back in features by 1932, doing tiny bits in such MGM fare as *Emma*, as one of the brood under housekeeper Marie Dressler's care, and *The Beast of the City*, as chief of police Walter Huston's son. And billed as Mickey (Himself) McGuire, he also had slum kid or orphan roles in several 1932 B's (*Sin's Pay Day* for Mayfair, *High Speed* for Columbia, *Officer Thirteen* for Allied and *The Information Kid* aka *Fast Companions* for Universal). At Universal he was rechristened Mickey Rooney after a legal challenge to the Mickey McGuire name was brought by the copyright owners of the *Toonerville Trolley* strip. His mother had attempted to change his name legally from Joe Yule, Jr.—of course, she always called him Sonny—to Mickey McGuire. Prevented by Fox, she switched to Mickey Rooney (named after a vaudevillian pal of hers, Pat Rooney).

Puck, Huck, Andy H. and Louis B.

The Second Decade

The Mick moved up a notch with costarring roles in 1932 opposite cowboy star Tom Mix and Tony, the Wonder Horse, in *My Pal, the King* (12-year-old Rooney had the title part, the seven-year-old King of Alvania, saved by Tom Mix from the clutches of an evil count) and famed big game hunter and circus star Clyde Beatty in *The Big Cage*. For the Mix movie, Rooney has noted, he got his first mention in *The New York Times* "whose reviewer spelled my name right and said I did 'quite well.'" Universal paid him $250 for the ten-day shoot.

In 1934, barely teen Mickey Rooney played Shakespeare! It was the now-famous L.A. production of *A Midsummer Night's Dream* under noted Austrian director Max Reinhardt, who even in the early '30s had seen the handwriting on the wall and found that Vienna of the day was really no place for a Jew. Reinhardt wanted to direct movies, so he headed first to New York and became part of the large German immigrant community — but he spoke hardly a word of English. Not long afterward, though, he found himself in Los Angeles, where the Chamber of Commerce was to put on a production of Shakespeare at the Hollywood Bowl and Max — in decidedly broken English, of course — made a pitch to do it.

According to the second of Rooney's two autobiographies, *Life Is Too Short*, Reinhardt dispatched his son Gottfried (later also to be a Hollywood film director) to advance his (Max's) daring proposal to sign the biggest names in town for this Shakespeare: Charlie Chaplin for Bottom, Greta Garbo for Titania, Clark Gable for Demetrius, Gary Cooper for Lysander, John Barrymore for Oberon, W.C. Fields for Thisbe, Wallace Beery for the Lion, Walter Huston for Thesus, Joan Crawford for Hermia, Myrna Loy for Helena, and Fred Astaire for Puck. All would agree that even in that company town, newcomer Max had chutzpah. In any event, as Rooney said, "A lot of other stars and would-be stars wanted to work with Reinhardt [after all, he had been founder and director of the Salzburg Festival in Austria and director of the Deutsches Theatre in Berlin], and they started a stampede to the auditions at the Hollywood Roosevelt Hotel. Olivia de Havilland yearned to play Puck. She was a petite 18-year-old, and she could have passed for a boy. Mary Pickford, then 41 but still slight, also pitched for the part. I got it." De Havilland would be Hermia. The Mick later mused, "Not only how could a 13-year-old play Shakespeare, but also how could a 13-year-old who had never even read Shakespeare play Shakespeare?" But he proved himself a game, and quite talented, Puck.

Hollywood packed the Bowl for Reinhardt's Shakespeare. More than 24,000 people filled the amphitheater and the knolls above the stage, and searchlights scanned the skies that September night. The *Los Angeles Times* gave the smash show a thumbs up review, pointing to Rooney's Puck as

"one of the brightest moments of the performance." After 28 nightly performances, Reinhardt took the show on the road — Berkeley, San Francisco, the whole Bay Area, even a four-week stand at the Blackstone Theatre in Chicago (where Rooney had last seen his father a decade before), and to Kansas City (his adopted home town as a kid), Detroit and New York City. In January, Jack Warner decided to put Reinhardt's production on the screen — but basically without Reinhardt. William Dieterle, who once had been Reinhardt's assistant in Europe, was given the

Portrait shot of Mickey, circa 1934 (UPI).

director's megaphone. Warner Bros.' contract players rounded out the cast: James Cagney, Dick Powell, Joe E. Brown, Hugh Herbert, Arthur Treacher, Anita Louise, and others. Rooney and de Havilland (in her film debut) repeated their stage roles.

During rehearsals for the movie in January 1935, Rooney, as Puck, went tobogganing in the mountains, slammed into a tree, and broke his leg. While lying in his hospital bed recuperating, he wryly recalls that his reading matter stretched from *Variety* to the *Racing Form*—and nothing in between. That just about covered his main interests in life — other than, eventually, girls. However, filming ultimately went on with Mickey's injury concealed. And long since having found a way to steal a scene, he did his thing here. On the movie's East Coast premiere in October 1935, *New York Times* critic Andre Sennwald found that "Mickey Rooney's performance as Puck is one of the major delights of the work" and that he and Joe E. Brown (as Flute) "are the bright stars of the photoplay. They keep it awake and hammer it into liveliness." Four decades later, Rooney returned to *A Midsummer Night's Dream*, this time playing Bottom, at the Paper Mill Playhouse in New Jersey and other venues.

For all of his work in the prestigious stage and screen production of the Bard's play, the undeniably talented teenage Rooney continued to toil in minor roles as a contract player in an assortment of films, working with (and often stealing scenes from) the likes of Clark Gable, Jean Harlow, William Powell, Will Rogers, Joan Crawford, and Spencer Tracy. Louis B. Mayer, at the urging of his son-in-law, producer David O. Selznick (who reportedly put into a 16-page memo why Mickey Rooney should be hired at MGM in 1934), added the young dynamo to his stable of performers at $150 a week to start (he was making ten times that just by 1941), not really prescient that the kid would not many years later be the company's most valuable player. Mayer soon had Rooney stealing a version of Eugene O'Neill's family comedy *Ah, Wilderness!* from Beery (Wallace) and Barrymore (Lionel), loaned him out the independent Selznick to play opposite fellow teen actor Freddie Bartholomew in *Little Lord Fauntleroy*, and then teamed him with Spencer Tracy in Kipling's *Captains Courageous*, again with Bartholomew. Rooney often found himself on "loan out" during his first couple of years as an L.B. Mayer contractee. "MGM didn't lend me, it rented me out at two or three times my MGM salary," Mickey later said. "Of course I had no way of knowing this at the time." In fact they loaned him out three times more than they used him in 1934 ("They not only got my services free, but they made money on me to boot.... It was something like slavery, except that slaves, at least can feel the whip"). When he was loaned to Warners to play a jockey in the low-budget *Down the Stretch*, he

With pal Jackie Cooper (left) in 1935.

got $300 a week for four weeks, even though, as The Mick later observed, Warners' records showed that they paid MGM $600 a week for his services. But then he was a kid, making good bread at the time, and working steady. And becoming someone in Hollywood. It didn't matter to him — until years later, looking back.*

For his thirty-fifth feature, Rooney was cast once more with Lionel Barrymore in what was called a programmer, *A Family Affair*. It was loosely based on an undistinguished late '20s play called *Skidding*, and had the teenager cast as rambunctious high schooler Andrew Hardy. Who knew?

---

*Mickey's dad, Joe Yule, Sr., also worked in films as a character actor at MGM during the '30s and '40s. With his son suddenly making a name for himself in films, Joe Sr. soon began turning up on burlesque bills around L.A. in the late 1930s billing himself as "Mickey Rooney's Father." Louis B. Mayer was importuned by his lieutenants to buy off Yule with a player's contract at the studio. Later, between 1948 and 1950, Yule starred in Monogram's popular low-budget "Jiggs and Maggie" series, based on the cartoon strip, before he died on March 13, 1950. Mickey's mom passed away 16 years afterward. Rooney, in the late 1980s, had among his countless possible endeavors a "Jiggs and Maggie" Broadway musical, costarring with Martha Raye or, later, Cloris Leachman.

With chums Jackie Cooper (left) and Freddie Bartholomew (top) (1937) (UPI).

"Barrymore," Rooney has reminisced, "didn't really want to play wise old Judge Hardy in a 'B' movie, but he, like everyone else, was under contract, one of the many actors that MGM had on call. Since MGM had nothing else for Barrymore at the moment, he took the part." Mickey then pointed out that the studio had a young man named Frankie Thomas who was to have gotten the part of Andy, but he was growing too fast and at filming

With Margaret Marquis, the "original" Polly Benedict to Andy Hardy, in *A Family Affair* (1937) (MGM).

he was too tall. The Mick said: "Fate found Rooney, then 16 years old, with his height seemingly on hold." Although Rooney already had made nearly three dozen films, he had to screen test for the role of young Andrew Hardy — and footage from that test was incorporated into one of MGM's later "Romance of Celluloid" one-reel promotional shorts of the early 1940s.

    Under George B. Seitz's direction, *A Family Affair* was made in 15 days and came in $7,000 under budget. A funny thing happened, though: This little programmer, released in April 1937, managed to gross more than half a million dollars worldwide. The critics really weren't impressed with it, but the box office figures came to the attention of Louis B. Mayer, who had been preoccupied by the death of his popular young production chief Irving Thalberg, at age 37. Another thing that was said to have gotten Mayer to sit up was a wire from a Rochester, New York, motion picture exhibitor: "For God's sake, let's have more of that Rooney kid. Stop. He really wowed them. Stop. The way he tripped over that doormat and looked into the eyes of that Polly Benedict girl. That was really something.

Stop. The kid's a gold mine. Stop. And so is the rest of the cast. Stop. Please make another Hardy picture right away."

Mayer, it was speculated, didn't want to make another Hardy picture right away. Rooney wrote in *Life Is Too Short*, "During the spring of 1937, I am told, many a conference was held in Mr. Mayer's white-carpeted office to figure out what to do about 'the Hardy problem.' If the fans were turned on by little Andy Hardy and his little-boy romance with Polly Benedict, then maybe they were tired of the romantic leads. Maybe this was a trend that would depreciate MGM's investment in its Gables and its Tracys and its Taylors. That could be a disaster."

Barrymore, a member of theatrical royalty, was said to have bristled at doing a "B" picture at that point, but getting stuck in a "B" *series* was asking too much (although later he did get stuck in the "Dr. Gillespie" series). He told Mayer that he would continue as the Judge in future entries if the studio would tear up his current contract and, say, doubled his salary. Mayer, of course, was never one to be called cheap, but he decided he didn't want to double Barrymore's salary because he saw that he really didn't need Barrymore in the part. That young whippersnapper Rooney was what sold the picture. *He* was the star. So Barrymore was out of the cast (on his existing contract, which would go on until his death in 1954) and veteran character actor Lewis Stone was in, along with Fay Holden (replacing Spring Byington) as Andy's mom, Cecilia Parker as his sister Marian, Sara Haden as spinsterish Aunt Milly, and dimpled Ann Rutherford, a young starlet from Canada, as Polly Benedict.

Not long afterward, there was another cast addition to complicate Andy Hardy's (puppy) love life, girl-next-door Betsy Booth, played by Judy Garland. (Mickey and Judy already had teamed in a racehorse picture called *Thoroughbreds Don't Cry*, and, intriguingly, she was billed ahead of him.) The moneymaking "A" series of Andy Hardy films began in 1938 with *You're Only Young Once* and continued with 13 more entries through 1946 plus one ill-considered character revival in 1959 (with Mickey playing Judge Andy Hardy, and Rooney's own son as Andy). There also would be a syndicated radio series in 1949 called *The Hardy Family* with Rooney, Stone and Holden plus, occasionally, Judy Garland.

Mickey once said of the Hardy family: "Andy had a father who was a small-town judge as honest as Abe Lincoln, and a mother who was as sweet as my own. The Hardy family was so *clean* Andy only shook hands with her."

The impact of Andy Hardy and his screen family in the fictional Carvel — everytown USA — cannot be overstated in movie history. Author and film historian James Robert Parish noted in *The Great Movie Series*

(A.S. Barnes, 1971) that Andy Hardy flicks "were geared to have strong but restrained humor, set in a sensible and warm atmosphere. Slapstick and wisecracks were carefully avoided in the homey series. Judge Hardy's success with his children was due to his ability to be a guide, philosopher, and friend. In his heart-to-heart, fireside talks with his son, he moralized without being intolerably sentimental or sententious.... The teamwork of the repertory group among the Hardy clan was hard to beat."

Spring Byington, who played Andy's original "mom" (she also was Rooney's mother earlier in *Ah, Wilderness!* and more than a decade later in *The Big Wheel*, and she had him as a guest star on her '50s TV series, *December Bride*) always spoke fondly of this part of Hollywood history and Rooney's role in it. "His Andrew Hardy — that's how I always liked to refer to him — was the idealized small-town teenager of the day, respectful, honorable, eager to please his parents and to have those father-son chats with the Judge that were part of every film. Mickey was the perfect son that every mother of the time would have loved. That's not to say that his public offscreen life, as laid out in the movie magazines of the '30s and '40s and the Hollywood columnists like news hens Hedda Hopper and Louella Parsons and later, Earl Wilson, Ed Sullivan, and Sidney Skolsky, mirrored that of the Judge's son."

The Hardy Films also proved an ideal training ground for such studio starlets as Lana Turner, Donna Reed, Kathryn Grayson, and Esther Williams, in addition to Judy — or Jutes, as The Mick always affectionately has called her. And the tremendously popular entries would go on to make up the screen's most successful "A" series until James Bond came along. (Some might quibble that the Blondie movies with Penny Singleton and Arthur Lake, running to 28 titles, belonged there, but they were strictly "B" programmers.)

"Despite the Metro screenwriters shipping the Hardys frequently outside of Carvel's town limits to other destinations," Parish observed in *The Great Movie Series*, "the folksy homeside influence was always there. At the slightest infractions of social norms, Judge Hardy would be ready with his fatherly talks, and Andy, gulping in silent confusion and realization of his errors, would be a reformed boy-man. The fact that [toward the end] the 20-year-old plus Rooney was portraying a teenager bothered audiences little." (After all, later audiences gave Sidney Poitier a pass playing a rebellious teen in *Blackboard Jungle* in the 1950s when he actually was 31, and Sissy Spacek was also 31 when she played Loretta Lynn at age 13 in *Coal Miner's Daughter*.)

Rooney obviously had caught the public's fancy, whether roughhousing with fellow teen Freddie Bartholomew in their four movies

With Freddie Bartholomew (left) in *Little Lord Fauntleroy* (1936).

together or, as Andy Hardy, jumping into his roadster with pert Ann
Rutherford, or later staging backyard musicals with Judy Garland and
friends.

Rooney and Bartholomew were arguably the two most famous kid
actors on the screen during the '30s (excluding perhaps Shirley Temple,
but that's another story). And it could be argued also that Freddy's career
suffered at the hands of Rooney. Perhaps the audiences found the English
Bartholomew, initially, as described by Efraim Katz in *The Film Encyclo-
pedia*, "a curly-haired, dimpled, angelic boy star of Hollywood films,"
rather sissified as opposed to rough-and-tumble, swaggering Rooney, but
they were great friends as well as rivals on the MGM lot. Freddy, of course,
got the great title roles in *David Copperfield* and *Little Lord Fauntleroy*,
while Rooney got to play Tom Edison and Huck Finn. "Mickey and I used
to compete for roles ... I was kind of under the wing of David O. Selznick,
who had a love-hate relationship with L.B. Mayer, his father-in-law." The
grown-up and out-of-moviemaking Bartholomew felt: "L.B. apparently
wasn't as enamored with David because of his bent for somewhat more

highbrow pictures—taken from classics of British literature, Kipling and
Dickens and such—rather than the family fare which Mayer aimed at middle America. I ended up usually getting the role of the dandy, who was the
lead, and eventually I kind of grew out of a movie career in my teens, and
went to New York where I found another, quite satisfying one in the advertising game."

Andy's love interest in most of the films in the series was played by
Ann Rutherford—also well-remembered for her role as one of Scarlett
O'Hara's sisters in *Gone with the Wind*. Rutherford fits nicely into one of
those contemporary "seven degrees of separation from Kevin Bacon" routines: After playing Rooney's sweetie in the Hardy films, the young actress
found herself in the movie of Margaret Mitchell's famed story of the Old
South as a sibling of Evelyn Keyes, who later would be married to band-
leader/raconteur Artie Shaw, after he had wed Rooney costar Lana Turner
and then Ava Gardner after she and The Mick divorced. "In those days at
MGM," she remembered, "Mickey and I had our puppy-love flings in Andy
Hardy's jalopy, but of course never did anything untoward in the rumble
seat." (Rooney gallantly said in his autobiography that "I didn't date Ann
offscreen. Offscreen I had other things to do, other women to squire around.")

"Mickey was important enough and impetuous enough," Rutherford
has recalled, "for Louis B. Mayer to assign what could be called 'a minder'
to try to keep him on the straight and narrow and on his best offscreen
behavior—a man named Les Peterson, given the Mickey assignment by
Howard Strickling, L.B.'s head of publicity. Mickey was to be Les' one and
only job for many years. He actually could be called sort of an MGM vice-
president in charge of Mickey Rooney."

In *Life Is Too Short*, Mickey remembered: "Les Peterson could have
become a nuisance, but he had a nice, easy way about him. He seemed to
be there when I wanted him and invisible when I didn't want him." Rooney
also reminisced: "Les and Howard Strickling took it upon themselves to
go a bit beyond protecting my image and move on to creating a new one.
They wrote a studio biography for me that had little or nothing to do with
reality. Instead of collecting blondes, brunettes, and redheads, they had me
collecting stamps, coins, and matchboxes."

By the end of the '30s, Rooney, already a veteran trouper not yet out
of his teens, found himself propelled into the box office Top Ten behind
fellow MGM stars Gable and Tracy. During the 1940-42 period he was,
according to *Time* magazine, the top moneymaker in movies. And as a
bona fide—if height-challenged—superstar, he also found himself with
an invite to the White House and dinner with FDR (who professed to be
a genuine fan) and Eleanor.

With Ann Rutherford (left) and Judy Garland, as Andy Hardy's girlfriends Polly
Benedict and Betsy Booth (UPI).

"When he wasn't playing a scene," *Coronet*'s George Frazier wrote in
the late 1940s, "Rooney was seated at his piano on the set, composing popular songs and slaving over an opus which he'd speak of as 'my symphony.'
Judged by the fact that he had had only a dozen piano lessons in his life,
Rooney's in several respects a rather remarkable musician. His popular
songs, however, can be so called only by courtesy." Rooney's "symphony,"

At MGM's party celebrating Lionel Barrymore's sixty-first birthday in 1939. Left to right: Rooney, Norma Shearer, Robert Montgomery, Barrymore, Clark Gable, Louis B. Mayer, Rosalind Russell, and Robert Taylor.

though, was a different matter. Its first public performance, on the night of January 19, 1941, at the Inauguration Gala in Constitution Hall in Washington, was before an audience of approximately 3,450 and fellow celebrities Irving Berlin, Nelson Eddy, Ethel Barrymore, and others. People who came to know Mickey's screen persona, it was reported, initially began to titter, and their merriment grew louder as he pulled up his sleeves and announced that he was about to give the initial performance of his three-movement symphony, which he had labeled *Melodante*. But as he began to play, with the Washington Symphony Orchestra, the amusement began to subside and the hall hushed, and at the end of 19 minutes and *Melodante*, he arose and bowed to the wildest applause of the evening.

Andy Hardy was not Rooney's whole movie life by any means. Between these hugely popular family adventures, he starred in the memorable *Boys Town* with Spencer Tracy and was ideally cast in the lead in *The Adventures of Huckleberry Finn*. In *Young Tom Edison*, he was on the verge of inventing the light bulb in his basement lab. (In all, according to Rooney's figuring, he played in 19 pictures between 1936 and 1948 — but then, who's counting?)

He was cast opposite Judy Garland most famously in the musicals *Babes in Arms*, *Strike Up the Band* and *Babes on Broadway*, all directed by Busby Berkeley, and later *Girl Crazy*. The two also appeared together in person on the premiere bill of *The Wizard of Oz* at Loew's Capitol in New York in August 1939, and in several other cities where the picture opened. The two did seven or eight shows a day between screenings of the film. Such was the celebrity of Mickey and Judy at the time that, at their Broadway opening, more than 20,000 tried to storm the place, as seen in a famed photo from the *New York Post* under the headline: "Mick and Judy Wrap 'Em Round a Block." (Though booked for two weeks, Rooney and Garland were split up toward the end of the run when he was called back to the studio to start his next film. He was replaced in the Capitol act by Bert Lahr, the Cowardly Lion in *Wizard* to Judy's Dorothy.)

The Mick received a special Academy Award in 1938 for his achievements. The following year, for his role in *Babes in Arms* (the third of his ten movies with Judy), he was nominated as Best Actor in company with

With Judy Garland in *Love Finds Andy Hardy* (1938) (MGM).

With Judy Garland in *Babes on Broadway* (1941) (MGM).

Clark Gable, Laurence Olivier, James Stewart, and (the winner) Robert Donat. Rooney reminisced in *Life Is Too Short*: "Judy and I were both Hollywood kids, caring more about what other people thought than what we should have known in our hearts. We'd made Tinseltown's phony ways our own ways. It would take me years to see through them and years more to reject them completely. I doubt that Judy ever did."

In a lengthy Rooney piece in a 1938 *Photoplay* (one of the leading movie magazines of the time), the writer made this observation regarding an on-set incident on his MGM movie *Love Is a Headache*: "When the scene was over, [star] Gladys George turned to the little impudent, yellow-haired guy who had stolen it. With a quizzical frown, she said: 'You're starting that a little early in life, aren't you?' Mickey grinned as politely as he could. If he had followed his natural inclinations and stuck strictly to facts, he might have answered like this: 'Shake yourself loose there, Toots. Whaddya mean, starting early? This is old stuff for me. After five hundred pictures, pinchin' scenes comes natural. Now less gab on the set and let's get this in the can. I'm a busy man.'"

With Judy Garland in *Girl Crazy* (1943) (MGM).

MGM boyhood pal Jackie Cooper — who acted with Mickey in such films as *Broadway to Hollywood* and *The Devil Is a Sissy* in the 1930s, and *Everything's Ducky* in the 1960s, worked with him on his (Cooper's) 1959–62 TV series *Hennesey*, and later directed him on TV in 1981 in *Leave 'Em Laughing*— often has attested to Rooney's "busy man" claim. Busy, though short, Casanova would be more like it in the days when The Mick was on his way to being the biggest little man in films. "I was out there going on high school dates with Judy [Garland], and Mickey was romancing everyone else. Or at least going on the town. There were the babes of the day, and the ponies. Mickey's passions. All of those reported money problems in his life were for another time. Same for his one-at-a-time parade of Mrs. R's. He beat me by five."

Famed syndicated

Above: With Judy Garland on the set of *Words and Music* (1948) (MGM).

'30s–'40s entertainment columnist (and later film producer) Sidney Skolsky, in his unique, punchy style, profiled Rooney in mid–1938: "He is an intelligent young star and speaks a little French, German, Spanish, and Japanese. His ambition is to be a movie director. He dresses like a page out of *Esquire*, only with more color. He favors porkpie hats and loudly checked sports shirts. He's a great ladies man and has a colored valet, Sylvester, who takes care of him." Skolsky also pointed out that Rooney wrote music and was into trap drumming. Among the songs he wrote in the 1930s were "Oceans Apart" and "I Can't Afford to Fall in Love"—the title of the latter certainly to be prophetic in Mickey's subsequent life. And with teenage Sidney Miller, he composed "That's What Love Will Do for You," "Mister Heartbreak" and "Have a Heart," among others. None quite made it into the so-called Great American Songbook.

Opposite: With Judy Garland on The Judy Garland Show (1962) (CBS-TV).

"Babes in Arms" and on His Arms, Then Uncle Sam

The Third Decade

By the time of *Babes in Arms*, Rooney was pulling down an estimated $3,000 a week and was reportedly establishing himself as Hollywood No. 1 Casanova, making the social scene with leggy girls on one or both arms. "Yes I had affairs with some beautiful women," he told *Interview* magazine in May 1992. "I had a great passion for Lana Turner, and I was always attracted to Norma Shearer ... that was way before Ava." With Norma (hardly the leggy beauty that young Mick was seen dating at the time almost nightly) at her suite in the Waldorf Astoria, "I became more of a man than I thought I was ... it was my first, wonderful, lovely experience with a woman. Not counting the brothel. I was 19 ... she was 38. It wasn't one of those quickies with the clothes off and things." Here he was, he said he thought, kanoodling with Marie Antoinette!

Another pal of both Rooney and Cooper, Sidney Miller (who died in early January 2004) made appearances in a number of Mickey's films in the '30s and wrote songs with him — before later becoming sidekick of many years to Donald O'Connor. Miller confirmed a *Playboy* magazine story (June 1997), in which writer James R. Pearson asserted that "in real life, Mickey Rooney had a much more interesting sex life than did his on-screen persona, Andy Hardy." Miller said: "[Mickey, Jackie and I] used to hang out together, and one day we took up Phil Silvers' challenge that we get a hooker and then bet who of the four of us could last the longest." As *Playboy* printed it: "The girl arrived and went into the bedroom. One after another, Miller, Silvers and Cooper went in — and each emerged in three

At a March of Dimes event in 1940 with Jack Benny (middle) and Orson Welles (ACME/UPI).

minutes flat. Rooney went in last. Twenty minutes passed; the three outside heard all sorts of assorted shrieks. Rooney finally emerged, acknowledged his victory and left. When the hooker came out, Silvers asked, 'Was Mickey really in the saddle 20 minutes?' 'Are you kidding? Four minutes of f—king and 16 minutes of imitations.'" Miller recalled that Mickey was famous not only for his champion moves on the tennis courts and his musicianship, but also for his impersonations of Gable, FDR, Lionel Barrymore, even Mae West, and penchant for entertaining bedmates—and everyone else — with the best lines and moves. (Coincidentally, Sidney died within one week of another Miller whose life was entwined with Rooney — Ann, from *Sugar Babies*.) Regarding the above incident, Mickey added in his book that the lady (of the evening) in question had the numbers correct — but in the wrong order. "I've always found that it's better to get a woman laughing first."

The Mick admitted that he must have inherited in some gene a drive that pushed him harder and harder. "The more successful I was, the more successful I had to become. I'd acted, sung, danced, drunk, gambled. I'd met President Roosevelt and Henry Ford. My face was plastered all over America."

The second of the four memorable Mickey and Judy musicals—following *Babes in Arms* and preceding *Babes on Broadway* and *Girl Crazy*: the never-a-dull-moment *Strike Up the Band*. When it opened at the Capitol in New York, *The Times* hurrah-ed, "Roll out the red carpet, folks, and stand by. That boy is here again, the Piped Piper of the box office, the eighth or ninth wonder of the world, the kid himself—in short, Mickey Rooney.... Call him cocky and brash, but he has the exuberant talent that keeps your eyes on the screen, whether he's banging the trap-drums, prancing through a conga, or hamming the old ham actors."

And then, for Rooney, along sauntered Ava.

"The first time I saw Ava Gardner," he told one reporter, "was on the set of *Babes on Broadway* in 1941. Ava was dressed like a princess and I was dressed like Carmen Miranda. I walked over in my samba skirt, my wedge shoes, my bodice blouse, and my fruity hat, and asked her for a date." After a three-month courtship, during which time he reportedly proposed nightly, she, at 19, became the first Mrs. Mickey Rooney on January 10, 1942, at a nondenominational church in Bellwood, between Los Angeles and San Francisco. (Rooney, in his first autobiography, seems to have forgotten the date of his first, very well publicized marriage, moving it back a year to 1941.) An extremely unhappy Mayer, it is said, sent a press agent along on their honeymoon. Also not wildly enthusiastic about the Mickey-Ava union, reportedly, were the groom's mother, stepfather, and father. Arthur Marx described the ceremony in his book *The Nine Lives of Mickey Rooney* (Stein and Day, 1986): "Rooney, in a new charcoal-gray, double-breasted suit with a green polka-dotted tie, was visibly nervous as he stood between Gardner and best man Les Peterson, who also wrote the press releases. Rooney stumbled through most of the ceremony and almost dropped the ring while trying to slide it onto Gardner's finger."

As Carmen Miranda in *Babes on Broadway* (1941) (MGM).

On Lifetime TV's *Intimate Portrait* in the 1990s, critic Kenneth Turan discussed the difficulties faced by both Gardner, a down-home girl from North Carolina who'd been in Hollywood for just a few months and wanted seemingly just to "play house" as a wife, and Mickey, who was far from a homebody. Ava's close friend of 40 years, confidante and housekeeper

Mearene Jordan, told the Lifetime camera that Ava told her: "I married him because he wanted to get in my britches, and I wasn't going to let him in there until we were married." And Mickey himself, talking about the marriage on camera, said: "I fell madly in love with Ava the first night I went out with her, and later I asked her to marry me, and she wouldn't have any part of it — like the problem I had getting her to give me her phone number, until I wore her down." Rooney admitted that, after they wed, they would go out partying and Ava would catch him talking to any woman in the room, and she'd turn around and walk out. "There was a lot of jealousy on Ava's part." Mearene pointed out that "Ava got even by stepping out with her friend, Lana Turner, who was newly divorced from bandleader Artie Shaw." Said The Mick: "She had an awfully fiery temper. You had to watch out what you said around her. Her sister Barb told me. I should have listened."

Sixteen months later, in May 1943, the two were divorced. "We remained friends," Rooney said. "She never asked me for a dime." Actually, she did get a couple of things in the settlement (a car, her furs, jewelry he had bought her, and about $25,000 in cash), although she probably could have taken him to the cleaners — possibly at the expense of her Hollywood career, Rooney being an important MGM commodity and she being an out-of-work starlet. (Gardner went on to marry, equally briefly, musically inclined Artie Shaw and Frank Sinatra. The latter, in a down point in his life and career, was reportedly far from happy at being referred to as "Mr. Ava Gardner.")

With the leading man ranks being depleted by wartime duty, Mickey Rooney inherited the role of King at MGM, alternating Andy Hardy films with Judy Garland musicals. In 1943, for his poignant performance as the telegraph messenger in *The Human Comedy* with Frank Morgan (Judy's Wizard of Oz) and young Van Johnson, Rooney received his second Best Actor Oscar nomination. Just how big a star Rooney had become at MGM is illustrated by his billing on the ads for *The Human Comedy*. Although he was listed below the title, his name was twice the size of Frank Morgan's and five times the size of all the other significant players. And there was this legend beneath his name: "In his greatest role since *Boys Town*."

The following year, after teaching below-the-title Elizabeth Taylor to ride horses in *National Velvet*, The Mick got the call from Uncle Sam, and Private Mickey Rooney found himself stationed at Camp Sibert near Gadsden, Alabama, eventually to be assigned to the 6817th Special Services Battalion. In Alabama, he would meet, woo, and, on September 30, 1944, after a seven-day engagement, wed "Miss Birmingham," 17-year-old Betty Jane Rase. Like most of his wives, she towered over him. This marriage was to last three years and two months and produced two sons — Mickey Jr.

The second and first husbands of Ava Gardner (Artie Shaw and Mickey Rooney) in the 1940s (UPI).

(actually Joe Yule III), on July 4, 1945, and Timothy on January 6, 1947. The settlement to B.J., as M.R. called her: $12,500-a-year alimony for ten years, $25,000 down payment on a new home for her, $750 a month in rent until she moved from Encino into that new home, $5,000 a year for child support, one Mercury and one Chrysler. Remember, this was just 1947. Costs were low.

In his Mickey biography, Arthur Marx — Groucho's screenwriter-author son — wrote, "Rooney proposed to Betty Jane Rase on an intoxicated whim." He went on about a later Mrs. R. "Only bride number four, actress Elaine Mahnken, seems to have put much effort into their marriage, but even she gave up when all her efforts to pay off her husband's debts couldn't counteract his spendthrift ways."

Decades later, Rooney told *People Weekly* (July 26, 1993) that Rase "was totally oblivious to anything that was going on outside our home,

Private Mickey Rooney and Clark Cable, MGM's king, in 1944 (UPI).

we just weren't compatibly compatible." Omitted from this reminiscence was the fact that for most of the marriage, Mickey was away in uniform — overseas, entertaining the troops as a member of the famed Jeep Theatre. He — usually as emcee — and several others put on Mickey and Judy–type backyard musicals all over the western front.

The Jeep Shows, as the dwindling number of World War II vets recall, brought show biz to the troops, generally right up on the front lines. Joshua Logan, the Broadway producer, then a major in the army, was the man behind the popular venture, bringing GI entertainers like Mickey Rooney, Bobby Breen (a kid star at Universal), soldier comic Red Buttons, big band sax player Jimmy Cook, and others— at least in The Mick's mix — along with the troops, armed with battery-powered megaphones and musical instruments (drums, saxes, clarinets, accordions). The guys were split up into touring groups of four and five, and each team generally had a musician or two, a singer and an emcee who told jokes. Rooney recalled, "'The only real problems you'll have,' Logan told me and some of the others, 'is finding (or improvising) your own stages.' I did my old numbers from vaudeville, pieces of Mickey McGuire, bits from my best movies, imitations and such." Mickey remembered putting on their first show between two Sherman tanks in a Belgian snowstorm three miles from the front, with about 60 guys in the audience. They sometimes did seven shows in one evening. This definitely was no USO troupe. Rooney and gang reportedly covered something like 150,000 miles that first year.

In 1944, prior to his call from Uncle Sam, another Sam had come into Mickey's life. He was Sam Stiefel, a promoter from Philly who pitched The Mick about being his manager. Rooney bit, and the two set up a corporation known as Rooney, Inc. Mickey was president, Sam the secretary-treasurer, and Mort Briskin, a longtime friend of Sam's, legal counsel. The Mick later took pride in having been one of the first movie stars to become his own producer. The venture, though it lasted into the early '50s, was— like Rooney's assorted marriages— a very contentious relationship that ultimately cost him very big bucks.*

Mickey came home from the war a sergeant. He was in the army, he reckoned, one year, eight months and 21 days— and returned, as he said, older, wiser, and still in one piece. He had one Bronze Star, a good conduct medal, a World War II victory medal, seven bronze campaign buttons on his European Theater of Operations ribbon, and a sharpshooter

---

*Among his low-budget, post–MGM melodramas of the era were The Big Wheel (with Spring Byington, his first Andy Hardy mom, and his mom again here) and Quicksand. "The less said about Quicksand the better," Rooney later recalled, "except to note that it was aptly titled. We sank it." But those particular nothing-for-his-career flicks were yet to come.

badge with an automatic rifle bar. And wartime memories. And a wife he almost didn't recognize. That's deadly. They really didn't have much more in common (except one kid, and later a second) than on the day they met back in Alabama in 1944 — when she as a then-teenager was several inches shorter before becoming a statuesque beauty who Mickey would have to now stand on his tiptoes to kiss. "Later, B.J. married again. Still later she was divorced again. She has again remarried," Mickey said several years after their split. "I wish her happiness. I was a lousy husband to her and she wasn't the greatest wife to me, but she's been a good mother to two wonderful sons."

Back in postwar Hollywood, a now-mature 26-year-old Rooney tried to recapture the old teenage vivacity with the Hardy family in *Love Laughs at Andy Hardy*. He and Louis B. Mayer — discovered that while he was away, the public's tastes were changing. He made three more films at MGM, in his first truly adult one (*Killer McCoy*) playing a boxer; it was a remake of the 1938 film *The Crowd Roars*. He then returned to his adolescent image, starring (with a pal from the old MGM days, Gloria De Haven) in *Summer Holiday*, a musical redo of *Ah, Wilderness!* in which he had appeared 13 years before. He then impersonated composer Lorenz Hart (to Tom Drake's Richard Rodgers) in the all-star pseudo-biopic of Rodgers and Hart, *Words and Music*. In it, he even got to do one last musical screen number with Judy Garland.

It has been said that *Words and Music* was The Mick's last lead role in an "A" flick — that he simply was too short to play a romantic lead as an adult. In *Bright Lights Film Journal*, Alan Vanneman wrote, "His talents as a singer and dancer if not as an actor, are on full display here. Although naturally 'ebullient,' to make up for his lack of height, Rooney could shift gears when he wanted to." Vanneman felt that Rooney "gives a lovely, quiet rendering of the quintessential Manhattan song, 'Manhattan,' [and] 'I Wish I Were in Love Again,' his last film duet with Garland, is one of the best things he (and Garland) ever did." The writer concluded, "[Lorenz] Hart, Rooney and Garland all knew a lot about unhappy affairs, but for three minutes on the big screen at least, there are no regrets."

The Rooney-MGM era then ended after 14 years with Mick squaring off with his onetime mentor Louis B. Mayer over money, only to discover that the whole Metro contretemps would be costing him nearly a half-million clams on top of the alimony bills that were piling up on the home front. It went something like this, according to Rooney: "I had to forgo my $5,000 a week salary and my pension (I could start drawing $49,000 a year in four years). And I had to pay Metro $500,000 besides, which I was to work off at a rate of $100,000 a picture (and keeping only $25,000

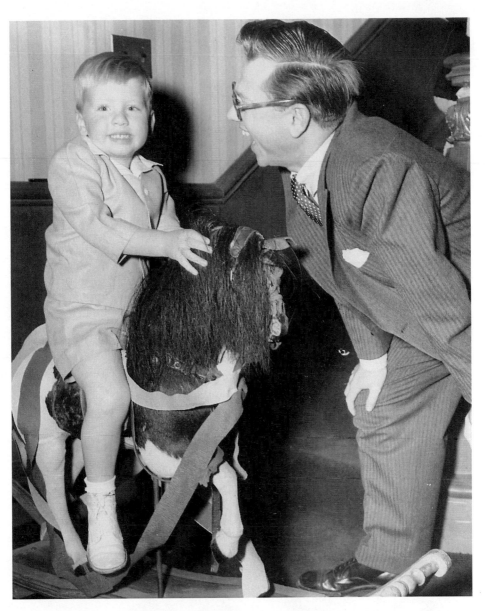

With Mickey Jr. in 1948 (ACME/UPI).

for myself).” Basically, Sam Stiefel negotiated him down to $25,000 a pic-
ture, and Mickey had collected nearly $170,000 for his work on *Words and
Music*—which, despite too many words but all that great music, turned
not to be a happy shoot, sending The Mick into the same kind of boozing
as the character he was playing, Lorenz Hart. (Pal and costar Judy Garland also was having her troubles at the time.) So, staying at MGM, he had

With Mickey Jr. in 1962 (ACME/UPI).

to do five pictures at $25,000 per, minus Stiefel's 50 percent off-the-top cut, and also minus Uncle Sam's share. "That would bring me down to less than $10,000 a picture — not even enough to pay me upcoming alimony and child support," Rooney wrote in *Life Is Too Short*. "And who knew if I'd ever make a picture?"

Stiefel had Mickey go the independent route with his own movie production company. He did some personal appearances (the Hippodrome Theatre in Baltimore for two weeks in December 1949 at $10,000 a week and another two in Hartford at $12,000), toured in what was left of vaudeville and made his film directing debut with a "B" melodrama for Columbia, *My True Story* with Helen Walker. (He directed — or co-directed — just one more time some years later.) Rooney also starred in a couple of radio series: the 1948 *Shorty Bell*, in which he played a cub reporter writing obituaries who'd like to be covering the crime beat (one of the cast regulars was his dad, Joe Yule, Sr.), and then *The Hardy Family* in 1949 with Lewis Stone and Fay Holden. *Variety*'s review (Nov. 23, 1949) noted: "While the films were handicapped by Mickey Rooney's aging out of his part, *The Hardy Family* on the air has no such hurdles. He is still cast as the irrepressible adolescent, hamming up his lines in his usual ingratiating manner."

His efforts, however, failed to change the direction of his screen career, hampered by a series of duds of his company's own making. And by his own admission, he was becoming increasingly less disciplined.

"I Do!" "I Do!" "I Do!" "I Do ... Not!" — and the Boob Tube

The Fourth Decade

The legendary marital merry-go-round of Mickey Rooney, which provided lots of material for his Vegas club act and well as his various autobiographies, continued. From 1949 to 1951, actress Martha Vickers was Mrs. R. (they wed June 3, 1949. just hours after he picked up his final divorce papers from the Betty Jane Rase union), and they had a son, Teddy, born April 13, 1950. "Mart," as The Mick called her, was a Warner Bros. contract player who'd made a splash, of sorts, as a bad girl in Humphrey Bogart's *The Big Sleep* and a couple of other lesser movies; young Teddy would costar with his dad in Rooney's futile attempt to resurrect the Andy Hardy series in the late 1950s. He later told *People Weekly* (July 26, 1993): "She drank too much, and we couldn't go on."

A year after this marriage ended (the divorce was on September 25, 1951), Rooney wed statuesque 23-year-old Elaine Mahnken, a Montana beaut from Butte, Montana (as the legendary comic duo Bob and Ray used to say), who as Elaine Davis had appeared with him in the film *The Atomic Kid*. The march down the now well-worn aisle — this time at Las Vegas' Wee Kirk on the Heather — took place on November 15, 1952. Elaine wasn't really keen on the races, or about Mick's gambling, either. Turns out that gambling had been an addiction of her ex-husband Dan Ducich, who'd been convicted in 1949 of armed robbery, put on five years probation afterward, and couldn't stop playing the tables in Vegas. A few months after her marriage to Mick, Ducich was rubbed out by the Mob for welshing on unpaid markers.

On their divorce six years later, she would charge Rooney with being an incurable horseplayer and gambler. He admitted in the above-mentioned *People Weekly* piece that he "overtly cheated on Elaine with future wife number five."

The next Rooney wedding took place on May 18, 1959, only hours after he was divorced by wife number four. Phoenix-born model Barbara Ann Thomason — then 22 Miss Muscle Beach of Santa Monica, who'd acted in a couple of low-budget films in the late '50s as Carolyn Mitchell — was the new bride, except that it turned out that she and Mickey secretly had been married in Mexico since December 1, 1958, making him, technically, a bigamist. (The New York *Daily News* joked in its headline: "Half Pint Takes a Fifth.") According to an Internet website on "Carolyn Mitchell," in March 1959, while Mickey still was legally married to Elaine Mahnken and illegally to her, Barbara threatened suicide if Rooney wouldn't get a divorce and marry her officially as she was three months pregnant. There were four children from this union: daughters Kelly Ann (born September 13, 1959), Kerry Yule (December 29, 1960), and Kimmy Sue (September 13, 1963), and son Michael Joseph Kyle (April 2, 1962).

In January 1966, Rooney sued Barbara for divorce, naming as corespondent a Yugoslavian chauffeur and sometimes actor, 25-year-old Milos Milosevic. At the end of January, Mickey returned early from film location in the Philippines and found the two of them dead in his bedroom, a murder-suicide. The New York *Daily News* headline of Tuesday, February 1, 1966: "Mick Rooney's Wife No. 5 Slain"; the subhead: "Find Jealous Lover a Suicide." (Milosevic's brother was later found dead in Paris, touching off a sex scandal that was said to implicate his employer, actor Alain Delon, as well as then-members of the French government.) Rooney's mom, Nell Carter Pankey, was to die at age 69 only just over a month after Barbara's death — on March 3, 1966.

On the performing front, between movie assignments, Mickey had gone to London in 1949 for an less than successful engagement at the Palladium (reportedly Danny Kaye had to be called in to shore up the floundering Rooney gig); did a nightclub act with his then-partner, Joey Forman; was invited to be a presenter at the Oscar ceremonies in 1951, and then was disinvited when the Motion Picture Academy had second thoughts because of his offscreen image (read marital and monetary track record); did some vaudeville turns in Chicago in July 1953 with Dick Winslow as his sidekick and in Miami in March 1954 with Danny Morton; and, later in the decade, managed a couple of weeks with Forman at the Copacabana in the Big Apple. "It's a turn," *Variety* reported in November 1958, "that encompasses a wide range of material including even the

Rooney as director, putting Wilton Graff and Helen Walker through their paces in *My True Story* (1950) (ACME/UPI).

thespic, and although Rooney starts out slowly, he winds up far in the lead."

In March 1951, there was this in, of all places, *The New York Times*: a pocket review of a show caught in Phoenix, Arizona. "Mickey Rooney made his debut on the legitimate stage as a Don Juan in *Sailor, Beware* last night [the 14th] at the Sombrero Playhouse. His mugging and clowning dominated every scene he was in." This "debut" notice failed to take into account that The Mick was Puck on stage at the Hollywood Bowl and other touring venues more than 15 years earlier. And in 1953, it was announced that Mickey would be making his Broadway debut in a musical called *Ankles Aweigh*, for his former MGM producer Fred Finklehoffe. Monetary squabbles apparently scotched the plan, and instead ex-vaudevillian Lew Parker opened in it in early 1955, along with Betty and Jane Kean and Gabe Dell of the East Side Kids/Bowery Boys. It wasn't much of a success.

With his old studio MGM now under new management (Dore Schary was in charge), Rooney returned briefly in 1951 for a low-budget mini-musical called *The Strip,* somewhat glumly playing a jazz drummer accused of a racketeer's murder. Best part of the film: Louis Armstrong doing a cameo introducing the song "A Kiss to Build a Dream On," which was Oscar-nominated. But with the exception of roles in *Off Limits,* a military comedy with Bob Hope ("Rooney is fine in a subdued role, which finds him floundering and helpless unless Hope is in his corner," said *The New York Times*), and *The Bridges at Toko-Ri,* playing a helicopter jockey in Korea, he did not have a part in a major film for seven years.

He did a batch of forgettable "B" pictures at Columbia with his boyhood pal and now director, Richard Quine (several written by an up-and-coming Blake Edwards). He was quite good, however, as a traveling parson in a minor Western that he produced for Republic, *The Twinkle in God's Eye* (1955). He then gave an energetic, jive-talking, allegedly ad libbed performance that not only saved a routine war movie for RKO, *The Bold and the Brave* (1956), but also earned him an Academy Award nomination as Best Supporting Actor.

Rooney mistakenly thought that his old fans might like to visit with Andy Hardy again, and talked the powers that be at MGM to let him produce a flick called *Andy Hardy Comes Home.* He brought Cecilia Parker, Fay Holden, and Sara Haden back as his sister, mother, and aunt, and cast his own son Teddy as Andy's son. "I went to MGM and asked the brass to bring Andy Hardy back as a young man," The Mick has reported. "I was to be a young judge myself, married to my high school sweetheart, Polly Benedict. Ann Rutherford was supposed to play Polly, but she nixed that. She was happily married to a very successful studio head, Bill Dozier, and she had not wish to do films again." Rooney wrote in his autobiography, "I came back to Carvel in [the film], but the trouble was, nobody noticed. The public simply didn't care what happened to Andy Hardy."

Rooney also later garnered attention—though not of the positive kind—for his role as a myopic, buck-toothed Japanese neighbor of "good-

On the drums; with Jack Teagarden (left), Barney Bigard and Louis Armstrong in *The Strip* (1951).

time girl" Audrey Hepburn in *Breakfast at Tiffany's* (1961). Oddly, in these days of political correctness that caused the Charlie Chan films of the 1930s and 1940s and the Amos 'n' Andy TV series of the early 1950s to become targets of the P.C. segments of the Asian and black communities, nothing ever is said of Rooney's quite visible and rather funny but archly stereotypical portrayal of "Mr. Yunioshi," considering that the film was much less obscure than the earlier Chans. But then again, The Mick has survived films in which gabby ducks, talking mules, and helpful pelicans were his costars.

Television provided him with the opportunity to show, as he periodically has done brilliantly through his convoluted career, his exceptional dramatic abilities. He made his acting debut in a 1952 TV version of Maxwell Anderson's *Saturday's Children* (which, unfortunately, did not go too well, in the eyes of the critics of the time). Things really got going after this, and he starred memorably in Rod Serling's *Playhouse 90* drama *The Comedian* (1957), receiving an Emmy nomination for his portrait of

As George M. Cohan (1957), a role he later repeated on the Bob Hope Chrysler Theatre and in a summer tour of Broadway's *George M!* (RCA Records).

arrogant, unscrupulous TV personality Sammy Hogarth. (The show itself won the Emmy as the Outstanding Single Program of the Year.) In 1958 he again earned a nomination, this time as a down-on-his-luck gambler in *Eddie,* a one-man show displaying his remarkable versatility. He received a third Best Actor nomination in 1961 for his portrayal of a lonely seaman

With son Timmy in 1957.

looking for friendship in *Somebody's Waiting* on *The Dick Powell Show*. Rooney gave an another extraordinary one-man performance on Serling's *The Last Night of a Jockey* (1963) on *The Twilight Zone*, playing a middle-aged jockey who prays to be bigger — only to have his wish granted and he finds himself too big physically for the only occupation he knows.

    The Mick finally won the Emmy as Best Actor for the 1981 made-for-

TV movie *Bill*, playing real-life Bill Sackter, a man forced to face life on the outside after being institutionalized for 44 years. (He later reprised the role of Sackter in the sequel *Bill: On His Own*.)

Rooney also went into series television, starring during the 1954-55 season in his own series with Forman, *Hey Mulligan* (aka *The Mickey Rooney Show*), playing a page at a broadcasting studio. The show wasn't half bad; but it had tough competition: NBC aired it on Saturday nights opposite Jackie Gleason. His second TV series a decade later, *Mickey*, had him playing an accidental hotel owner. His real-life son, Tim, played his teenage son, Timmy. It ran for 13 weeks at the beginning of the 1964-65 season. Unfortunately for the series, its direct competition was *The Dick Van Dyke Show*. It would be more than 15 years before The Mick did another series.

However, Rooney the entertainer was seen on TV as George M. Cohan in *Mr. Broadway*, directed by Sidney Lumet, and he had the title role in a new musical version of *Pinocchio*, both in 1957. He again played Cohan in Bob Hope's 1964 TV version of *The Seven Little Foys*, and in 1969 and 1970 he was doing the summer strawhat circuit in the Broadway musical *George M!* Rooney's Cohan was just one of a career gallery that had him playing Huck Finn, Thomas Edison, '30s gangster Baby Face Nelson, Broadway lyricist Lorenz Hart, Pinocchio, and others. One wag noted that Rooney didn't become them, they became Mickey Rooney.

Down and Out — and Up
The Fifth Decade

During this time, other bad days beset Rooney. As his boyhood chum, director Richard Quine, told Rooney biographer Arthur Marx in *The Nine Lives of Mickey Rooney*, "Let's face it. It wasn't all that easy to find roles for a 5-foot-3 man who'd passed the age of Andy Hardy." In 1962, at age 42, debts piled high enough to cause him to file for bankruptcy. Mickey could well have used one of those standard Andy Hardy father-son talks (set pieces that were in every one of the Hardy movies) and taken some sage advice from Judge Hardy. As journalist David Gelman wrote at the time in the *New York Post*, "There were reportedly some in Hollywood who were enjoying Mickey's plight. As Andy Hardy, Rooney was America's favorite adolescent, but in the film capital his popularity was somewhat dimmer. A performer from the time he could talk, Rooney grew up to be one of the great, many-sided talents of show business. At the same time, his egotism, brashness and belligerence earned him a host of enemies."

Rooney once estimated that's he'd made in excess of $12 million in his heyday. He'd not been plagued by the tribulations of fellow child actors Jackie Coogan and Freddie Bartholomew, whose parents had been in control of their munificent early earnings and had frittered much of them away, leading to dragged-out court cases and family ruptures. Take Coogan, whose career, like Rooney's, began when he was less than two years old, and who became the most successful child actor of his time — ironically, until Sonny Yule came along and became Mickey "Himself" McGuire. Coogan, who played his last role as a child star in 1927, and later made a comeback of sorts as the screen's Tom Sawyer and then Huckleberry Finn (a part, of course, that Rooney also was to play years later), was in 1935 to have received $4 million he had earned as a kid, but which

50

had been placed in a trust until his twenty-first birthday. He found, though, that his mother and stepfather were in no hurry to turn over his own money to him and he was obligated to file suit against the family. The case dragged on and on; his assets reportedly had dwindled to about $250,000, and he was given just half of that. The legal issue led to the passage of California's Child Actors Bill. "The Coogan Act" is how it became known popularly, designed to create court-administered trust funds for juvenile actors. Jackie Coogan never recovered from the litigation, nor did his career move much beyond taking character parts until later generations rediscovered him as Uncle Fester on TV's *The Addams Family*. Coogan died in 1970.

Then there was Freddie Bartholomew, Mickey's studio pal at MGM. He became embroiled in not one but two debilitating court cases in the late 1930s while he was still a child star. First his parents tried vainly to wrest him from the guardianship of his aunt, who had raised him after he had come to the United States from his native England in the early '30s. Next his aunt, who still maintained control, tried unsuccessfully to have him released from his MGM contract, which involved a substantial amount of money. During the period, his own career went into decline and he eventually retired from films—though he found a successful second career in the East in advertising and then as a producer of the CBS soap opera *As the World Turns*. He died in 1992.

Rooney's monetary woes were of his own making. Since his mother had married an accountant in 1937, and he happened to work for MGM, Mickey's cash affairs were well handled, but as a self-styled man about town and admirer of horse racing (both before and since reaching the age when he could lay down a legal bet), Rooney found that money literally slipped through his fingers. And with the revolving door of wives over a 30-year period, there were the alimony woes and the child support bills—especially with nearly a dozen kids. He also decided he had been working for slave wages while the likes of L.B. Mayer were raking in big bucks. And there were those bundles of dough he left at the craps tables in Vegas and Tahoe and Reno. By the '50s and '60s, when he admitted to making a comeback every two weeks, he was in bankruptcy.

One of the popular entertainment magazines of 1982 reported, in a multi-page piece on The Mick (by writer Chuck Jamieson), that "in a petition of involuntary bankruptcy filed in the Federal Court of Los Angeles in June, pint-size, gravel-voiced Mickey Rooney listed debts of $464,914 and assets of just $500—mostly household goods and old clothes." ... "Among his principal creditors he cited the United States Internal Revenue Bureau, with a claim totaling $106,686; the State of California, which also wants a big hunk of lettuce for back

With wife Ava Gardner in 1942 (UPI).

taxes; and three of his pretty ex-wives, who have been clamoring for back alimony and child support.*

How muddle-headed can a little guy get?" And then there were liabilities like a personal loan for $168,600 from Fryman Enterprises, one of the production companies in which he was involved with then-partner Red Dorff; $25,000 to the Citizen's National Bank; $38,230 to six lawyers; $37,500 or so to four professional agencies; $4,800 in hotel bills in Quebec, New York City, Palm Springs, and Honolulu, and assorted other debts— according to articles in both *Variety* and *The New York Times.*

Alimony-wise, Mrs. R. No. 2, Betty Jane Rase, received a $100,000 settlement plus child support for their two young boys. No. 3, movie starlet turned "B" actress Martha Vickers, also got a generous settlement: the house, the family furniture, child support for son Teddy and alimony which would rise gradually from $2,000 per month in 1951 to $3,000 per

*Actually, there were only two doing the clamoring; his settlement with Ava, his first, was amicable and as he admitted, she never asked for a dime.

With wife Betty Jane Rase in 1944 (UPI).

month in 1959 — providing she didn't marry again. She was taken off the alimony rolls when she ran off and remarried in 1954.

By the time his marriage (childless) to Elaine Mahnken, wife No. 4, ended, he found he was paying her more support than all of his previous spouses and children together. "Sure, Elaine spent a lot of money," Rooney

With wife Martha Vickers in 1949 (UPI).

recalled, "but she also tried to get all of my old bills paid, including a tax bill from the IRS for $32,000." The *Los Angeles Times*, at the time, headlined, to his humiliation, "Wife Dumps Rooney for $381,750." That included a $100,000 home in Studio City and another house at Lake Arrowhead, plus all the furniture, and an agreement to pay her $21,000 a year for the next decade. In fact, alimony payments and property settlements

With wife Elaine Mahnken in 1953 (UPI).

gobbled up more than $1 million a year. It was Chapter 11 for Mick in 1962, but three years later he was solvent again. (He did have, it turns out, a $250,000 trust fund on proceeds from the Hardy movies, thanks to his accountant stepfather — but he hadn't been able to draw on it until he turned 65!) All of this ended up as self-deprecating fodder for his club act. "How short am I?" he tells interviewers of his marriages — pre Jan. "Since

With wife Barbara Thomason in 1961 (UPI).

the last divorce, about $250,000. My marriage license is made out to 'To Whom It May Concern.'"

Beginning in the late 1940s, assorted agents and managers led to more of Mick's monetary missteps, as did a variety of entrepreneurial enterprises that turned out to be business blunders. With Daniel Tabas he

With wife Margie Lane in 1966 (UPI).

co-owned from 1969 through 1983 the Dowingtown (Pennsylvania) Motor Inn, with an eye to bring big league golf there and build a motion picture studio; he also co-owned the City Line Dinner Theatre at the Tabas Hotel. (The Tabas closed in mid–July 1999.) Also there were Mickey Rooney's Talentown U.S.A., Inc., a franchise operation, formed in 1971 and devoted to teaching creative arts to children from three to 16 years of age; a series of one-nighters leading a 17-piece orchestra, and singing, playing piano, signing autographs, and selling his latest album on his own label.

Then there were Mickey Rooney's S.S.A.C. (Self-Study Acting Course), a mail-order enterprise; Mickey Rooney's Motion Picture Commemorative

Society, where he had hoped to mint coins honoring the likes of Judy Garland, Charlie Chaplin, James Dean, and Marilyn Monroe; a movie company "dealership" called Galaxy Films (announced at a major Hollywood press conference) which "will make 30 films a year and play only in theaters that buy into the franchise-like operation"; a restaurant chain called Mickey Rooney's Delicious Inc., which began in Fort Lee, New Jersey, in 1985 (but didn't get too far); a food line headed by Mickey Rooney Macaroni—moving into competition with Paul Newman's salad dressing and popcorn for Newman's Own; and an endless number of other abortive stage and screen projects.

And most boisterously, there was his outrage on learning that he had no residuals from any of the hundred-plus movies he'd made before 1960. Ted Turner, who had bought the MGM film library, was not obligated to pay residuals to anyone whose earlier contracts did not specify payments—and in the old Hollywood studio system, the moguls were (rightly, they felt) quite tight-fisted about sharing the riches. Rooney sought legal relief in a class action suit. He told *Variety* in 1987: "SAG screwed us and I am mad about it." This whole thing has been what Rooney considered "a game of greed." At assorted press conferences over the years, he often would spend time lambasting various things like studio management and pornography, and taking up the cause of older actors and actresses who never see any residuals for films made before the SAG cutoff. He elaborated to the West Coast theatrical publication *Drama-Logue*, "What I am angry about and will always be angry about is the terrible blow actors were dealt when our supposed union negotiated our rights away from receiving monetary compensations for all the work done before 1960. Why didn't the union protect us? Ted Turner gets the money and the performer gets an actors' home to get sick and die in."

Rooney took his case all the way to the U.S. Supreme Court, where he was rebuffed. They wouldn't hear it.

But beyond money, marriage, and macaroni, Mickey Rooney trouped on through the year, with a bottomless bag of show biz projects and motivational talks, an autobiography entitled "*i.e.*" (G.P. Putnam's Sons, 1965), which it turns out was ghost-written by Roger Kahn, other business ventures and, along the way, some big dates at the Moulin Rouge in Hollywood Las Vegas at the Riviera and the Dunes in the late 1950s and early 1960s. "I was a smash at the Riviera, where I drew $17,500 a week—and lost twice that on the crap table," The Mick remembers. And with Bobby Van, he did three weeks at the Latin Quarter in the Big Apple, just prior to the murder of Barbara and the death of his beloved mom.

There also were still more movies, television, and wives to come. His

With wife Caroline Hockett in 1969 (AP Wirephoto).

future trips down the aisle included a Las Vegas one on September 19, 1966, to his dead wife Barbara's best friend, 45-year-old Margie Lane, but they split after just 100 days. Next was an "I Do!" on May 27, 1969, with former Miami secretary Carolyn Hockett, 23 years younger than The Mick and the seventh Mrs. R. At the time, Mickey had moved his financial ventures and his life to Fort Lauderdale. With her there were two more children, Jonell (born January 11, 1970) and Jimmy, from Carolyn's earlier marriage, whom Mickey adopted. As Rooney's official online site delicately put it in his biography, "financial instability ended the relationship," and in 1974 she filed for divorce; Rooney was saddled with more crushing alimony and child support payments. "I never married Judy Garland," he has joked, "I didn't want to ruin her life."

The Rooney parade of nuptials has produced ten children (plus one adopted and two stepsons) who have given him a number of grandchildren. It was reported in *The Star* (October 2, 1990) that he'd cut all of them out of his will. "None will get a dime when he kicks the bucket," wrote

With wife Jan Chamberlin (1975 to the present) (UPI).

the tabloid. "The truth is, there's no love lost between him and his kids. He's feuded constantly over with years with his eldest son Mickey Jr. [who towers over dad by more than a foot], and he thinks some of the others are just lazy." Whatever transpired in the decade or so after those printed comments remains unresolved.

In 1963, Mickey had a memorable television reunion with Judy Garland on her classic (single season) CBS musical series. The erstwhile Joe Yule, Jr., first met the equally erstwhile Frances Gumm in the Hollywood School for Professional Children when he was eight and she was seven. They would play in three Andy Hardy films together and six MGM musicals. In later years, he always would call her "Mommy," and on TV, at their professional get-together (their last), he told her, "Hey, legend, we should have made *Days of Wine and Roses* together." In *Rainbow* (1978), the first of two TV-movie biographies of Judy Garland — this one book-ended by two of Judy's signature songs, "I'm Always Chasing Rainbows" and "Over the Rainbow" — Mickey Rooney was impersonated by teenager Moosie Drier. It was directed by longtime pal and onetime Rooney castmate, Jackie Cooper, who, as a fellow teen on the lot, frequently dated Judy. Cooper also was portrayed in the film, which starred Andrea McArdle (Broadway's original *Annie*) as Judy. One of the dozens of projects that The Mick still keeps in his hip pocket is a musical based on their lives, called "Mickey and Judy"—although with Rooney in his mid-eighties, it seems unlikely that this one ever will materialize.

Judy Garland, of course, always comes up as a topic in Rooney interviews. *New York Times* columnist Alex Witchel chatted him up in 1993 as he was readying himself for another go at Broadway, and asked if he keeps in touch with Judy's daughter, Liza Minnelli: "We're not what you'd call buddy-buddy. She's off doing her thing, being Liza. But I miss Judy every day. She was part of me. I loved her. I think Judy Garland was without any equivocation one of the greatest actresses, entities, who ever lived and will be for the next two centuries. And that's quite a statement."

Beginning in the 1960, the indefatigable Mickey was on stage—regionally and in dinner theatre—in such fare as *Tunnel of Love* (1963) with Bobby Van, another MGM albeit somewhat younger studio veteran; *A Funny Thing Happened on the Way to the Forum* (regionally in 1965); a 1967 gig at Caesars Palace in Las Vegas playing Oscar Madison to Tony Randall's Felix Unger in *The Odd Couple*; and the previously mentioned *George M!*

It came out in the early '60s that The Mick also wrote a play, a comedy called *The Difference Between Night and Day* which he hoped to bring to Broadway in 1964. It was a takeoff on murder mysteries with Agnes Moorehead as a dowager, and Rooney and Jonathan Winters as a couple of private eyes. Aside from a news conference announcing it (reported in the *New York Herald Tribune* on September 7, 1964), no further word ever was heard of it.

W.C., Jan C., "Sugar Babies" and Rebirth

The Sixth Decade

Fort Lauderdale was his new home base starting in 1971. Pal Eddie Bracken, then running the Coconut Grove Playhouse in Miami, gave him a job in a sex farce called *Three Goats and a Blanket* in 1971. Recalling The Mick in a 1995 A&E *Biography*, Bracken noted: "This comedy was about alimony, and Mickey Rooney's the perfect guy for that. The first night, only 15 people paid to get in to see him. That's how dead he was at the time. But Mickey tirelessly hustled the show on local television, and soon it was sold out, and then he went on to become the king of dinner theatres."*

The comedy, concocted by a couple of Gleason writers, was hardly the greatest vehicle to come down the pike — or *up* it, since it was promoted as being Broadway bound. Mickey took it on the regional theatre circuit with his usual boundless energy — one critic along the way wrote, "It's great to see Rooney running riot again," and called the show "a new comedy gem." Then he toured tirelessly in similar early 1970s farces like *Hide and Seek*, *Goodnight Ladies*, and *See How They Run*, Phillip King's hoary British sex romp from the late 1940s that never did play Broadway, and later, *Alimony* and *Go Ahead and Laugh*, both actually reworkings of *Three Goats and a Blanket*.

He also starred as W.C. Fields in 1971 in a musical called *W.C.* (book by Milton Sperling and Sam Locke, adapted from Robert Lewis Taylor's Fields biography; music and lyrics by Al Carmines) that also was intended for Broadway. Diminutive Rooney actually made audiences believe him to

Bracken's memory of the first night crowd was somewhat at odds with the critic for Variety *who, catching the show in Miami in early April, wrote, "Opening night, before a celebrity audience which included Jackie Gleason, Rooney dominated the stage, mugging and miming, doing bits within the play, getting more laughs out of it than the material contains."*

be Fields by donning an exaggerated top hat that added about six inches to his height. (As a kid, Mickey crossed paths many times on the old MGM lot with the erstwhile William Claude Dukenfield, but never worked with him.) *W.C.* tryouts started in Baltimore; *Variety*'s critic wrote after its mid–July Albany opening: "Virtually the only satisfying part of the show is Rooney, who brings Fields to life in physical appearance, voice and characteristics. He is greeted enthusiastically by the audience, a response engendered by his own personality."

When *W.C.* next opened at the Westbury Music Fair on Long Island, *Newsday* critic Leo Seligsohn responded to "an engaging Fields impersonation by Rooney." Later the reviewer noted that "despite Rooney's impressive efforts (mugging excused, Fields did it all the time), Fields come off as one-dimensional — his alcoholism is treated as a barrel of laughs until, too suddenly, he is a melodramatically tragic figure." ... A bit more sensitive treatment here and there, plus an imaginative set, and the entire production could match the level of Rooney's fine impersonation." The show, which also starred Bernadette Peters as Carlotta Monti, never made it to the Great White Way. It closed in Detroit in mid–October 1971.

In the mid–'70s, never-a-dull-moment Mickey was to be found crisscrossing the country in a major revival of *Show Boat* as Cap'n Andy Hawks. When *Show Boat* docked at the Opera House at Washington's Kennedy Center 1974, critic Ward Morehouse III wrote: "Mickey Rooney makes a sprightly Cap'n Andy, and with the energy of a Mississippi paddlewheel, spins adroitly through comic relief and poignant melodrama. Frequent ad-libs about his own pint-size only add a light, self-effacing and personal touch to what is written as a flamboyant role." (Rooney's old MGM buddy and brief Andy Hardy girlfriend Kathryn Grayson originally was to have been in this production, repeating her 1951 film role of Magnolia, but dropped out of the tour early on.)

In 1978, at his then-agent Ruth Webb's place, into his life came a 25-year-old Nashville country singer named Janice Darlene Chamberlin (or Chamberlain, depending on which of Rooney's autobiographies and dozens of articles about him and her in the intervening years mentions her). They wed on July 28 in the Conejo Valley Church of Religious Science, about 30 miles northwest of Hollywood. She seems to have brought The Mick stability, and he found religion with her. (In his book, he writes about a life-altering experience at a coffee shop at Harrah's in Lake Tahoe, California, which turned out to him to be an epiphany. And in a 1993 interview with *The New York Times*, he said, "I believe God gave me my career. I was sent here to do my Father's work.")

The Mickey and Jan Rooney marriage continues apace after more

With wife Jan in 1983.

than 25 years. In 2003–04, they were touring the country in what he dubbed "A One Man, One Wife Show," which they also put out on CD.

He has written in *Life Is Too Short*: "In many ways I haven't changed a bit. I am still the same self-absorbed guy I was when I married Ava. I like to do what I want, when I want, where I want, without much thought for the wants of others. The people around me fare best when they do not challenge me. But Jan challenged me and she's still doing it, years later. The challenge is good for me."

In early 1979, Rooney signed on to star in a theatrical burlesque review for the whole family, called *Sugar Babies*, along with another onetime MGM bright light, dancer Ann Miller (they never before had worked together). Rooney and Miller opened in San Francisco in May and then went to L.A. with it in June, and read basically mediocre reviews of the show. But The Mick, of course, was never one to be kept down and, knowing a good vehicle when he saw one based on all those years of experience, he trouped on with Miller. Making their way East to Broadway, they turned the show into a smash. At 59, Mickey Rooney was reincarnated as a baggy-pants comedian — back as a top banana in show biz in his belated Broadway debut.

"When *Sugar Babies* opened," Mickey is fond of saying, "I was the most famous has-been in the entertainment business." *Time* magazine wrote: "Mickey Rooney has greasepaint in his blood and the house in his pocket.... He has lungs of iron and feet that skitter like a sandpiper's." The *New York Post*'s Clive Barnes called Rooney "Broadway's most promising newcomer ... the true icing on *Sugar Babies*, a Top Banana if we ever had one."

Mickey made the cover of *Life* magazine following *Sugar Babies*' premiere on the Great White Way. Rooney and Miller did the show for 1,208 performances in New York and then toured with it for five years, including eight months later on in London's West End. (In his autobiography, Mickey admitted to knocking down 10,000 bucks a week initially, raised by the producers to 15,000, then 20,000 and, after the show went into the black, 30,000 — and finally ended up getting one percent of the producer's share forever, no matter where the show was produced. There were later versions with Carol Channing and Robert Morse; Eddie Bracken and Mimi Hines; Juliet Prowse and Rip Taylor.) While on Broadway from October 1979 through August 1982, Rooney found time for other movie and television projects— and never missed a performance. He also, according to costar Ann Miller, never missed a chance to ad-lib or read the lines the same way twice, if he even stuck to the script.

The Kid's Still Trouping
The Seventh Decade

Mick's third TV series, *One of the Boys* (with Dana Carvey, Nathan Lane, and a young Meg Ryan), aired between January and August 1982. He also, for a while, was a regular with Sammy Davis, Jr., in the short-lived 1973 vaudeville-style series *NBC Follies*.

In 1985–86, Rooney found himself being portrayed in a short-lived and rather mediocre musical on London's West End, *Judy*, about Judy Garland, as he was nearly a decade earlier in a TV movie about her, *Rainbow*, which was directed by their mutual pal, Jackie Cooper.

Returning to Sondheim, Rooney headed the 1987 national tour of *A Funny Thing Happened on the Way to the Forum*, which he had played in the '60s. ("This is clearly Rooney's show as he cavorts and struts around the stage," *Variety* wrote in a relatively tepid review when this *Forum* played the Pantages Theatre in Los Angeles.) While talking to the press promoting the show, the Mick passed the word that he was contemplating starring next in a new tour of the musical *The King and I*—in the Yul Brynner part!

The Mick's second *Forum* was followed by a tour of his one-man show *Mickey Rooney in Mickey Rooney*, with engagements in the early '90s in Australia and New Zealand. On its stop in San Francisco in mid–1988, the *Chronicle* critic was underwhelmed, to say the least. Under the headline: "Mickey Takes His Ego for a Stroll," he wrote: "After being trapped in Theatre on the Square for two-and-one-half hours without intermission, I think we need a law against yelling 'Mickey Rooney' in a crowded theater. At the very start of this most peculiar, almost endless, one-man show, modesty called *Mickey Rooney in Mickey Rooney*, the star says he hopes he fits the part. In fact, he's been badly miscast, playing the role of a windy old showbiz bore, the one thing Mickey Rooney has never been."

66

Next up: teaming in the late '80s with longtime friend Donald O'Connor, costarring in a musical revue called *Two for the Show*. The closest they ever came to working together previously was the very first time they met, in 1933, at the Orpheum Theatre in L.A. "It was one of those talent nights, when the young people get up and try to make people laugh — just like today's comedy clubs," O'Connor told the New York *Daily News'* Bruce Chadwick in 1989, when they first paired. "I was working with the O'Connors, our family vaudeville troupe [Mickey was 13 and Donald, eight], and a few minutes after we were done, Mickey came out. Boy, was he funny! I remember it vividly." *Variety* caught the Mickey-Donald show at the Riviera in Las Vegas and wrote (August 23, 1989): "The 90-minute razzle-dazzle of the two showbiz vets heralds a new nitery team sorely needed in these times in Las Vegas. The matching of talent was exemplary, exhibiting both entertainers in song, dance, comedy, and plenty of theatrics."

Still "Girl Crazy"
After All These Years
The Eighth Decade

Rooney and O'Connor followed *Two for the Show* with a 14-city tour in a 1990 production of Neil Simon's *The Sunshine Boys* as feuding, aging vaudevillians, at odds over a onetime-only comeback reprising their long ago act on *The Ed Sullivan Show*. Then he joined the long-running Chicago production of playwright Ken Ludwig's hit of a couple of years earlier, *Lend Me a Tenor*, prior to returning to Broadway in mid–1993 and almost single-handedly revitalizing the Tommy Tune–directed musical *The Will Rogers Follies*, succeeding Dick Latessa as Rogers' dad Clem (around the time country star Larry Gatlin succeeded Keith Carradine and Mac Davis in the lead), and very nearly turning the show into "The Mickey Rooney Follies." (As a kid, The Mick had costarred with Rogers in the 1935 film *The County Chairman*.)

"From his first entrance, it's clear that the audience is in love with Mickey Rooney," critic Howard Kissel wrote in the New York *Daily News*. "The affection they beam onto the stage he sends back in spades. His comic skills are as spiffy as ever." Clive Barnes, in the *New York Post*, wrote: "Rooney is no shrinking violet, but here — unlike his shticks in *Sugar Babies* — this happily shuffling performance by one of the last, indeed perhaps *the* last, of the glorious old vaudevillians, is restrained, touching, rhythmic, and brilliant. Quite marvelous!"

He followed his *Will Rogers Follies* stint with the London production of *Sugar Babies* with Ann Miller at the Savoy, beginning in September 1988. It was Rooney's first stage gig in Old Blighty since the one at the Palladium four decades earlier, and *The Times*' critic wrote: "Time has left no mark on Mr. Rooney's fast footwork and timing." Reviewer Clive Hirschhorn in the *Sunday Express* felt that "Rooney, the little man with the outsized showmanship, pilfers every sketch he is in, suggestively flicking his tongue like a salacious adder, and doing a pretty good imitation of a sex-obsessed Peck's Bad Boy. His drag routine is a knockout." Both Rooney and Miller were nominated for the 1988 Laurence Olivier Awards as Outstanding Actor and Actress in a Musical.

"I came here 40 years ago, to the London Palladium just after the war, and it was not a good idea," Rooney told Sheridan Morley in an interview for *The Times of London*. "They had never had a Hollywood star there before, and one of the papers ran a headline: 'American here to take our money.' I think they thought I was supposed to appear without a fee. Anyway, the reviews were terrible, but I survived the two weeks; it was a touchy time, but then, I've had a lot of those. In the 1960s, the work was very sparse indeed; there was just no demand for me and Hollywood, anyway. We all moved to Fort Lauderdale to live with my wife's parents."

In the West End version of *Sugar Babies*, Rooney reportedly received $40,000 weekly plus $3,000 in expenses, but *Variety* reported (March 29, 1989) that he failed to pay agent Ruth Webb her ten percent for "arranging" for his participation. On the television front, from 1990 through 1992, The Mick starred in the Canadian-made family series, *The Adventures of the Black Stallion*, repeating the role of Henry Dailey, the grumpy but lovable horse trainer, which he first played (and won an Oscar nomination for) in the 1979 film *The Black Stallion*.

One Man, One Wife
The Ninth Decade

As the twentieth century waned, the indefatigable Mick's live performing agenda included a continuing tour of *Mickey Rooney in Mickey Rooney* and guest star gigs not only in the long-running Chicago production of Ken Ludwig's zany Broadway hit *Lend Me a Tenor*, but also opposite Great Britain's popular Ruthie Henshall, the lead in the London production of another Ludwig smash, *Crazy for You*, in a 1995 Toronto staging of that show — which was inspired by his 1940s movie *Girl Crazy* with Judy Garland. And the Judy connection continued with Mickey's touring for several years at the end of the '90s in *The Wizard of Oz*, a shortened version of Britain's Royal National Theatre production that found its way to New Jersey's popular Paper Mill Playhouse. It became a delightful, popular family touring vehicle running about 90 minutes with Rooney as the Wiz, Eartha Kitt, Jo Anne Worley, and others as the Wicked Witch of the West, and newcomer Jessica Grové as Dorothy. It also played several engagements in New York at Madison Square Garden.

He told Pete Hamill of the New York *Daily News*, "We're doing 12 *Oz* shows a week at the Garden; Judy and I did 12 shows a day at the Capitol Theatre. She would could come out and do songs—'I Got Rhythm'—and I'd come out and do a funny skit, some impressions, a dance or something. They had long lines around the block all day long. This was '38, and I remember when Judy and I arrived at Grand Central to play the gig, there were 24,000 people waiting. Then later, of course, she started taking those pills—and when she died it just broke my heart, and I still haven't gotten over it."

Rooney's screen career never flagged, either. During the last three decades he appeared in more than 50 films, some, of course, bigger and/or more prestigious than others. They effectively could be classified as the

Good (*The Black Stallion* in 1979, *That's Entertainment,* as one of the hosts, in 1974, and Carl Reiner's *The Comic,* as baggy-pants comic Dick Van Dyke's one-eyed sidekick); the Bad (*Silent Night, Deadly Night 5: The Toy Maker,* as an evil, often drunk toy maker, Tim Robbins' Viking grandpa in *Erik the Viking,* and *Rachel's Man,* with Rooney as a smart-mouthed biblical figure) and the Ugly (a critical slammed Western, *Outlaws: The Legend of O.B. Taggart,* for which he wrote the screenplay and in which he stars, and *La Vida Lactea,* playing a rich old codger dressed solely in a diaper and suckling at the breast of plus-sized German actress Marianne Sagebrecht).

A renaissance show biz legend, Mickey at one point or another in his career led a 17-piece band in one-nighters in the Fort Lauderdale area (in 1972); appeared in at least one porno flick (no, The Mick never got naked — it was a documentary on blue movies, and he was one of the talking heads being interviewed!); eked out a living in the late 1960s in Florida (according to his autobiography, showing up at parties as a rented celebrity); played a free-form gig, a solo cabaret act, at the famed jazz club Michael's Pub in the Big Apple (in 1993), which ended up in the newspapers after a contract dispute caused him to walk out — like a walk he took several decades earlier in the midst of a turn at Hollywood's Moulin Rouge (and that one cost him six grand!); did a turn as a novelist with *The Search for Sonny Skies* (Birch Lane Press, 1994); toured with current wife Jan in a dual musical act, "The One Man, One Wife Show" (playing, for instance, at the Tropicana in Atlantic City at Christmas 2003); managed to cram his entire life into a 337 page autobiography; and was even Richard Nixon's guardian angel in a bizarre screen fantasy. And in 1993. Mickey Rooney finally won his Oscar — an honorary one, "in recognition of his 60 years of versatility in a variety of memorable film performances."

Pete Hamill wrote of his May 1998 sit-down with Mickey while preparing for his interpretation of the Wonderful Wizard of Oz.: "He turns his chair, and regales you with a nonstop two hours of showbiz anecdotes and observations on life, religion, age, friendship, love and work."

In addition to his current work, and of course Judy Garland, Hamill said: "He talks of another old friend named Marilyn Monroe, a screen name Rooney claims he invented. ('I told Norma Jeane Baker she needed someone she could trust, an agent, because there was gonna be a line of people trying to jump her bones. I told her she also needed a new name. At the time, there was a great stage actress named Marilyn Miller. So I told Norma Jeane she should be a Marilyn. Then I got a call from a screenwriter named Monroe Manning. And it clicked.')"

Rooney also related to Hamill: "I'd discovered a lot of people. I found

Mickey and Jan Rooney: One Man, One Wife (2003) (Mickey Rooney collection).

Sammy Davis, Jr., I brought Red Skelton to MGM and [not yet 20] directed his first screen test [Red, who already had a long career in vaudeville as a clown, was touring for years in presentation houses, had made an abortive screen debut for RKO in 1938, and had done some Vitaphone shorts], found Ann Jillian and put her in *Sugar Babies*. Walt Disney even named Mickey Mouse after me."

He also reminisced, not really in anger: "I think of the good old days and I smile. Gable got $100,000 for *Gone with the Wind*, and today Jim Carrey and Tom Cruise get $20 million and 15 percent of the gross. God bless them, but it isn't even comparable. And directors make movies for like $300 million. The cook in the kitchen could make a movie for $300 million if he learned a few key lines like 'Roll 'em!,' 'Cut,' 'One more,' 'Print that one,' 'Lunch' and 'Wrap.'

"But look I come from vaudeville, I come from burlesque, I come from heartaches, I come from sadness, I come from gladness, I come from work, and sweat and respect for the craft."

The Mick also was well-nigh ubiquitous on television in 2003, talking about his friend and colleague, Bob Hope, first on the assorted celebrations of Hope's centennial in May and not long afterward reminiscing following the legendary performer's death. The two had worked together on television on *Bob Hope Chrysler Theatre*, had costarred in one feature film and appeared together in several Hollywood shorts. Actually, Hope had been of Joe Yule, Sr.'s vaudeville generation, and Rooney was quick to make that association — in effect, bringing his dad back into the spotlight for an added moment.

As he once wrote, "Had I been brighter, had the ladies been gentler, had the Scotch been weaker, had the gods be kinder, this could have been a one-sentence story: once upon a time Mickey Rooney lived happily ever after."

Filmography

(In the following filmography, the bit of shorthand used is MR for Mickey Rooney.)

Not to Be Trusted, Fox, 1926

Director: Thomas Buckingham; *Writer:* Murray Roth, from a story by Mabel Herbert Turner.

Featuring Matt Moore, Bud Jamison, June La Vere and MR as a midget con man, out on a heist with "partner" Jamison.

The Mickey (Himself) McGuire Shorts

(1926–28, released by F.B.O.; 1929–33, released by Radio Pictures; 1934, released by Columbia Pictures)

All were produced by Larry Darmour and directed variously by Albert Herman, Earl Montgomery and J.A. Duffy

In the first, MR was billed as Mickey Yule. In the others, his billing was Mickey (Himself) McGuire. Beginning with *Mickey's Race* (1933), it became "Mickey McGuire, now known as Mickey Rooney."

1927: *Mickey's Circus; Mickey's Pals; Mickey's Battle; Mickey's Eleven*

1928: *Mickey's Parade; Mickey in School; Mickey's Nine; Mickey's Little Eva; Mickey's Wild West; Mickey in Love; Mickey's Triumph; Mickey's Babies; Mickey's Movies; Mickey's Rivals; Mickey the Detective; Mickey's Athletes; Mickey's Big Game Hunt*

1929: *Mickey's Great Idea; Mickey's Explorers; Mickey's Menagerie; Mickey's Last Chance; Mickey's Brown Derby* (the first talkie in the series); *Mickey's Northwest Mounted; Mickey's Initiation; Mickey's Midnight Follies; Mickey's Surprise; Mickey's Mix-up; Mickey's Big Moment*

1930: *Mickey's Champs; Mickey's Strategy; Mickey's Mastermind; Mickey's Luck; Mickey's Whirlwind; Mickey's Warrior; Mickey the Romeo; Mickey's Merry Men; Mickey's Winners, Mickey's Musketeers; Mickey's Bargain*

1931: *Mickey's Stampede; Mickey's Crusaders; Mickey's Rebellion; Mickey's Diplomacy; Mickey's Wildcats; Mickey's Thrill Hunters; Mickey's Helping Hand; Mickey's Sideline* (Mickey and the Toonerville Kids get boxing pointers from heavyweight champ Jim Jeffries)

1932: *Mickey's Travels; Mickey's Holiday; Mickey's Golden Rule; Mickey's Busy Day; Mickey's Charity; Mickey's Big Business*

1933: *Mickey's Ape Man*; *Mickey's Race*; *Mickey's Big Broadcast*; *Mickey's Disguises*; *Mickey's Touchdown*; *Mickey's Tent Show*; *Mickey's Covered Wagon*

1934: *Mickey's Minstrels*, *Mickey's Rescue*; *Mickey's Medicine Man*

In 1934, Mickey (Himself) McGuire also hosted one in a series of Columbia's "Screen Snapshots," a one-reel short with Lloyd Hughes, Marie Prevost, Mary Pickford, Dolores Del Rio, Douglas Fairbanks, Louis Wolheim and others.

In 1945, a number of the Mickey (Himself) McGuire talkies were resurrected and, with some new footage added along with the thoughts of Shirley Jean Rickert, one of his now-grown female costars of the series, became the focus of a five-reel film compilation called *Mickey the Great*.

As Mickey "Himself" McGuire.

The Feature Films

1. Orchids and Ermine, First National, 1927

Director: Alfred Santell; *Original screenplay:* Carey Wilson; Comedy construction: Mervyn LeRoy

Cast: Colleen Moore, Jack Mulhall, Sam Hardy, Gwen Lee, Jack Duffy, Hedda Hopper, Fred Kelsey, Frank Hagney, Kate Price and MR playing a swaggering, cigar-smoking midget with a cane who makes a pass at comely hotel switchboard operator Moore. In his 1970s–80s film series at the New School in Manhattan, the esteemed writer and movie authority William K. Everson called *Orchids and Ermine* "a typically gay [in the original sense of the word] Cinderella story of the flapper era, with few surprises in plot, but plenty of surprises in terms of incident." He went on to observe: "Few things date quite as much as the wisecrack subtitles of '20s comedies; many of them must have seemed impossibly labored even at the time, but even here, *Orchids and Ermine* is a delight…. Although it clicks largely because of the charm and personality of its star, one should mention in passing the remarkable film debut of Mickey Rooney, playing an ultra self-confident midget!"

2. Emma, MGM, 1932

Director: Clarence Brown; *Screenplay:* Frances Marion

Cast: Marie Dressler (*Emma Thatcher*), Richard Cromwell (*Ronnie Smith*), Jean Hersholt (*Mr. Frederick Smith*), Myrna Loy (*Isabelle Smith [Countess Marlin]*), John Miljan (*District Attorney*), Purnell B. Pratt (*Haskins*), Leila Bennett (*Matilda*),

Putting the make on Colleen Moore in *Orchids and Ermine* (1927).

Barbara Kent (*Gypsy Smith*), Kathryn Crawford (*Sue Smith*), George Meeker (*Bill Smith*), Dale Fuller (*Maid*), Wilfred Noy (*Drake*), André Cheron (*Pierre [Count Marlin]*), Dorothy Peterson (*Mrs. Winthrop*), and MR, unbilled, as one of the brood of kids under the care of Dressler, beloved faithful housekeeper for many decades in the home of wealthy Cromwell, son of self-styled inventor but now absentminded Hersholt.

3. The Beast of the City, MGM, 1932

Director: Charles Brabin; *Screenplay:* John Lee Mahin, from a story by W. R. Burnett

    Cast: Walter Huston (*Jim Fitzpatrick*), Jean Harlow (*Daisy Stevens*), Wallace Ford (*Edward Fitzpatrick*), Jean Hersholt (*Sam Belmonte*), Dorothy Peterson (*Mary Fitzpatrick*); Tully Marshall (*Michaels*), John Miljan (*District Attorney*), Emmett Corrigan (*Chief of Police Burton*), Warner Richmond (*Tom*), J. Carrol Naish (*Pietro Cholo*), Sandy Roth (*Mac*), Edward Brophy (*Police Dispatcher*); Edgar Dearing (*Policeman*), Robert Homans (*Policeman*), George Chandler (*Reporter*), Nat Pendleton (*Robber Abe Gorman*), Clarence Wilson (*Coroner*), Julie Haydon (*Woman in Police Lineup*), Murray Kinnell (*Judge*), Arthur Hoyt (*Witness*), Morgan Wallace (*Police Captain*) and MR (billed as Mickey McGuire), seen briefly as the son of Huston, a police chief in a war against gangster Hersholt. Huston's weak-willed detective brother Ford has enraged the crime kingpin after falling for the latter's mistress Harlow.

    Variety called it "a gang story for rural and home circle consumption, preaching the gospel of civic righteousness. They even made Harlow keep her skirts down." A *Hollywood Reporter* news item indicated that the rather violent film was made as the result of conferences between Louis B. Mayer and President Herbert Hoover about the need to educate the public to have a greater respect for law enforcement officers.

4. Sin's Pay Day, Mayfair, 1932

Director: George B. Seitz; *Screenplay:* Gene Morgan and Betty Burbridge

    Cast: Dorothy Revier (*Iris Markey*), Forrest Stanley (*James Markey*), Harry Semels (*Louie Joe*), Hal Price (*Jack Bernheim*), Alfred Cross (*David Lee*), Lloyd Whitlock (*Robert Webb*), Bess Flowers (*Jane Webb*) and third-billed MR (again billed as Mickey McGuire) as Chubby Dennis, a slum kid who befriends underworld attorney Stanley. Stanley has hit the skids after his wife leaves him when he refuses to abandon his practice. When the kid is killed by a gangster's stray bullet, the lawyer vows revenge, works his way back to District Attorney and reconciles with his wife. (Later rereleased in 1938 as *Slums of New York*, with Rooney given star billing under his new name after legally changing it from Mickey McGuire.)

5. High Speed, Columbia, 1932

Director: D. Ross Lederman; *Screenplay:* Adele Buffington, from a story by Harold Shumate

    Cast: Buck Jones (*Bill Toomey*), Loretta Sayers (*Peggy Preston*), Wallace MacDonald (*Tom Carlis*), Dick Dickinson (*Kane*), William Walling (*Preston*), Edward LeSaint (*Police Captain*), Ward Bond (*Ham*), Pat O'Malley (*Buddy Whipple*), Ed

Chandler (*Bowers*), Joe Bordeaux (*Jim*), Martin Faust (*Kelly*) and fourth-billed MR (credited as Mickey McGuire) as auto racer Jones' crippled pal Buddy Whipple, son of the former's dead racing companion, O'Malley. Jones, a hugely popular cowboy star of the day, finds himself disqualified from the track thanks to the schemes of MacDonald's crooked gang, but stages a comeback, unmasks the gang leader, saves the girl and wins the race, natch.

6. Officer Thirteen, Allied, 1932

Director: George Melford; *Screenplay:* Frances Hyland, from a story by Paul Edwards

    Cast: Monte Blue (*Tom Burke*), Lila Lee (*Doris Dane*), Charles Delaney (*Sandy Marlowe*), Robert Ellis (*Jack Blake*), Frances Rich (*Joan Thorpe*), Joseph Girard (*Chief of Police*), Seena Owen (*Trixi DuBray*), Jackie Searl (*Sammy*), Lloyd Ingraham (*Judge Dane*), Florence Roberts (*Granny*), Charles O'Malley (*Fruit vendor*), Alan Cravan (*Capt. Reed*), Edward Cooper (*Butler*) and eighth-billed MR (credited as Mickey McGuire) as Buddy Malone, the son of motorcycle cop Delaney, whose death at the hands of politically connected (and acquitted) motorist Ellis partner Blue vows to avenge.

7. Fast Companions (aka The Information Kid), Universal, 1932

Director: Kurt Neumann; *Screenplay:* Earl Snell, from a story by Gerald Beaumont

    Cast: Tom Brown (*Marty Black*), James Gleason (*Silk Henley*), Maureen O'Sullivan (*Sally*), Andy Devine (*Information Kid*), Berton Churchill (*Committee Chairman*), Morgan Wallace (*"Cueball" Kelly*), Russell Hopton (*Jack*), Arletta Duncan (*Dora*) and fifth-billed MR as Midge, a smart-alecky orphan stable boy living with bookie Gleason. This racetrack programmer is packed with shady characters including the lead (Brown), who ultimately reforms for the love of a good woman. The film's alternate title, incidentally, referred to the character played by Devine. Many of the exterior scenes were shot at the Agua Caliente racetrack in Tijuana, Mexico, where youngster Rooney got his introduction to one of his later lifestyle passions— playing the ponies.

8. My Pal, the King, Universal 1932

Director: Kurt Neumann; *Screenplay:* Jack Natteford and Tom Crizer, from a story by Richard Schayer

    Cast: Tom Mix (*Tom Reed*), Tony the Wonder Horse, James Kirkwood (*Count De Mar*), Wallis Clark (*Prof. Lorenz*), Noel Francis (*Princess Elsa*), Stuart Holmes (*Baron Kluckstein*), Finis Barton (*Gretchen*), Paul Hurst (*"Red"*), James Thorpe (the famed Native American athlete) (*Black Cloud*), Christian Frank (*Etzel*), Clarissa Selwynne (*Dowager Queen*), Ferdinand Schumann-Heink (*Gen. Wiedeman*) and third-billed MR — after Tony, the Wonder Horse — as Charles V, boy king of Alvonia, whom cowboy star Tom Mix, on a rodeo tour of the Balkans, saves from evil regent Holmes.

    New York Times critic Mordaunt Hall pointed out: "Little Mickey Rooney appears as King Charles and he does quite well." This was Mick's first movie notice in *The Times.*

9. *The Big Cage*, Universal, 1933

Director: Kurt Neumann; *Screenplay:* Edward Anthony and Ferdinand Reyher, from the 1933 book by Clyde Beatty and Anthony, adapted by Dale Van Every.

With Tom Brown in *Fast Companions* (1932).

Cast: Clyde Beatty (*Himself*), Anita Page (*Lillian Langley*), Andy Devine (*"Scoops"*), Vince Barnett (*"Soupmeat"*), Wallace Ford (*Russ Penny*), Raymond Hatton (*Timothy O'Hara*), Reginald Barlow (*John Whipple*), Robert McWade (*Henry Cameron*), Edward Peil, Sr. (*Glenn Stoner*), Wilfred Lucas (*Bob Mills*), James Durkin (*Silas Warner*) and fifth-billed MR as Jimmy O'Hara, son of former trainer-turned-drunk Hatton, taken in by Beatty after his dad is killed in a tiger cage trying to prove his lost prowess. The subplot of this film, Beatty's feature debut, involves a love affair between aerialist Page and lion tamer Ford, who has lost his nerve following a mauling.

Of this decidedly minor league showcase for Beatty playing a circus tiger tamer, *The New York Times* critic noted: "Mickey is very clever as Jimmy O'Hara, the orphan aspiring to be an animal trainer."

10. The Life of Jimmy Dolan, Warner Bros., 1933

Director: Archie Mayo; *Screenplay:* David Boehm and Erwin Gelsey, from the 1933 play *The Sucker* by Bertram Millhauser and Beulah Marie Dix.

Cast: Douglas Fairbanks, Jr. (*Jimmy Dolan/Jack Dougherty*), Loretta Young (*Peggy*), Aline MacMahon (*Auntie [Mrs. Moore]*), Guy Kibbee (*Phlaxer*), Lyle Talbot (*Doc Woods*), Fifi D'Orsay (*Budgie*), Harold Huber (*Reggie Newman*), Shirley Gray (*Goldie West*), George Meeker (*Charles Magee*), David Durand (*George*),

With Tom Mix (left) and Wallis Clark in *My Pal, the King* (1932).

Farina (*Samuel*), Dawn O'Day [later Anne Shirley] (*Mary Lou*), Arthur Hohl (*Trainer*), John Wayne (in a bit part as a boxer) and twelfth-billed MR, playing Freckles, a kid at a farm for underprivileged children where prize fighter Fairbanks, on the lam from a crime committed while drunk, hides out. The film was remade in 1939 as *They Made Me a Criminal*, a vehicle for John Garfield.

11. The Big Chance, Eagle Pictures, 1933

Director: Albert Herman; *Screenplay:* Mauri Grashin, adapted without credit from Charles Saxton's original story "Fighting in the Dark" (which was the film's title during production).

    Cast: John Darrow (*"Knockout" Frankie Morgan*), Merna Kennedy (*Mary Wilson*), Natalie Moorhead (*Babe*), Mathew Betz (*Flash McQuaid*), J. Carrol Naish (*John Wilson*), Hank Mann (*Tugboat*), Eleanor Boardman (*Singer*) and fourth-billed MR as Arthur Wilson, kid brother of Kennedy, girlfriend of boxer Darrow, who has double-crossed his crooked manager by winning a fixed fight and now faces retribution from gangsters.

    Variety observed that the film "evidently was given rush production following a major studio trend to a pugilistic cycle [with] pictures of real fights cleverly worked into the plot."

12. Broadway to Hollywood, MGM, 1933

Directors: Willard Mack and Harry Rapf; *Screenplay:* Edgar Allan Woolf and Mack.
    Cast: Alice Brady (*Lulu Hackett*), Frank Morgan (*Ted Hackett*), Jackie Cooper

(*Ted Hackett, Jr., as a child*), Russell Hardie (*Ted Hackett, Jr.*), Madge Evans (*Anne Ainsley*), Eddie Quillan (*Ted Hackett III*), Jimmy Durante (*Jimmy*), Fay Templeton (*Singer*), May Robson (*Actress*), The Albertina Rasch Dancers (*Specialty Act*), Edward Brophy (*Joe Mannion*), Edwin Maxwell (*Rockwell*), Tad Alexander (*David*), Ruth Channing (*Wanda*), Jean Howard (*Grace*), Robert Greig (*"Diamond Jim" Brady*), Una Merkel (*Chorus Girl*); As themselves: Muriel Evans, Marie Dressler, Joe Weber, Lou Fields, Nelson Eddy (in his screen debut), William Collier, Sr., and De Wolf Hopper. Sixth-billed MR (in his first major MGM film) plays a third generation vaudevillian — Quillan has the role as an adult — in this epic 40-year saga of a show biz family.

13. The World Changes, Warner Bros., 1933

Director: Mervyn LeRoy; *Screenplay:* Edward Chodorov, from the novel *America Kneels* by Sheridan Gibney.

Cast: Paul Muni (*Orin Nordholm, Jr.*), Aline MacMahon (*Anna Nordholm*), Mary Astor (*Virginia Nordholm*), Donald Cook (*Richard Nordholm*), Jean Muir (*Selma II [Petersen]*) (film debut), Guy Kibbee (*James Claflin*), Patricia Ellis (*Natalie*), Theodore Newton (*Paul*), Margaret Lindsay (*Jennifer Clinton*), Gordon Westcott (*John*), Alan Dinehart (*Ogden Jarratt*), Henry O'Neill (*Orin Nordholm, Sr.*), Anna Q. Nilsson (*Mrs. Peterson*), Willard Robertson (*Mr. Peterson*), Douglass Dumbrille (*Buffalo Bill*), William Janney (*Orin Nordholm III*), Arthur Hohl (*Patten*), Sidney Toler (*Hodgens*), Alan Mowbray (*Sir Phillip Ivor*), Marjorie Gateson (*Mrs. Clinton*), William Burress (*Kraus*), Wallis Clark (*Mr. McCord*), Clay Clement (*Capt. Custer*), Jackie Searl (*John as a boy*), and MR (billed twenty-seventh in the cast) as young Otto Petersen, the son of pioneers Nilsson and Robertson, in this panorama of seven decades from frontier Dakotas to the Wall Street crash in 1929.

14. The Chief, MGM, 1933

Director: Charles F. Riesner; *Screenplay:* Arthur Caesar and Robert E. Hopkins.

Cast: Ed Wynn (*Henry Summers*), Charles "Chic" Sale (*Uncle Joe*), Dorothy Mackaill (*Dixie Dean*), William (Stage) Boyd (*Danny O'Rourke*), Effie Ellsler (*Ma Summers*). C. Henry Gordon (*Clayton*), Bradley Page (*Dapper Dan*), Purnell B. Pratt (*Al Morgan*), George Givot (*Clothing Merchant*), Nat Pendleton (*Mike*), Tom Wilson (*Blink*), Bob Perry (*Frank*), Jackie Searl (*Boy in Department Store*), Graham McNamee (*Himself*) and MR (unbilled) as Willie, a local youth in this vehicle for Ed Wynn, son of a dead fire hero on the old Bowery, who becomes an honorary fire chief through a series of accidental heroic deeds. Wynn re-created the popular "Fire Chief" character from his hit Texaco radio show of the day.

15. Beloved, Universal, 1934

Director: Victor Schertzinger; *Screenplay:* Paul Gangelin and George O'Neill, from a story by Gangelin.

Cast: John Boles (*Carl Hausmann*), Gloria Stuart (*Lucy Tarrant Hausmann*), Morgan Farley (*Eric Hausmann*), Ruth Hall (*Patricia Hedley*), Albert Conti (*Baron Franz von Hausmann*), Dorothy Peterson (*Baroness Irene von Hausmann*), Edmund Breese (*Maj. Tarrant*), Louise Carter (*Mrs. Tarrant*), Anderson Lawler (*Tom Rountree*), Richard Carle (*Judge B.T. Belden*), Lucile Webster Gleason (*The Duchess*), Mae Busch (*Marie*), Jimmy Butler (*Charles Hausmann as a youngster*), Edward

Woods (*Charles Hausmann*), Oscar Apfel (*Henry Burrows*), Jane Mercer (*Helen*), Lester Lee (*Carl, age ten*), Holmes Herbert (*Lord Landslake*), Lucille La Verne (*Mrs. Briggs*), Mary Gordon (*Mrs. O'Leary*), Wallis Clark (*Yates*), James Flavin (*Wilcox*), Fred Kelsey (*Mulvaney*), Clara Blandick (*Miss Murfee*). Peggy Terry (*Alice*), Margaret Mann (*Countess von Brandenburg*), Montague Shaw (*Alexander Talbot*), Walter Brennan (*Stuttering boarder*) and MR as Tommy, a violin student (billed eighteenth) in this little epic spanning 90 years, in which musician Boles has devoted his life to writing a symphonic portrait of America. Several songs, including the title one, were written by the film's director, a Tin Pan Alley composer.

16. I Like It That Way, Universal, 1934

Director: Harry Lachman; *Screenplay:* Chandler Sprague and Joseph Santley, from a story by Harry Sauber.

Cast: Roger Pryor (*Jack Anderson*), Gloria Stuart (*Ann Rogers/Dolly LaVerne*), Marian Marsh (*Jean Anderson*), Shirley Gray (*Peggy*), Onslow Stevens (*John*), Lucile Webster Gleason (*Mrs. Anderson*), Noel Madison (*Jimmy Stuart*), Clarence Hummel Wilson (*The Professor*), Gloria Shea (*Trixie*), Mae Busch (*Elsie*), Merna Kennedy (*Information girl*), John Darrow (*Harry Rogers*), Eddie Gribbon (*Pupil*), Virginia Sale (*Old Maid*) and ninth-billed MR as a Western Union messenger boy in this programmer about a hotshot insurance agent (Pryor) who falls for Stuart, a nightclub singer whose background his sister Marsh is rather leery about.

17. Love Birds, Universal, 1934

Director: William A. Seiter; *Screenplay:* Doris Anderson, from a story by Clarence Marks and Dale Van Every.

Cast: Slim Summerville (*Henry Whipple*), ZaSu Pitts (*Araminta Tootle*), Dorothy Christy (*Kitten*), Emmett Vogan (*Jameson Forbes*), Frederick Burton (*Barbwire*), Maude Eburne (*Madam Bertha Smith*), Gertrude Short (*Burlesque Girl*), Clarence Hummel Wilson (*Blewitt*), Arthur Stone (*Janitor*), Hugh Enfield (*Bus Driver*), Ethel Mandell (*Teacher*), John T. Murray (*Dentist*) and third-billed MR as precocious Gladwyn Tootle, the Bible-quoting nephew of schoolmarm Pitts, in this rural comedy in which she and Summerville, longtime enemies, are duped into buying the same shack miles from nowhere, that it turns out to be located in the center of a gold rush.

18. Half a Sinner, Universal, 1934

Director: Kurt Neumann; *Screenplay:* Earle Snell and Clarence Marks, from the 1925 play *Alias the Deacon* by John B. Hymer and LeRoy Clemens.

Cast: Sally Blane (*Phyllis*), Joel McCrea (*John Adams*), Berton Churchill ("*The Deacon*" *Caswell*) [re-creating the title role which he played on Broadway], Alexandra Carlisle (*Mrs. Mary Clark*), Guinn Williams ("*Bull*" *Moran*), Russell Hopton ("*Slim*" *Sullivan*), Spencer Charters (*Noel Cunningham*), Reginald Barlow (*Sheriff John King*), Henry Armetta (*Barber*), Gay Seabrook (*Louella*), Theresa Maxwell Conover (*Mrs. Gregory*), Fred Kohler, Sr. (*Brick*), Fred "Snowflake" Toones (*Snowflake*), Clarence Hummel Wilson (*Collector*), Bert Roach (*Bloomfield*), Maurice Black (*Mike*), Walter Brennan (*Announcer*) and fifth-billed MR as Willie Clark, the rapscallion son of Carlisle, the owner of a small town hotel where Blane is working after riding the rails with boyfriend McCrea, now the local garage mechanic and coach of MR's football team. The couple earlier had exposed a card shark posing as Churchill's character of The Deacon. It had been filmed before as a silent, *Alias the Deacon* (1927), with Jean Hersholt; later it would be remade (1940) under that title with Bob Burns.

19. The Lost Jungle, Mascot, 1934.

Directors: Armand Schaefer and Dave Howard; *Screenplay:* Colbert Clark and John Rathmell, based on a story by Sherman Lowe and Al Martin.

   Cast: Clyde Beatty (*Himself*), The Hagenback Wallace Animals, Cecilia Parker (*Ruth Robinson*), Syd Saylor (*Larry Henderson*), Edward LeSaint (*Capt. Robinson*), Warner Richmond (*Sharkey*), Wheeler Oakman (*Kirby*), Lou Meehan (*Flynn*), Max Wagner (*Slade*), Maston Williams (*Thompson*), J. Crauford Kent (*Prof. Livingston*), Lloyd Ingraham, Lloyd Whitlock, Jack Carlyle, Wally Wales, Ernie Adams, Harry Holman and last-billed MR as a youngster named Mickey. Feature version of the 15-chapter Clyde Beatty serial (also featuring MR) about a wild animal expedition and search for a lost treasure on a tropic isle. The leading lady, Cecilia Parker, later would play MR's older sister in the Andy Hardy series.

20. Upper World, Warner Bros., 1934

Director: Roy Del Ruth; *Screenplay:* Ben Markson, from a story by Ben Hecht.

   Cast: Warren William (*Alex Stream*), Mary Astor (*Mrs. Hettie Stream*), Ginger Rogers (*Lilly Linder*), Andy Devine (*Oscar*), Dickie Moore (*Tommy Stream*), Ferdinand Gottschalk (*Marcus*), Robert Barrat (*Commissioner Clark*), J. Carrol Naish (*Lou Colima*), Sidney Toler (*Moran*), Henry O'Neill (*Banker*), Frank Sheridan (*Inspector Kellogg*), Theodore Newton (*Rocklen*), Robert Grieg (*Butler*), John Qualen (*Chris*), Willard Robertson (*Capt. Reynolds*), Nora Cecil (*Housekeeper*), Lester Dorr (*Steward*), Edward LeSaint (*Henshaw*), Milton Kibbee (*Pilot*), Douglas Cosgrove (*Johnson*), Howard Hickman (*Judge*) and MR as a youngster named Jerry McDonald. The character seems to be missing from the release print, despite his photo being seen in extant Warners publicity stills; it probably ended on the cutting room floor. Plot deals with a love triangle involving a wealthy railroad magnate (William), his social-climbing wife (Astor) and a chorus girl (Rogers).

21. Manhattan Melodrama, MGM, 1934

Director: W.S. Van Dyke (and, unbilled, George Cukor); *Screenplay:* Oliver H.P. Garrett and Joseph L. Mankiewicz, from an original story by Arthur Caesar.

   Cast: Clark Gable (*Blackie Gallagher*), William Powell (*Jim Wade*), Myrna Loy (*Eleanor*), Leo Carrillo (*Father Joe*), Nat Pendleton (*Spud*), George Sidney (*Poppa Rosen*), Isabel Jewell (*Annabelle*), Muriel Evans (*Tootsie Malone*), Thomas Jackson (*Richard Snow*), Claudelle Kaye (*Miss Adams*), Frank Conroy (*Defense Attorney*), Noel Madison (*Manny Arnold*), Jimmy Butler (*Jim Wade as a boy*), Shirley Ross (*Black Singer in the Cotton Club*), Sam McDaniel (*Black Death Row Prisoner*), Samuel S. Hinds (*Warden*), Herman Bing (*German Proprietor*), Leonid Kinskey (*Trotsky Aide*), Leo Lange (*Leon Trotsky*), Edward Van Sloan (*Skipper of Yacht*), Emmett Vogan, Lee Phelps, Wade Boteler, Garry Owen, Oscar Apfel, Henry Roquemore, Stanley Blystone, Lee Shumway and thirteenth-billed MR as a scrappy youngster who grows up with street pal Butler to become big-time gambler Gable and district attorney Powell respectively.

   The Rodgers and Hart evergreen "Blue Moon" was introduced in this movie

With Jimmy Butler (seated) in *Manhattan Melodrama* (1934); they'd grow up in the flick to be Clark Gable and William Powell (MGM).

under its original title "The Bad in Every Man" (with somewhat different lyrics). Jean Harlow was supposed to have sung it in an earlier film, but Shirley Ross performed it (in modified blackface) in the Cotton Club sequence.

This movie, produced by David O. Selznick, became legendary as the one John Dillinger had just seen when he was gunned down by the Feds leaving the Chicago theater where it was playing on July 22, 1934. Remade as a set-in-the-Canadian Rockies Western called *Northwest Rangers* in 1942.

22. Hide-Out, MGM, 1934

Director: W.S. Van Dyke; *Screenplay:* Frances Goodrich and Albert Hackett, from a story by Mauri Grashin.

Cast: Robert Montgomery (*Lucky Wilson*), Maureen O'Sullivan (*Pauline Miller*), Edward Arnold (*Lt. MacCarthy*), Elizabeth Patterson (*Ma Miller*), Whitford Kane (*Pa Miller*), C. Henry Gordon (*Tony Berrelli*), Muriel Evans (*Babe*), Edward Brophy (*Britt*), Henry Armetta (*Louis Shuman*), Herman Bing (*Jake Lillie*), Louise Henry (*Millie*), Harold Huber (*Dr. Warner*), Roberta Gale (*Hat Check Girl*), Bobby Watson (*Emcee*), Virginia Verrill (*Singer*), Arthur Belasco, Billy Arnold, Louis Natheaux, Frank Leighton, Frank O'Connor, Lucile Browne and sixth-billed MR as young Willie Miller, whose schoolteacher sister becomes the love interest for

With Maureen O'Sullivan (Mia Farrow's mom) in *Hideout* (1934) (MGM).

playboy-racketeer Montgomery, hiding out from the cops on their Catskills farm.

Variety reported: "Rooney well-nigh steals the picture." Leading lady O'Sullivan left the project early on to be with her seriously ill father in Ireland and was replaced during production by Loretta Young, who then was hospitalized and replaced by the original O'Sullivan. The songs "All I Do Is Dream of You" and "The Dream Was So Beautiful" were written by Arthur Freed and Nacio Herb Brown. Remade in 1941 as *I'll Wait for You* with Virginia Weidler and Paul Kelly.

23. Chained, MGM, 1934

Director: Clarence Brown; *Screenplay:* John Lee Mahin, from a story by Edgar Selwyn.

Cast: Joan Crawford (*Diane Levering Field*), Clark Gable (*Mike Bradley*), Otto Kruger (*Richard Field*), Stuart Erwin (*Johnnie Smith*), Marjorie Gateson (*Mrs. Louis Smith*), Una O'Connor (*Amy*), Akim Tamiroff (*Pablo*), Hooper Atchley, Phillips Smalley, Edward LeSaint (*Steamship Officers*), Theresa Maxwell Conover (*Secretary*), Ward Bond (*Sailor*), Lee Phelps (*Bartender*), Louis Natheaux (*Steward*), Ernie Alexander, Nora Cecil, Grace Hayle, Delmar Watson, Chris Pin Martin, Gino Corrado, Sam Flint, Frank Parker, Wade Boteler and MR (billed twenty-second) in a tiny role as a young swimmer on the ship where a romance blossoms between smooth-talking South American rancher Gable and the mistress (Crawford) of wealthy shipping magnate Kruger. Originally this was to have been titled *Sacred and Profane* and to have costarred Crawford with Preston Foster.

24. Blind Date, Columbia, 1934

Director: Roy William Neill; *Screenplay:* Ethel Hill, based on the 1931 novel by Vida Hurst.

    Cast: Ann Sothern (*Kitty Taylor*), Neil Hamilton (*Bob Hartwell*), Paul Kelly (*Bill Lowry*), Spencer Charters (*Charlie Taylor*), Jane Darwell (*Ma Taylor*), Joan Gale (*Flora Taylor*), Geneva Mitchell (*Dot*), Theodore Newton (*Tom*), Tyler Brooke (*Emy*), Henry Kolker (*J.W. Hartwell*), Ben Hendricks, Jr. (*Burt Stearns*), Billie Seward (*Barbara Hartwell*), Mary Forbes (*Mrs. Hartwell*), Selmer Jackson (*Martin*), Sam Hayes (*Radio Announcer*), Henry Roquemore (*Sugar Daddy*), Claire du Brey (*Head Saleslady*), Carol Tevis (*Dumb Dora*), Charles King (*Red*), Lee Phelps (*Attendant*) and fourth-billed MR as Freddy Taylor, the smart-mouthed kid brother of Sothern, a pretty switchboard operator torn between her auto mechanic boyfriend Kelly and her boss' son Hamilton.

25. Death on the Diamond, MGM, 1934

Director: Edward Sedgwick; *Screenplay:* Harvey Thew, Joseph Sherman and Ralph Spence, based on the 1934 novel *Death on the Diamond: A Baseball Mystery Story* by Courtland Fitzsimmons.

    Cast: Robert Young (*Larry Kelly*), Madge Evans (*Frances Clark*), Nat Pendleton (*"Truck" Hogan*), Ted Healy (*Terry "Crawfish" O'Toole*), C. Henry Gordon (*Joe Karnes*), Paul Kelly (*Jimmie Downey*), David Landau (*Pop Clark*), DeWitt Jennings (*Patterson*), Edward Brophy (*Grogan*), Willard Robertson (*Lt. Cato*), Robert Livingston (*Frank Higgins*), Joe Sawyer (*Dunk Spencer*), James Ellison (*Cincinnati Pitcher*), Ray Mayer (*Sugar Kane*), Pat Flaherty (*Coach*), Ralph Bushman (*Briscoe*), Charles Sullivan (*Taxi Driver*), Pat O'Malley (*Cashier*), Lee Phelps (*Cigar Clerk*), Tom McGuire (*Chief of Police*), Walter Brennan (*Hot Dog Vendor*), Howard Hickman (*Doctor*), Fred "Snowflake" Toones (*Porter*), Ward Bond (*Policeman*), Alice Lake (*Mrs. Briscoe*), John Hyams (*Henry Ainsley*), Billy Watson, Heinie Conklin, Max Wagner, Frank Marlowe. Gertrude Short, Wilbur Mack, Marc Lawrence, Kane Richmond, Ernie Alexander, Frank Layton, Herman Brix, Garry Owens, Don Brodie, Louis Natheaux and eleventh-billed MR as Mickey, the batboy of the St. Louis Cardinals baseball team that is plagued by snipers in the bleachers, stranglers in the locker room, poisoners in the commissary and booby-trapped spitballs. Thanks to upstanding rookie pitcher Young, they overcome the odds to win the pennant. (Franchot Tone initially was cast in Young's role.)

26. The County Chairman, Fox, 1935

Director: John Blystone; *Screenplay:* Sam Hellman and Gladys Lehman, based on the 1903 play by George Ade.

    Cast: Will Rogers (*Jim Hackler*), Evelyn Venable (*Lucy Rigby*), Kent Taylor (*Ben Harvey*), Louise Dresser (*Mrs. Mary Rigby*), Berton Churchill (*Elias Rigby*), Frank Melton (*Henry Cleaver*), Robert McWade (*Tom Cruden*), Russell Simpson, (*Vance Jimmison*), William V. Mong (*Uncle Eck*), Jan Duggan (*Abigail Trewsbury*), Gay Seabrook (*Lorna Cruden*), Charles Middleton (*Riley Cleaver*), Erville Alderson (*Wilson Prewitt*), Stepin Fetchit (*Sassafras*), Alfred James (*Ezra Gibson*), Francis

Ford (*Cattle Rancher*), Harlan Knight, Carl Stockdale, Sam Flint, Frank Austin, Anders Van Haden, Eleanor Wesselhoeft, Ernie Shields, Carmencita Johnson and fifth-billed MR as a local kid named Freckles in this bucolic tale about a rural Wyoming country chairman (Rogers) who helps get partner Taylor elected public prosecutor, though the latter's future father-in-law is his powerful political rival. (Rooney decades later would play Will Rogers' dad on Broadway in *The Will Rogers Follies*.) There had been an earlier (silent) film adaptation of the Ade play in 1914 with Maclyn Arbuckle in the lead.

27. Reckless, MGM, 1935

Director: Victor Fleming; *Screenplay:* P.J. Wolfson, from a story by Oliver Jeffries.

Cast: Jean Harlow (*Mona Leslie*), William Powell (*Ned Riley*), Franchot Tone (*Bob Harrison*), May Robson (*Granny*), Ted Healy (*Smiley*), Rosalind Russell (*Josephine Mercer*), Nat Pendleton (*Blossom*), Henry Stephenson (*Col. H. Harrison*), Robert Light (*Paul Mercer*), Allan Jones (*Allan*), Louise Henry (*Louise*), James Ellison (*Dale Every*), Nina Mae McKinney (*Herself*), Man Mountain Dean (*Himself*), Leon Waycoff [Ames] (*Ralph Watson*), Alice Weaver (*Dancer*), Farina (*Gold Dust*) and eighth-billed MR as Eddie, the young pal of sports promoter Powell, rival to millionaire Tone for the affections of Broadway showgirl Harlow in this soap opera produced by David O. Selznick. It reportedly was inspired by the life of torch singer Libby Holman and the headline-making mystery surrounding the death of her tobacco heir husband Zachary Smith Reynolds II (she was accused of his murder.

Jerome Kern and Oscar Hammerstein II wrote the title song, and Burton Lane and Harold Adamson composed "Hear What My Heart Is Saying."

28. The Healer (aka Little Pal), Monogram, 1935

Director: Reginald Baker; *Screenplay:* George Waggner, adapted by James Knox Miller and John Goodrich from the 1911 novel by Robert Herrick.

Cast: Ralph Bellamy (*Dr. Holden*), Karen Morley (*Evelyn Allen*), Judith Allen (*Joan Bradshaw*), J. Farrell MacDonald (*Applejack*), Robert McWade (*Mr. Bradshaw*), Bruce Warren (*Dr. Gordon Thornton*), Vessie Farrell (*Martha*) and third-billed MR as "Soldier" Jimmy, a youngster who has lost the use of his legs and is under the care of a doctor (Bellamy) known as "The Healer," at a small camp near a therapeutic mineral pool in the Adirondacks. When the film later was reissued as *Little Pal*, Rooney was given billing above the title, to capitalize on his new-found popularity.

29. A Midsummer Night's Dream, Warner Bros., 1935

Directors: Max Reinhardt and William Dieterle; *Screenplay:* Charles Kenyon and Mary C. McCall, adapted from the play by William Shakespeare.

Cast: James Cagney (*Bottom, the Weaver*), Dick Powell (*Lysander*), Joe E. Brown (*Flute*), Jean Muir (*Helena*), Hugh Herbert (*Snout, the Tinker*), Ian Hunter (*Thesus,*

Opposite, top: With "Doc" Ralph Bellamy in *The Healer* (1935). **Bottom:** As Puck, with Olivia de Havilland as Hermia, in *A Midsummer Night's Dream* (1935).

Duke of Athens), Frank McHugh (*Quince, the Carpenter*), Victor Jory (*Oberon, King of the Fairies*), Olivia de Havilland (*Hermia*), Ross Alexander (*Demetrius*), Grant Mitchell (*Egeus*), Dewey Robinson (*Snug, the Joiner*), Helen Westcott (*Cobweb*), Nini Theilade (*Fairie*), Verree Teasdale (*Hippolyta*), Anita Louise (*Titania*), Hobart Cavanaugh (*Philostrate*), Otis Harlan (*Starveling, the Tailor*), Sara Haden (*Bottom's Wife*), Fred Sale, Jr. (*Moth*), Arthur Treacher (*Epilogue*), Billy Barty (*Mustard-Seed*), Sheila Brown (*Indian Prince*), Katherine Frey (*Pease-Blossom*) and fourteenth-billed MR, repeating his stage performance as Puck, or Robin Goodfellow, a fairy, from the famed Hollywood Bowl production.

This film marked 18-year-old Olivia de Havilland's movie debut, although her name twice was misspelled in the credits.

30. Ah, Wilderness! MGM 1935

Director: Clarence Brown; *Screenplay:* Frances Goodrich and Albert Hackett, based on the 1933 Theatre Guild play by Eugene O'Neill.

Cast: Wallace Beery (*Sid Miller*), Lionel Barrymore (*Nat Miller*), Aline MacMahon (*Lily*), Eric Linden (*Richard Miller*), Cecilia Parker (*Muriel*), Spring Byington (*Essie Miller*), Charley Grapewin (*Mr. McComber*), Frank Albertson (*Arthur Miller*), Edward Nugent (*Wint Selby*), Bonita Granville (*Mildred Miller*), Helen

With Bonita Granville (left) and Spring Byington in *Ah, Wilderness!* (1935) (MGM).

Flint (*Bette*), Helen Freeman (*Miss Hawley*), Edward LeSaint (*Minister*), Eily Malyon (*Maid*), Buddy Messinger (*George Danforth*), Leigh De Lacy (*Mrs. Danforth*), Jed Prouty, Norman Phillips, Jr., Tommy Dugan, Mary Russell, James Donlan, Harry C. Bradley, George Offerman, Jr., and seventh-billed MR as the youngest son, Tommy Miller, in this American family portrait (circa 1906) about teen Linden's relationship with his father Barrymore and his tippling uncle Beery. Barrymore, Byington and Parker would be back as part of MR's Andy Hardy family a couple of years later. In the 1948 musical remake *Summer Holiday*, Rooney would have the role of the older son, Richard.

31. Riffraff, MGM, 1936

Director: J. Walter Rubin; *Screenplay:* Frances Marion, H.W. Hanemann and Anita Loos, from an original story by Marion.

Cast: Jean Harlow (*Hattie Muller*), Spencer Tracy (*Dutch Muller*), Una Merkel (*Lil*), Joseph Calleia (*Nick Lewis*), Victor Kilian (*"Flytrap"*), J. Farrell MacDonald (*"Brains" McCall*), Roger Imhof (*"Pops"*), Juanita Quigley (*Rosie*), Vince Barnett (*Lew*), Paul Hurst (*Belcher*), Dorothy Appleby (*Gertie*), Judith Wood (*Mabel*), George Givot (*Markis*), Arthur Housman (*"Ratsy"*), Helen Flint (*Sadie*), Helen Costello (*Maisie*), Wade Boteler (*Bert*), Al Hill (*"Speed"*), Lillian Harmer (*Mrs.*

With "big sister" Jean Harlow in *Riffraff* (1936) (MGM).

McCall), Sam McDaniel (*Porter*), Joe Phillips, William Newell, Edward Peil, Sr., Harry Cording, Lee Phelps, Harry C. Bradley, Frank Darien and sixth-billed MR as Jimmy, the kid brother of waterfront belle Harlow and Merkel. The former becomes involved in a fisherman's strike led by Tracy against tuna king Calleia.

The New York Times said of this film: "When it is content to be a robust comedy of bad manners, *Riffraff* is a free-wheeling vehicle for the amusing talents of the illustrious Jean Harlow, the toast of the tuna fleet, the belle of the waterfront, and Miss Hook and Ladder Company No. 7." Clark Gable and Gloria Swanson initially were announced as the leads, though it's hard to picture the latter age-wise in the Harlow role.

32. Little Lord Fauntleroy, Selznick International/United Artists, 1936

Director: John Cromwell; *Screenplay:* Hugh Walpole, based on the 1886 novel by Frances Hodgson Burnett.

Cast: Freddie Bartholomew (*Ceddie Errol*), Dolores Costello Barrymore (*"Dearest" [Mrs. Errol]*), C. Aubrey Smith (*Earl of Dorincourt*), Guy Kibbee (*Mr. Hobbs*), Henry Stephenson (*Havisham*), Constance Collier (*Lady Lorridaile*), E.E. Clive (*Sir Harry Lorridaile*), Una O'Connor (*Mary*), Jackie Searl (*Tom*), Jessie Ralph (*The Applewoman*), Ivan Simpson (*Reverend Mordaunt*), Helen Flint (*Minna*), Eric Alden (*Ben*), May Beatty (*Mrs. Mellon*), Virginia Field (*Miss Herbert*), Reginald Barlow (*Newick*), Lionel Belmore (*Higgins*), Tempe Pigott (*Mrs. Dibble*), Gilbert Emery (*Purvis*), Lawrence Grant (*Lord Chief Justice*), Walter Kingsford (*Mr. Sande*), Eily Malyon (*Landlady*), Fred Walton (*Landlord*), Montague Shaw (*Mr. Semple*), Robert Emmett O'Connor, Elsa Buchanan, Mary Gordon, Dickie Jones, Alec Craig, Daisy Belmore, Joseph Tozer, Jack Cameron and sixth-billed MR as Brooklyn bootblack Dick, Bartholomew and Kibbee's friend. This was Selznick's first independent production after leaving MGM, run by his father-in-law, Louis B. Mayer. There had been earlier versions of the film: a British one in 1914 starring Gerald Royston and Jane Wells, and the famed Mary Pickford one in 1921.

33. The Devil Is a Sissy (aka The Devil Takes the Count), MGM, 1936

Director: W.S. Van Dyke; *Screenplay:* John Lee Mahin and Richard Schayer, from a story by Rowland Brown.

Cast: Freddie Bartholomew (*Claude Pierce*), Jackie Cooper (*"Buck" Murphy*), Ian Hunter (*Jay Pierce*), Peggy Conklin (*Rose Hawley*), Katherine Alexander (*Hilda Pierce*), Gene Lockhart (*Mr. Murphy*), Kathleen Lockhart (*Mrs. Murphy*), Jonathan Hale (*Judge Holmes*), Etienne Girardot (*Principal Crusenberry*), Sherwood Bailey (*"Bugs"*), Buster Slavin (*"Six Toes"*), Grant Mitchell (*Paul Krump*), Harold Huber (*Willie*), Frank Puglia (*"Grandma"*), Stanley Fields (*Joe*), Etta McDaniel (*Molly*), Dorothy Peterson (*Jennie Stevens*), Charles Coleman (*Doorman*), Ian Wolfe, Rollo Lloyd (*Pawnbrokers*), Stanley Andrews (*Doctor*), Jason Robards [Sr.] (*Kraus*), Mary Doran (*Mrs. Robbins*), Andrew Tombes (*Mr. Muldoon*) and third-billed MR as junior tough guy "Gig" Stevens, whose dad is about to go the electric chair for murder, and, with surly pal Cooper, cons young English lad Bartholomew, who has come to school in America, into falling in with them.

The critic for *The New York Times* found of Rooney: "His is, without question, one of the finest performances of the year." Arthur Freed and Nacio Herb Brown wrote the song "Say Ah!" for the film.

34. Down the Stretch, Warner Bros.–First National, 1936

Director: William Clemens; Story and *Screenplay:* William Jacobs.

Cast: Patricia Ellis (*Patricia Barrington*), Dennis Moore (*Cliff Barrington*), Willie Best (*Noah*), Gordon Hart (*Judge Adams*), Gordon Elliott (*Robert Bates*), Virginia Brissac (*Aunt Julia*), Charles Wilson (*Tex Reardon*), Joseph Crehan (*Secretary Burch*), Mary Treen (*Nurse*), Robert Emmett Keane (*Nick*), Charles Foy (*Arnold Roach*), Crawford Kent (*Sir Oliver*), Edward Keane (*Fred Yates*), Raymond Brown (*Col. Carter*), Andre Beranger (*Cooper*), Ferdinand Schumann-Heink (*Clerk*), Frank Faylen (*Ben the Bookie*), Jimmy Eagles (*Sunny Burnett*), Tom Wilson (*Officer*), Emmett Vogan (*Lawyer*), Billy McClain (*Uncle Lew*), Milton Kibbee (*Veteran*), Ralph Dunn (*Starter*) and second-billed MR as Snapper Sinclair, a jockey who has come out of the reformatory and becomes the ward of horsewoman Ellis out of pity because his dad rode her dad's mounts and became involved in his racing scandal. Original title: *Blood Lines.*

35. A Family Affair, MGM, 1937

Director: George B. Seitz; *Screenplay:* Kay Van Riper, based on the 1928 play *Skidding* by Aurania Rouverol.

Cast: Lionel Barrymore (*Judge James K. Hardy*), Cecilia Parker (*Marian Hardy*), Eric Linden (*Wayne Trent III*), Charley Grapewin (*Frank Redmond*), Spring Byington (*Mrs. Emily Hardy*), Julie Haydon (*Joan Hardy Martin*), Sara Haden (*Aunt Milly*), Allen Vincent (*Bill Martin*), Margaret Marquis (*Polly Benedict*), Selmer Jackson (*Hoyt Wells*), Harlan Briggs (*Oscar Stubbins*), Robert Emmett Keane (*J. Carroll Nichols*), William Soderling (*Adams*), Erville Alderson (*Dave*), O.G. "Dutch" Hendrian (*Delegate*), Virginia Sale (*Social News Editor*), George Chandler (*Waiter*), Arthur Housman (*Drunk*), Sam McDaniel (*Chauffeur*) and fourth-billed MR as Andy Hardy for the first time. In this "B" film, his dad Judge Hardy (Barrymore) faces election woes after signing an order halting an aqueduct that would be a boon to the county.

Lionel Barrymore and Spring Byington (replacing the initially cast Janet Beecher) were Andy's parents, succeeded in the next Hardy entry by Lewis Stone and Fay Holden. Margaret Marquis played Andy's girl friend Polly Benedict, replaced in the many remaining films in the subsequent series by Ann Rutherford. Richard Thorpe initially was scheduled to direct.

Frank Nugent, critic for *The New York Times*, wrote, "Mickey Rooney is the epitome of all 14-year-olds who hate girls until they see a pretty one in a party dress."

36. Captains Courageous, MGM, 1937

Director: Victor Fleming; *Screenplay:* John Lee Mahin, Marc Connelly and Dale Van Every, based on the 1897 novel by Rudyard Kipling.

Cast: Freddie Bartholomew (*Harvey Cheyne*), Spencer Tracy (*Manuel*), Lionel Barrymore (*Capt. Disko Troop*), Melvyn Douglas (*Mr. Cheyne*), Charley Grapewin (*Uncle Salters*), John Carradine (*"Long Jack"*), Jack LaRue (*Priest*), Oscar O'Shea (*Cushman*), Walter Kingsford (*Dr. Finley*), Donald Briggs (*Tyler*), Sam McDaniel (*"Doc"*), Leo G. Carroll (*Burns*), Billy Burrud (*Charles*), Billy Gilbert (*Soda Jerk*), Charles Trowbridge (*Dr. Walsh*), Roger Gray (*Nate Rogers*), Jimmy Conlin (*Martin*), Christian Rub (*Old Clement*), Dave Thursby (*Tom*), Katherine Kenworth

(*Mrs. Disko*), Frank Sully (*Taxi driver*), Bobby Watson (*Reporter*), Lloyd Ingraham, Edward Peil, Sr., Charles Coleman, Murray Kinnell, Lester Dorr, Wade Boteler, Myra Marsh, Gene Reynolds, Monte Vandergrift, Herman Ainsley, Myra McKinney and sixth-billed MR as Dan Troop, pal of spoiled rich kid Bartholomew, who learns something about life from Portuguese fisherman Tracy (in his first of two consecutive Oscar-winning roles) on a whaling schooner. Original songs composed by Franz Waxman (who wrote the film's stirring score) and Gus Kahn. The movie was Oscar-nominated as Best Picture of the Year, with another nomination going to the screenwriters.

37. Slave Ship, 20th Century–Fox, 1937

Director: Tay Garnett; *Screenplay:* Sam Hellman, Lamar Trotti and Gladys Lehman, from the story by William Faulkner, based on the 1933 novel *The Last Slaver* by George S. King.

  Cast: Warner Baxter (*Jim Lovett*), Wallace Beery (*Jack Thompson*), Elizabeth Allen (*Nancy Marlowe*), George Sanders (*Lefty*), Jane Darwell (*Mrs. Marlowe*), Joseph Schildkraut (*Danelo*), Miles Mander (*Corey*), Arthur Hohl (*Grimes*), Douglas Scott (*Boy*), Minna Gombell (*Mabel*), Billy Bevan (*Atkins*), Francis Ford (*Scraps*), J. Farrell MacDonald (*Proprietor*), Jane Jones (*Ma Belcher*), Paul Hurst (*Drunk*), Dorothy Christy (*Blonde*), Charles Middleton (*Slave Dealer*), Holmes Herbert, Dewey Robinson, DeWitt Jennings, Arthur Aylesworth, Scotty Beckett, Stymie Beard, Tom Kennedy, Anita Brown, Eddie Dunn, John Burton, Lionel Pape, Lon Chaney, Jr., Russ Clark, Fred Kelsey and fourth-billed MR as Swifty, cabin boy on a slave ship whose captain (Baxter) falls for a woman, abandons the ivory trade and faces mutiny.

  John Ford and then Howard Hawks were initially scheduled to direct. Peter Lorre had been signed to play the part ultimately played by Joseph Schildkraut. In his autobiography, director Tay Garnett wrote that Clark Gable was to costar with Beery and Rooney, but MGM would not let Gable go.

  The New York Times' Frank S. Nugent described Mickey's character "a terrible-tempered cabin boy, a sort of Donald Duck with a retroussé nose."

38. Hoosier Schoolboy, Monogram, 1937

Director: William Nigh; *Screenplay:* Robert Lee Johnson, based on the 1883 novel by Edward Eggleston.

  Cast: Anne Nagel (*Mary Evans*), Frank Shields (the famed tennis star) (*Jack Matthews*), Edward Pawley (*Capt. Carter*), William Gould (*John Matthews, Sr.*), Dorothy Vaughan (*Miss Hodges*), Harry Hayden (*Mr. Townsend*), Helena Grant (*Vilma Rose*), Bradley Metcalf (*Roger Townsend*), Doris Rankin (*Millicent*), Maude Philby (*Mrs. Townsend*), Walter Long, Mary Field, Cecil Weston, Fred Kelsey, Zita Moulton, Anita Deniston and first-billed (alone above the title) MR as Shockey Carter, a farm boy ridiculed for his loyalty to his alcoholic, shell-shocked dad (Pawley). He is helped by pretty teacher Nagel, who gets the old man a job driving a milk truck, and then is adopted by her when her own dad is killed during a milk strike.

  Reviewing the film on its New York premiere at the Brooklyn Paramount, *The New York American* wrote: "Bobbing and weaving in and out of scenes, but mostly in, is Mickey Rooney, who is excellent as always." When reissued in 1941 to cash in on Rooney's celebrity as the No. 1 star on the screen, this movie was retitled *Forgotten Hero.*

39. Live, Love and Learn, MGM, 1937

Director: George Fitzmaurice; *Screenplay:* Charles Brackett, Cyril Hume and Richard Maibaum, from a story by Marion Parsonnet.

Cast: Robert Montgomery (*Bob Graham*), Rosalind Russell (*Julie Stoddard*), Robert Benchley (*Oscar*), Helen Vinson (*Lily Chalmers*), Monty Woolley [screen debut] (*Mr. Charles C. Bawtitude*), E.E. Clive (*Mr. Palmiston*), Charles Judels (*Pedro Filipe*), Maude Eburne (*Mrs. Crump*), Harlan Briggs (*Justice of the Peace*), June Clayworth (*Mrs. Annabella Post*), Barnett Parker (*Alfredo*), Al Shean (*Prof. Fraum*), Ann Rutherford (*Class President*), Billy Gilbert (*Newsboy*), Winifred Harris (*Mrs. Colfax-Baxter*), Dorothy Appleby (*Lou*), James Flavin, Jack Pennick, Russ Clark, Frank Sully, George Cooper, John Quillan, Chester Clute, Wilbur Mack, Frank Marlowe, Robert Emmett Keane, Minerva Urecal, Zeffie Tilbury, Maxine Elliott Hicks, Virginia Sale and seventh-billed MR as Jerry Crump, a pesky neighborhood kid in this romantic comedy. MR keeps bothering struggling artist Montgomery at work, after the latter has wed wealth-weary heiress Russell, who finds herself back on the Park Avenue she desperately wanted to escape when hubby hits the big time though the aid of society matron Vinson.

40. Thoroughbreds Don't Cry, MGM, 1937

Director: Alfred E. Green; *Screenplay:* Lawrence Hazard, from a story by Eleanore Griffin and J. Walter Rubin.

Cast: Judy Garland (*Cricket West*), Ronald Sinclair (*Roger Calverton*), C. Aubrey Smith (*Sir Peter Calverton*), Sophie Tucker (*Mother Ralph*), Forrester Harvey (*Wilkins*), Charles D. Brown (*"Click" Donovan*), Frankie Darro (*"Dink" Reid*), Henry Kolker (*Doc Godfrey*), Helen Troy (*Hilda*), Elisha Cook, Jr. (*Boots Maguire*), Francis X. Bushman, Pierre Watkin (*Racing Stewards*), James Flavin (*Timmie's Agent*), Marie Blake (*Operator*), George Chandler (*Usher*), Jack Norton (*Man with Monocle*), Edgar Dearing (*Policeman*) and second-billed MR (with Judy Garland in their first film together) as jockey Timmie Donovan, recruited by proper English sportsman Smith to ride his champion mount, and then bribed by his own dad (Brown) to throw the race. Judy plays Cricket West, niece of the owner of the racetrack boarding house (Sophie Tucker).

Smith and Tucker replaced the originally cast Lewis Stone and Edna May Oliver. Freddie Bartholomew initially was scheduled to play the role taken here by Ronald Sinclair.

"Little Mr. Rooney, as the jock, manages to streak with a brilliant performance which lends a certain quality to the whole picture," *The New York Times* reported. Arthur Freed and Nacio Herb Brown wrote "Got a Pair of New Shoes" for Judy.

41. You're Only Young Once, MGM, 1938

Director: George B. Seitz; *Screenplay:* Kay Van Riper, based on characters created by Aurania Rouverol.

Cast: Lewis Stone (*Judge Hardy*), Cecilia Parker (*Marian Hardy*), Fay Holden (*Mrs. Emily Hardy*), Frank Craven (*Frank Redman*), Ann Rutherford (*Polly Benedict*), Sara Haden (*Aunt Milly*), Eleanor Lynn (*Geraldine Lane*), Ted Pearson (*Bill*

The Hardy family: Fay Holden (seated), Cecilia Parker (rear left), Lewis Stone, Sara Haden, and Rooney in *You're Only Young Once* (1938) (MGM).

Rand), Charles Judels (*Capt. Swenson*), Selmer Jackson (*Hoyt Wells*), Ruth Hart (*Mary*), Mary Gordon (*Mary's Mother*), Oscar O'Shea (*Sheriff*), Norman Phillips, Jr., Jack Baxley, Garry Owen, Phillip Terry, Dick Webster, Wilson Benge and third-billed MR as Andrew Hardy—as the credits indicated, joining his (new) family on a fishing vacation in Santa Catalina. He and his older sister each find a summer romance, while the Judge is preoccupied with a financial question. Stone, Holden and Rutherford came aboard here as the regular cast, along with Parker and Holden. Originally this was to have been titled *A Family Vacation*.

42. Love Is a Headache, MGM, 1938

Director: Richard Thorpe; *Screenplay:* Marion Parsonnet, Harry Ruskin and William R. Lipman, suggested by a story by Lou Heifetz and Herbert Klein.

Cast: Gladys George (*Carlotta "Charlie" Lee*), Franchot Tone (*Peter Lawrence*), Ted Healy (*Jimmy Slattery*), Frank Jenks (*Joe Cannon*), Ralph Morgan (*Reggie O'Dell*), Virginia Weidler (*Jake O'Toole*), Jessie Ralph (*Sheriff Janet Winfield*), Fay Holden (*Mary, Peter's Secretary*), Barnett Parker (*Hotchkiss, Carlotta's Butler*), Julius Tannen (*Mr. Hillier*), Henry Kolker (*Sam Ellinger*), Oscar O'Shea (*Pop Sheeman*), Sarah Edwards (*Mrs. Warden*), Ernie Alexander (*Reporter Johnson*), Robert Middlemass (*Police Commissioner*), Marie Blake (*Hillier's secretary*), Chester Clute,

Phillip Terry, Jack Norton, June Brewster, Leigh De Lacey, Edgar Dearing, Don Brodie. Howard Hickman and fourth-billed MR, playing young Mike O'Toole, an orphaned waif who, with sister Weidler, is adopted by Broadway star George as a publicity stunt and is defended in her "kidnapping" by her boyfriend, society columnist Tone.

The critic for *The New York Times* felt: "[Rooney's] comic sense is so perfect, his characterization so sure that every time he flashes on the screen, the magnificent tad had the floor [and] whatever breath of life there is in *Love Is a Headache* must be attributed to Mickey (Himself) Rooney."

43. Judge Hardy's Children, MGM, 1938

Director: George B. Seitz; *Screenplay:* Kay Van Riper, based on characters created by Aurania Rouverol.

Cast: Lewis Stone (*Judge Hardy*), Cecilia Parker (*Marian Hardy*), Fay Holden (*Mrs. Emily Hardy*), Ann Rutherford (*Polly Benedict*), Ruth Hussey (*Margaret Lee*), Betty Ross Clarke (*Aunt Milly*), Jacqueline Laurent (*Suzanne Cortrot*), Robert Whitney (*Wayne Trenton*), Jonathan Hale (*John Lee*), Janet Beecher (*Miss Budge*), Leonard Penn (*Steve Prentice*), Sarah Edwards (*Miss Adams*), Erville Alderson (*Deputy Sheriff*), Boyd Crawford (*Radio Announcer*), Don Douglas (*J.O. Harper*), Charles Peck (*Tommy MacMahon*), George Revanent (*Monsigneur Cortot*), Edward Earle (*Penniwill*) and second-billed MR as Andy Hardy, in Washington with his family where the Judge is serving as chairman of a special committee. MR finds himself succumbing to the charms of a young French mam'selle, while his sister Marian's head is turned by the rich social life.

44. Hold That Kiss, MGM, 1938

Director: Edwin L. Marin. Story and *Screenplay:* Stanley Rauh.

Cast: Maureen O'Sullivan (*Jane Evans*), Dennis O'Keefe (*Tommy Bradford*), George Barbier (*J. Westley Piermont*), Jessie Ralph (*Aunt Lucy McCaffey*), Fay Holden (*Mrs. Evans*), Edward S. Brophy (*Al*), Frank Albertson (*Steve Evans*), Phillip Terry (*Ted Evans*), Ruth Hussey (*Nadine Piermont*), Barnett Parker (*Maurice*), Jack Norton (*Mallory*), Edgar Dearing, Monte Vandergrift (*Policemen*), Morgan Wallace (*Mr. Wood*), Tully Marshall (*Mr. Lazarus*), Charles Judels (*Otto Schmidt*), Evelyn Beresford (*Mrs. Townley*), Ernie Alexander (*Maurice's Chauffeur*), Oscar O'Shea (*Pop*), Betty Blythe, Betty Ross Clarke, William Benedict, Forbes Murray, Eric Wilton, Leonard Carey, Ben Taggart, Buddy Messinger and third-billed MR as the young brother of working model O'Sullivan, who is pretending to be a debutante to impress travel agency clerk O'Keefe — who is pretending to be rich to impress *her!*

45. Lord Jeff, MGM, 1938

Director: Sam Wood; *Screenplay:* James Kevin McGuinness, from a story by Bradford Ropes, Val Burton and Endre Bohem.

Cast: Freddie Bartholomew (*Geoffrey "Lord Jeff" Braemer*), Charles Coburn (*Capt. Briggs*), Herbert Mundin (*"Crusty" Jelks*), Terry Kilburn (*Albert Baker*), Gale Sondergaard (*Doris Clandon*), Peter Lawford (*Benny Potter*), Walter Tetley (*Tommy Thrums*), Peter Ellis (*Ned Saunders*), George Zucco (*Jim Hamstead*), Matthew Boulton (*Inspector Scott*), John Burton (*John Cartwright*), Emma Dunn

(*Mrs. Briggs*), Monty Woolley (*Jeweler*), Gilbert Emery (*Magistrate*), Walter Kingsford (*Superintendent*), Rex Evans (*Commissionaire*), Charles Coleman (*Hotel Clerk*), May Beatty (*Mrs. Frimley*), C. Montague Shaw, Winifred Harris, Doris Lloyd, Charles Irwin, Wilson Benge, Olaf Hytten, Evan Thomas, Eric Wilton and second-billed MR playing Terry O'Mulvaney, an Irish-brogued mate, covering for an American delinquent and spoiled brat (Bartholomew) who goes to an English naval training school, rebels and runs away.

Although this was Bartholomew's picture, it was MR's jaunty photo that accompanied *The New York Times'* review when the film opened at the Capitol Theatre on Broadway. Critic Frank S. Nugent observed: "Against Lord Jeff's precise English, we have the fine Irish brogue of Mickey (Himself) Rooney, the thistle burr Scots of Terry Kilburn, and the rasping cockney of Peter Lawford."

46. Love Finds Andy Hardy, MGM, 1938

Director: George B. Seitz; *Screenplay:* William Ludwig, from a story by Vivien R. Bretherton, based on characters created by Aurania Rouverol.

Cast: Lewis Stone (*Judge Hardy*), Cecilia Parker (*Marian Hardy*), Fay Holden (*Mrs. Emily Hardy*), Judy Garland (*Betsy Booth*), Lana Turner (*Cynthia Potter*), Ann Rutherford (*Polly Benedict*), Betty Ross Clarke (*Aunt Milly*), Mary Howard (*Mrs. Mary Tompkins*). Gene Reynolds (*Jimmy MacMahon*), Don Castle (*Dennis Hunt*), Marie Blake (*Augusta*), George Breakston (*"Beezy"*), Raymond Hatton (*Peter Dugan*), Frank Darien (*Barnes*), Rand Brooks (*Young Man on Bandstand*), Erville Alderson (*Court Attendant*) and second-billed MR as Andy Hardy, looking for the final eight dollars he needs to purchase a jalopy in time for the Christmas dance at Carvel High and then finding a date when regular girlfriend Polly Benedict (Rutherford) goes out of town to visit her grandmother. He zeroes in on girl-next-door Betsy Booth (Judy Garland) after considering beauty Cynthia Potter (Lana Turner).

Despite Judy having received top billing ahead of MR only a year earlier in *Thoroughbreds Don't Cry*, she was credited fifth here, just ahead of up-and-coming starlet Turner. The film's title card reads "Metro-Goldwyn-Mayer Presents Judge Hardy's Family in *Love Finds Andy Hardy.*" Judy sang a pair of original songs by Mack Gordon and Harry Revel: "Meet the Beat of My Heart" and "It Never Rains but It Pours," and one by Roger Edens, "In Between." Her renditions of Cole Porter's "Easy to Love" and the novelty "Bei Mir Bist Du Shoen" were cut before the film's release.

"Based on her showing," *Variety* wrote, "they will have to find a permanent place for Miss Garland in future Hardys." (Her very next screen appearance would be in *The Wizard of Oz*.)

47. Boys Town, MGM, 1938

Director: Norman Taurog; *Screenplay:* Dore Schary and John Meehan, from an original story by Eleanore Griffin and Schary.

Cast: Spencer Tracy (*Father Edward Flanagan*), Henry Hull (*Dave Morris*), Leslie Fenton (*Dan Farrow*), Gene Reynolds (*Tony Ponessa*), Edward Norris (*Joe Marsh*), Addison Richards (*The Judge*), Minor Watson (*The Bishop*), Jonathan Hale (*John Hargraves*), Bobs Watson (*Pee Wee*), Martin Spellman (*Skinny*), Mickey Rentschler (*Tommy Anderson*), Frankie Thomas [MGM's initial choice to play Andy Hardy]

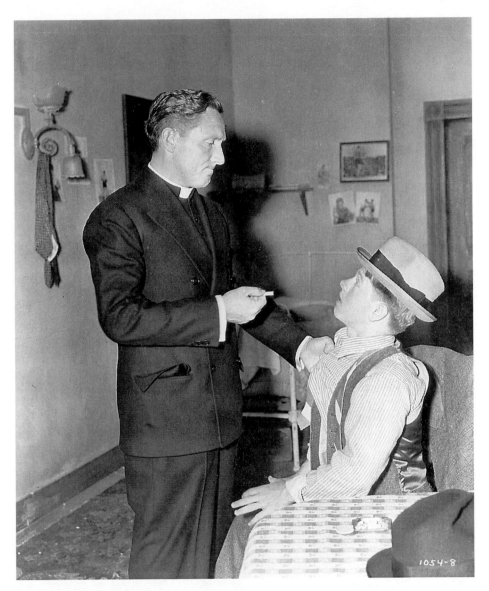

With Spencer Tracy in *Boys Town* (1938) (MGM).

(*Freddy Fuller*), Jimmy Butler (*Paul Ferguson*), Sidney Miller (*Mo Kahn*), Robert Emmett Keane (*Burton*), Victor Kilian (*The Sheriff*), John Hamilton (*The Warden*), Murray Harris, Jay Novello, Tom Noonan, Al Hill, Stanley Blystone, Phillip Terry, Helen Dickson, Nell Craig, Arthur Aylesworth, Kane Richmond, Donald Haines, Ronald Paige, Edward Hearn, Boys Town A Capella Choir, St. Luke's Choristers and second-billed MR playing cocky street kid Whitey Marsh who is sent swaggering to the famed Nebraska city for wayward boys and falls under the influence of Father Flanagan (Tracy, in his second consecutive Oscar-winning role).

"Father Flanagan's Boys Town," critic Frank Nugent wrote in *The New York Times*, "probably never had such a tough little mugg on its guest list as Mickey (Himself) Rooney, who plays Juvenile Delinquent #1.... Mickey is the Dead End gang rolled into one. He's Jimmy Cagney, Humphrey Bogart and King Kong before they grew up or knew a restraining hand.... [His] descent upon Boys Town is frightening to behold ... a pack of butts in his left-hand pocket, a deck of cards in his right, a Tenth Avenue homburg cocked over one ear, and his mind made up to blow up the joint." Tracy and Rooney later would costar in the film's sequel, *Men of Boys Town.*

48. Stablemates, MGM, 1938

Director: Sam Wood; *Screenplay:* Leonard Praskins and Richard Maibaum, from a story by William Thiele and Reginald Owen.

Cast: Wallace Beery (*Tom Terry*), Arthur Hohl (*Mr. Gale*), Margaret Hamilton (*Beulah Flanders*), Minor Watson (*Barney Donovan*), Marjorie Gateson (*Mrs. Shepherd*), Oscar O'Shea (*Pete Whalen*), Sam McDaniel (*Black Bookie*), Frank Hagney (*Poolroom Owner*), Cliff Nazarro (*Himself*), Johnnie Morris, James C. Norton,

With Wallace Beery in *Stablemates* (1938) (MGM).

Spencer Charters, Stanley Andrews, Al Herman, Charles Dunbar and second-billed MR as Mickey, a homeless jockey who becomes pals with down-and-out veterinarian-turned-racetrack tout Beery and talks him into operating on the foot of a prospective race winner.

The New York Times' B.R. Crisler praised "good old Wally, scratching himself and yawning, and Mickey (the boy Bernhardt) turning on the tears, the laughs, the hysterics, at will, like the perfect little screen virtuoso he is." (Judy Garland initially had been assigned to this film.)

49. Out West with the Hardys, MGM, 1938

Director: George B. Seitz; *Screenplay:* Kay Van Riper, William Ludwig and Agnes Christine Johnston, based on characters created by Aurania Rouverol.

Cast: Lewis Stone (*Judge Hardy*), Cecilia Parker (*Marian Hardy*), Fay Holden (*Mrs. Emily Hardy*), Ann Rutherford (*Polly Benedict*), Sara Haden (*Aunt Milly*), Don Castle (*Dennis Hunt*), Virginia Weidler (*"Jake" Holt*), Gordon Jones (*Ray Holt*), Ralph Morgan (*Bill Northcote*), Nana Bryant (*Dora Northcote*), Tom Brown (*Aldrich Brown*), Thurston Hall (*H.R. Bruxton*), Anthony Allan (*Cliff Thomas*), Mary Colcord (*Mrs. Foster*), George Douglas (*Mr. Carter*), Erville Alderson (*Deputy*), Mary Bovard, Marilyn Stuart, Joe Dominguez, Charles Grove, Eddy Waller and second-billed MR as Andy Hardy, vacationing with his family on an Arizona ranch owned by the Judge's childhood sweetheart (Bryant), who has asked him to help save the place from creditors.

50. The Adventures of Huckleberry Finn, MGM, 1939

Director: Richard Thorpe; *Screenplay:* Hugo Butler, based on the 1884 novel by Mark Twain.

Cast: Walter Connolly (*The King*), William Frawley (*The Duke*), Rex Ingram (*Jim*), Lynne Carver (*Mary Jane*), Jo Ann Sayers (*Susan*), Minor Watson (*Capt. Brandy*), Elisabeth Risdon (*Widow Douglas*), Victor Kilian (*Pap Finn*), Clara Blandick (*Miss Watson*), Anne O'Neal (*Miss Bartlett*), Harlan Briggs (*Mr. Bucker*), Sarah Edwards (*Mrs. Bucker*), Janice Chambers (*Mary Adams*), Harry Watson (*Ben Donaldson*), Billy Watson (*Eliot*), Delmar Watson (*Joe*), Wade Boteler (*Captain*), Irving Bacon (*Tad*), Robert Emmett Keane (*Lawyer*), Roger Imhof (*Judge*), Arthur Aylesworth (*Riverboat Pilot*), Erville Alderson (*Sheriff*), E. Alyn Warren (*Mr. Shackleford*), Nora Cecil (*Mrs. Shackleford*), Mickey Rentschler (*Harry*), Jessie Graves, Leni Lynn, Johnny Walsh, Frank Darien, Sarah Padden, Harry Cording, Roger Gray, Edwin J. Brady, and top-billed MR as Huck Finn. This was the first time Rooney got top billing at MGM.

51. The Hardys Ride High, MGM, 1939

Director: George B. Seitz; *Screenplay:* Kay Van Riper, William Ludwig and Agnes Christine Johnston, based on characters created by Aurania Rouverol.

Cast: Lewis Stone (*Judge Hardy*), Cecilia Parker (*Marian Hardy*), Fay Holden (*Mrs. Emily Hardy*), Ann Rutherford (*Polly Benedict*), Sara Haden (*Aunt Milly*), Virginia Grey (*Consuela McNeish*), Minor Watson (*Mr. Archer*), Marsha Hunt (*Susan Bowen*), John King (*Philip Westcott*), John T. Murray (*Don Davis*), Don Castle (*Dennis Hunt*), Halliwell Hobbes (*Dobbs*), George Irving (*Mr. Bronell*), Aileen Pringle (*Miss Booth*), Donald Briggs (*Caleb Bowen*), William Orr (*Dick Bannersly*),

As Huckleberry Finn (MGM).

Truman Bradley (*Jewelry Clerk*), Erville Alderson (*Bailiff*), Mary Tanner (*Desk Clerk*), Ann Morriss (*Rosamond*), Hale Hamilton (*Mr. Archer*), Frances McInerney (*Hatcheck Girl*) and second-billed MR as Andy Hardy, who finds life in Carvel altered when the Judge is informed — erroneously, it turns out — that he is heir apparent to a fortune that has come down from an ancestor who fought in the War of 1812.

52. Andy Hardy Gets Spring Fever, MGM, 1939

Director: W.S. Van Dyke II; *Screenplay:* Kay Van Riper, based on characters created by Aurania Rouverol.

Cast: Lewis Stone (*Judge Hardy*), Cecilia Parker (*Marian Hardy*), Fay Holden (*Mrs. Emily Hardy*), Ann Rutherford (*Polly Benedict*), Sara Haden (*Aunt Milly*), Helen Gilbert (*Rose Meredith*), Terry Kilburn (*"Stickin' Plaster"*), John T. Murray (*Don Davis*), George Breakston (*"Beezy"*), Charles Peck (*Tommy*), Sidney Miller (*Sidney*), Addison Richards (*Mr. Benedict*), Olaf Hytten (*Mr. Higginbotham*), Erville Alderson (*Bailiff*), Robert Kent (*Ensign Charles Copley*), Stanley Andrews (*James Willis*), Byron Foulger (*Mark Hansen*), James Bush (*Bill Franklin*), Harry Hayden (*Mr. McMahon*), John Dilson (*Mr. Davis*), Barbara Bedford (*Miss Howard*), Arthur Gardner, Mitchell Lewis, Ivan Miller, Ralph Romley, Mildred Coles, Arthur Belasco, Gerald Pierce, Mary Bovard and first-billed MR as Andy Hardy, here being dumped — temporarily — by girlfriend Polly Benedict, falling in puppy love with his young high school drama teacher (Gilbert), and becoming involved with the class play — which he wrote. It takes all the Judge's wisdom to bring him back to earth.

53. Babes in Arms, MGM, 1939

Director: Busby Berkeley (also choreographer); *Screenplay:* Kay Van Riper and Jack McGowan, from the 1937 musical by Richard Rodgers and Lorenz Hart.

Cast: Judy Garland (*Patsy Barton*), Charles Winninger (*Joe Moran*), Guy Kibbee (*Judge John Black*), June Preisser (*Rosalie Essex*), Grace Hayes (*Florrie Moran*), Betty Jaynes (*Molly Moran*), Douglas McPhail (*Don Brice*), Rand Brooks (*Jeff Steele*), Leni Lynn (*Dody Martin*), John Sheffield (*Bobs*), Henry Hull (*Harry Maddox*), Barnett Parker (*William Bartlett*), Ann Shoemaker (*Mrs. Lillian Barton*), Margaret Hamilton (*Martha Steele*), Joseph Crehan (*Mr. Essex*), George McKay (*Brice*), Henry Roquemore (*Shaw*), Charles D. Brown (*Larry Randall*), Robert Emmett Keane (*Booking Agent*), Lon McAllister (*Lon*), Lelah Tyler (*Mrs. Brice*), Sidney Miller (*Sid*), Mary Treen (*Maddox Secretary*), Frank Darien, Joe Caits, Cyril Ring, Charles Smith, Leonard Sues, Libby Taylor and top-billed MR as Mickey Moran, son of vaudevillian troupers Winninger and Hayes and a would-be songwriter-producer who stages a backyard musical with Garland that ends up on Broadway.

Rooney received an Oscar nomination as Best Actor. With the exception of "Where or When," "The Lady Is a Tramp" and the title song, Rodgers and Hart's original score was dumped in favor of tunes by Arthur Freed (whose legendary producing career began with this film), Nacio Herb Brown, Harold Arlen and E.Y. Harburg. Mickey sings "Ida, Sweet as Apple Cider" and, with Judy, performs "Good Morning," "Oh! Susannah," "I'm Just Wild About Harry" and the famed Minstrel routine (in blackface), written by Roger Edens. There's also a Rooney spoof of FDR in the patriotic finale number called "God's Country," composed by Arlen and Harburg, who'd previously written the score to *The Wizard of Oz*.

54. Judge Hardy and Son, MGM, 1940

Director: George B. Seitz; *Screenplay:* Carey Wilson, based on characters created by Aurania Rouverol.

Cast: Lewis Stone (*Judge Hardy*), Cecilia Parker (*Marian Hardy*), Fay Holden

Out on the town with his mom, Nell Pankey, in 1941 (ACME/UPI).

(*Mrs. Emily Hardy*), Ann Rutherford (*Polly Benedict*), Sara Haden (*Aunt Milly*), June Preisser (*Euphrasia Clark*), Maria Ouspenskaya (*Mrs. Judith Volduzzi*), Henry Hull (*Dr. Jones*), Martha O'Driscoll (*Elvie Horton*), Leona Maricle (*Mrs. Horton*), Margaret Early (*Clarabelle Lee*), George Breakston (*"Beezy"*), Egon Brecher (*Anton Volduzzi*), Edna Holland (*Nurse Trowbridge*), Marie Blake (*Augusta*), Milton Parsons

With his dad, Joe Yule, in *Judge Hardy and Son* (1940) (MGM).

(*Florist*), Joe Yule (*Munk, the Tire Man*), William Tannen (*Officer*), Ernie Alexander (*Court Clerk*) Erville Alderson (*Bailiff*), Jack Mulhall (*Intern*), Eddie Marr (*Second Clerk*) and second-billed MR as Andy Hardy, growing up a tad in this somewhat lesser series entry dealing with the "senior" problem: The Judge is touched by the plight of an elderly destitute couple in danger of losing their house and agrees to look into their case. Meanwhile, Andy faces another youthful crisis, a desperate need to find money to fix his jalopy in time to take Polly Benedict to the Fourth of July fireworks. Rooney's dad, Joe Yule, has a small role as the local tire man.

55. Young Tom Edison, MGM, 1940

Director: Norman Taurog; *Screenplay:* Bradbury Foote, Hugo Butler and Dore Schary.

Cast: Fay Bainter (*Mrs. Nancy Edison*), George Bancroft (*Samuel Edison*), Virginia Weidler (*Tannie Edison*), Eugene Pallette (*Mr. Nelson*), Victor Kilian (*Mr. Dingle*), Bobby Jordan (*Joe Dingle*), Lloyd Corrigan (*Dr. Pender*), J.M. Kerrigan (*Mr. McCarney*), John Kellogg (*Bill Edison*), Clem Bevans (*Mr. Waddell*), Eily Malyon (*Miss Lavinia Howard*), Harry Shannon (*Capt. Brackett*), Wade Boteler (*Si Weaver*), Joe Whitehead (*Mr. Hodge*), Mickey Rentschler (*Johnny*), Sherwood Bailey (*Red*), Emory Parnell (*Bob*), Harry Strang, Olin Howland, Stanley Blystone, Lee Phelps, Forrest Taylor, Victor Potel, Eddy Chandler, Ernie Adams and top-

As *Young Tom Edison* in 1940 (MGM).

billed MR inventing the light bulb in his basement lab in the title role, playing
Edison as a teenager. (The second part of the film, released shortly thereafter,
starred Spencer Tracy as the adult Edison.)

"It is so much Mickey's show the rest scarcely matters," Frank Nugent wrote in
his *New York Times* review.

56. Andy Hardy Meets Debutante, MGM, 1940

Director: George B. Seitz; *Screenplay:* Thomas Seller and Annalee Whitmore, from a story by Carey Wilson, based on characters created by Aurania Rouverol.

Cast: Lewis Stone (*Judge Hardy*), Cecilia Parker (*Marian Hardy*), Fay Holden (*Mrs. Emily Hardy*), Judy Garland (*Betsy Booth*), Ann Rutherford (*Polly Benedict*), Diana Lewis (*Daphne Fowler*), George Breakston ("*Beezy*"), Sara Haden (*Aunt Milly*), Addison Richards (*Mr. Benedict*), George Lessey (*Underwood*), Cy Kendall (*Mr. Carrillo*), Clyde Wilson (*Francis*), Harry Tyler (*Jordan*), Gladys Blake (*Gertrude*), Tom Neal (*Aldrich Brown*), Edwin Stanley (*Surrogate*), Sam McDaniel (*Porter*), Dutch Hendrian (*Driver*), Lester Dorr (*Photographer*), Marjorie Gateson (*Mrs. Fowler*), Claire DuBrey (*Mrs. Hackett*), Charles Trowbridge, Charles Coleman, Charles Wagenheim, Emmett Vogan, Pat Flaherty, Russell Hicks, Herbert Evans, Arthur Belasco, Forbes Murray and first-billed MR as Andy Hardy, falling for Manhattan socialite Lewis, whose newspaper photo he'd seen. He asks Betsy Booth (Judy Garland) to set up an introduction when he tags along with the Judge to the Big Apple — before returning to tried-and-true sweetheart Polly Benedict. Judy sang Arthur Freed and Nacio Herb Brown's "Alone" and "I'm Nobody's Baby," as well as "All I Do Is Dream of You" and "Buds Won't Bud" (the last two cut from the film).

With Lewis Stone in one of the traditional heart-to-hearts between Andy Hardy and his father, the Judge (MGM).

57. Strike Up the Band, MGM, 1940

Director: Busby Berkeley (also choreographer); *Screenplay:* John Monks, Jr., and Fred Finklehoffe.

Cast: Judy Garland (*Mary Holden*), Paul Whiteman and His Orchestra (*Themselves*), June Preisser (*Barbara Frances Morgan*), William Tracy (*Philip Turner*), Larry Nunn (*Willie Brewster*), Margaret Early (*Annie*), Ann Shoemaker (*Mrs. Connors*), Francis Pierlot (*Mr. Judd*), Virginia Brissac (*Mrs. May Holden*), George Lessey (*Mr. Morgan*), Enid Bennett (*Mrs. Morgan*), Sarah Edwards (*Miss Hodges*), Howard Hickman (*Doctor*), Milton Kibbee (*Mr. Holden*), Helen Jerome Eddy (*Mrs. Brewster*), Virginia Sale (*Music Teacher*), Phil Silvers [film debut] (*Pitchman*), Don Castle (*Charlie*), Earle Hodgins, Harry Harvey, Sidney Miller, Jack Mulhall, Jack Albertson, Charles Smith, Dick Allen, Sherrie Overton, Margaret Seddon, Margaret McWade, Leonard Sues, Henry Roquemore and top-billed MR, as a teenage drummer who turns his high school band into a swing group. With girlfriend Garland as singer, he raises money for the gang to go to Paul Whiteman's Chicago auditions—and of course blows everyone away.

Mickey and Judy do several numbers together, including George and Ira Gershwin's title song, and Judy introduces composer Roger Edens' Oscar-nominated song "Our Love Affair." Hollywood newcomer Vincente Minnelli staged Judy's dance routines, brought by producer Arthur Freed from New York where he'd been designing Radio City Music Hall's stage presentations from that venerable palace's beginnings.

58. Andy Hardy's Private Secretary, MGM, 1941

Director: George B. Seitz; *Screenplay:* Jane Murtin and Harry Ruskin, from a story by Katherine Brush, based on characters created by Aurania Rouverol.

Cast: Lewis Stone (*Judge Hardy*), Fay Holden (*Mrs. Emily Hardy*), Ann Rutherford (*Polly Benedict*), Sara Haden (*Aunt Milly*), Kathryn Grayson (*Kathryn Land*), Ian Hunter (*Steven Land*), George Breakston (*"Beezy"*), Todd Karns (*Harry Land*), Addison Richards (*Mr. Benedict*), Margaret Early (*Clarabelle Lee*), Bertha Priestley (*Susan Wiley*), Joseph Crehan (*Peter Dugan*), Lee Phelps (*Barnes*), John Dilson (*Principal Davis*), Frederick Burton (*Governor Spaulding*), Donald Douglas (*J.O. Harper*), Erskine Sanford (*Mr. Bosinny*), Gene Reynolds (*Jimmy MacMahon*), Ken Christy (*Policeman*), Mary Field (*Saleswoman*), Hooper Atchley, Hal K. Dawson, Betty Jane Graham, George Guhl, Charles Smith and first-billed MR as Andy Hardy, now senior class president and treasurer at Carvel High. He innocently accepts a bad check from pretty coed Grayson's dad (Hunter), then proceeds to help him and gives her a job as senior committee secretary and to handle his extracurricular activities. He flunks his English exam and nearly fails to graduate. The Judge sits him down and convinces him that he become too big for his boots..

59. Men of Boys Town, MGM, 1941

Director: Norman Taurog; *Screenplay:* James Kevin McGuinness.

Cast: Spencer Tracy (*Father Edward Flanagan*), Bobs Watson (*Pee Wee*), Larry Nunn (*Ted Martley*), Darryl Hickman (*Flip Brier*), Henry O'Neill (*Mr. Maitland*), Mary Nash (*Mrs. Maitland*), Lee J. Cobb (*Dave Morris*), Anne Revere (*Mrs. Fenely*), Sidney Miller (*Mo Kahn*), Addison Richards (*The Judge*), Lloyd Corrigan (*Roger*

Gorton), George Lessey (*Bradford Stone*), Robert Emmett Keane (*Burton*), Arthur Hohl (*Gate Guard*), Ben Welden (*Superintendent*), Janet Beecher (*Spokeswoman*), Paul Stanton (*Dr. Trem Fellows*), Edwin Stanley (*Dr. Carlton*), Harry Bradley, Byron Shores, Milton Kibbee, John Dilson, Frank Coghlan, Jr., Buddy Pepper, Edward Keane, Edward Earle, Charles Smith, Leonard Sues, Edward Gargan, Aubrey Mather, Wade Boteler, Jack Pennick, John A. Butler, Vondell Darr, William Haade, Sammy McKim, Lew Kelly and second-billed MR, returning to Boys Town as one-time young wiseguy Whitey Marsh, protégé of Father Flanagan (Tracy), who asks him to help out when the city faces bankruptcy. Decades later, Rooney would graduate to the screen role of Father Flanagan.

60. Life Begins for Andy Hardy, MGM, 1941

Director: George B. Seitz; *Screenplay:* Agnes Christine Johnston, based on characters created by Aurania Rouverol.

Cast: Lewis Stone (*Judge Hardy*), Judy Garland (*Betsy Booth*), Fay Holden (*Mrs. Emily Hardy*), Ann Rutherford (*Polly Benedict*), Sara Haden (*Aunt Milly*), Patricia Dane (*Jennitt Hicks*), Ray McDonald (*Jimmy Frobisher*), George Breakston (*"Beezy"*), Pierre Watkin (*Dr. Waggonger*), Frances Morris (*Operator*), Tommy Kelly (*Chuck*), Byron Shores (*Jackson*), Hollis Jewell (*Ted*), Purnell B. Pratt (*Dr.

With Fay Holden (rear), Judy Garland and Ann Rutherford (next to him) at the Hollywood premiere of *Life Begins for Andy Hardy* (1941).

On the MGM lot with Clark Gable, Shirley Temple and Judy Garland in 1941 (UPI).

Storfen), Ralph Byrd (*Dr. Gallagher*), Charlotte Wynters (*Elizabeth Horton*), Lester Matthews (*Mr. Maddox*), Joseph Crehan (*Peter Dugan*), Ann Morriss (*Miss Dean*), Nora Lane (*Miss Howard*), John Eldredge (*Paul McWilliams*), Sidney Miller, Arthur Loft, Duke York, Paul Newlan, James Flavin, Don Brodie, Frank Ferguson, Leonard Sues, Robert Homans, Mira McKinney, Bess Flowers and first-billed MR as Andy

Hardy, spending a month in Manhattan visiting with his "other" girlfriend, Betsy Booth (Garland), following graduation from Carvel High, and getting taken by gold digging telephone operator Dane.

Judy, in her third and final Hardy film, performed four songs initially but none made the cut in the final print. Originally this was to be called *Andy Hardy Goes to College.*

61. Babes on Broadway, MGM, 1941

Director: Busby Berkeley (also choreographer); *Screenplay:* Fred Finklehoffe and Elaine Ryan, from an original story by Finklehoffe.

Cast: Judy Garland (*Penny Morris*), Fay Bainter (*Miss "Jonesy" Jones*), Virginia Weidler (*Barbara Jo Conway*), Ray McDonald (*Ray Lambert*), Richard Quine (*Morton "Hammy" Hammond*), Donald Meek (*Mr. Stone*), Alexander Woollcott (*Himself*), Luis Alberni (*Nick*), James Gleason (*Thornton Reed*), Emma Dunn (*Mrs. Williams*), Frederick Burton (*Theodore Morris*), Cliff Clark (*Inspector Morarity*), William Post, Jr. (*Woollcott's Announcer*), Donna Reed (*Jonesy's Secretary*), Jean Porter (*Jeannie*), Sidney Miller (*Tony*), Dorothy Morris, Lester Dorr, Arthur Hoyt, Anne Rooney, Charles Wagenheim, Roger Steele, Barbara Bedford, Maxine Flores, Tom Hanlon, Bryant Washburn and top-billed MR as Tommy Williams, a member of a song-and-dance-trio (with dancer McDonald and future director Quine). After meeting young singer Garland, he goes on to produce a show for the group. Highlights of the film include Rooney's assorted impersonations, including a turn as Carmen Miranda. He sings the Oscar-nominated song "How About You?" (written by Arthur Freed and Burton Lane) and several others with Judy, and "Yankee Doodle Boy" solo. Ava Gardner had a bit, as did Rooney's dad, Joe Yule, and future MGM star Margaret O'Brien (in her film debut). Shirley Temple initially also was to have been in the cast, but her role was eliminated before production began.

"If all the energy used by Mickey Rooney in making *Babes on Broadway* could be assembled in one place, there would be enough to sustain a flying fortress in the stratosphere from Hollywood to New York and return — nonstop. And there might be some left over," *Variety* wrote. "Rooney is as fresh as the proverbial daisy at the end of two hours of strenuous theatrical calisthenics. He dances, sings, acts, and does imitations— dozens of them."

62. The Courtship of Andy Hardy, MGM, 1942

Director: George B. Seitz; *Screenplay:* Agnes Christine Johnston, based on characters created by Aurania Rouverol.

Cast: Lewis Stone (*Judge Hardy*), Cecilia Parker (*Marian Hardy*), Fay Holden (*Mrs. Emily Hardy*), Ann Rutherford (*Polly Benedict*), Sara Haden (*Aunt Milly*), Donna Reed (*Melodie Nesbit*), William Lundigan (*Jeff Willis*), Frieda Inescort (*Olivia Nesbit*), Stephen Cornell (*Stewart Dwight*), Harvey Stevens (*Roderick O. Nesbit*), Betty Wells (Susie), Joseph Crehan (*Peter Dugan*), George Breakston ("*Beezy*"), Todd Karns (*Harry Land*), Erville Alderson (*Bailiff*), Frank Coghlan, Jr. (*Red*), Lois Collier (*Cynthia*), Barbara Bedford (*Elsa*), Charles Peck (*Tommy*), Jay Ward, Dick Paxton, Floyd Shackelford, Betty-Jean Hainey, John A. Butler, Ken Christy and first-billed MR as Andy Hardy, who, before leaving for college, has a fling with the daughter (Reed) of a couple seeking a divorce through the Judge, but of course ends up with girlfriend Polly Benedict.

63. A Yank at Eton, MGM, 1942

Director: Norman Taurog; *Screenplay:* George Oppenheimer, Lionel Houser and Thomas Phipps, from an original story by Oppenheimer.

Cast: Edmund Gwenn (*Principal Justin*), Ian Hunter (*Roger Carlton*), Freddie Bartholomew (*Peter Carlton*), Marta Linden (*Winifred Dennis Carlton*), Alan Mowbray (*Mr. Duncan*), Juanita Quigley (*Jane "The Runt" Dennis*), Peter Lawford (*Ronnie Kenvil*), Raymond Severn (*Inky Weeld*), Alan Napier (*Restaurateur*), Tina Thayer (*Flossie Sampson*), Minna Phillips (*M'Dame*), Terry Kilburn (*Hilspeth*), Florence Shirley (*Mrs. Sampson*), Byron Shores (*Mr. Brown*), Billy Bevan (*Guide*), Walter Tetley (*Newsboy*), Gregg Barton (*Coach*), Paul Matthews (*Graham*), Aubrey Mather (*Widgeon, the Butler*), Mickey Rentschler (*Student*), Harry Cording, Al Young, Valerie Cole, Paul Scanlon, Herbert Clifton, Cyril Thornton, Charles Irwin, Dick Baron, Charles Stroud and top-billed MR in the title role as, Timothy Dennis, a talented high school football player who gives up his dreams of following his late dad's footsteps by playing at Notre Dame and reluctantly ends up at Eton after his widowed mom (Linden) decides to marry Britisher Hunter. This was the last of Rooney's four films with fellow kid actor Bartholomew, whose career headed down as Rooney's went up — and in this movie found his billing dropped to fourth! The two, incidentally, were reunited with Terry Kilburn and Peter Lawford — all four having played school chums together in *Lord Jeff* several years before.

In *The New York Times*, critic Bosley Crowther reported: "*A Yank at Eton* is a reckless fiction which several Metro writers conceived when they thought of Mickey Rooney attending an English public school.... Mr. Rooney has a field-day all over the place, clowning like Eddie Cantor and jutting his jaw like Jack Holt. Andy Hardy at Eton is a fearful thing to see."

64. Andy Hardy's Double Life (aka Andy Hardy Steps Out), MGM, 1942

Director: George B. Seitz; *Screenplay:* Agnes Christine Johnston, based on characters created by Aurania Rouverol.

Cast: Lewis Stone (*Judge Hardy*), Cecilia Parker (*Marian Hardy*), Fay Holden (*Mrs. Emily Hardy*), Ann Rutherford (*Polly Benedict*), Sara Haden (*Aunt Milly*), Esther Williams (*Sheila Brooks*), William Lundigan (*Jeff Willis*), Susan Peters (*Sue*), Bobby Blake (*"Tooky" Stedman*), Robert Pittard (*"Botsy"*), Addison Richards (*Mr. Benedict*), Arthur Space (*Stedman's Attorney*), Howard Hickman (*Lincoln's Attorney*), Erville Alderson (*Bailiff*), Mary Currier (*Mrs. Stedman*), John Walsh (*Harry*), Charles Peck (*Jack*), Frank Coghlan, Jr. (*Red*), Mickey Martin (*Bud*), George Watts (*Mr. Binks*), Mantan Moreland (*Prentiss*), Frank Chalfant, Philip Van Zandt, Floyd Shackelford, Robert Emmet O'Connor, Roger Moore and first-billed MR as Andy Hardy, on his way out of Carvel for Wainwright College, regretting that his new school is not coed, but still managing a juggling of his dating routine between steady girl Polly Benedict and a new one, Sheila Brooks (future star Esther Williams in her feature film debut).

65. The Human Comedy, MGM, 1943

Director: Clarence Brown; *Screenplay:* Howard Estabrook, based on an original story by William Saroyan that later was novelized.

Cast: Frank Morgan (*Willie Grogan*), James Craig (*Tom Spangler*), Marsha Hunt (*Diana Steed*), Fay Bainter (*Mrs. Katie Macauley*), Ray Collins (*Matthew Macauley*),

With Frank Morgan in *The Human Comedy* (1943) (MGM).

Van Johnson (*Marcus Macauley*), Donna Reed (*Bess Macauley*), Jackie "Butch" Jenkins [film debut] (*Ulysses Macauley*), Dorothy Morris (*Mary Arena*), John Craven (*Tobey George*), Ann Ayers (*Mrs. Rose Sandoval*), Mary Nash (*Miss Hicks*), Henry O'Neill (*Charles Streed*), Katherine Alexander (*Mrs. Steed*), Alan Baxter (*Norman*), Darryl Hickman (*Lionel*), Barry Nelson (*Fat Norman*), Don DeFore ("*Texas*" *Anthony*), Robert Mitchum (*Quentin "Horse" Gilbert*), Rita Quigley (*Helen Elliot*), Clem Bevans (*Henderson*), Ernest Whitman (*Black Man on Train*), Mark Daniels, Don Taylor, James Warren (*Soldiers*), Byron Foulger (*Blenton*), Wallis Clark (*Principal*), Wally Cassell (*Flirt*), David Holt (*Hubert Ackley III*), Morris Ankrum (*Mr. Beaufrere*), Lynne Carver (*Daughter*), Carl "Alfalfa" Switzer (*Auggie*), Bertram Marburgh, Albert Conti, Hobart Cavanaugh, Emory Parnell, Ernie Alexander, Frank Jenks, Howard Freeman, Robert Emmet O'Connor, Jay Ward, James Craven, Hooper Atchley, Leigh Sterling, Jean Fenwick, Dora Baker, Otto Hoffman and top-billed MR in a memorable Academy Award–nominated turn as Homer Macauley, a local Western Union messenger boy through whose eyes is seen rural Americana at the start of World War II.

Kate Cameron, critic for the New York *Daily News*, judged: "Mickey Rooney doesn't attempt to run the show, as in the Andy Hardy films, and, therefore, he turns in the best performance of his young life."

Initial casting, it was reported in the *AFI Catalogue* for feature films of the '40s, included Gene Kelly and Keenan Wynn, both in unspecified parts, along with others, and Lionel Barrymore and Spring Byington (Andy Hardy's original screen parents) in the roles eventually played by Frank Morgan and Katherine Alexander. This was Robert Mitchum's (here billed as Bob) first role in a major film, after a passel of Hopalong Cassidy B Westerns.

66. Girl Crazy, MGM, 1943

Director: Norman Taurog; *Screenplay:* Fred Finklehoffe, based on the 1930 musical play by Guy Bolton and Jack McGowan with a score by George and Ira Gershwin.

Cast: Judy Garland (*Ginger Gray*), Gil Stratton (*Bud Livermore*), Robert E. Strickland (*Henry Lathrop*), "Rags" Ragland (*"Rags"*), June Allyson (*Specialty*), Nancy Walker (*Polly Williams*), Guy Kibbee (*Dean Phineas Armour*), Frances Rafferty (*Marjorie Tait*), Henry O'Neill (*Danny Churchill, Sr.*), Howard Freeman (*Governor Tait*), Tommy Dorsey and His Orchestra (*Themselves*), Eve Whitney, Charles Walters [later the MGM director and choreographer], Charles Coleman, Kathleen Williams, Roger Moore, Harry Depp, Henry Roquemore, Irving Bacon, William Beaudine, Jr., Don Taylor, Peter Lawford, Bess Flowers, Harry C. Bradley, Sarah Edwards, William Bishop, Helen Dickson, Barbara Bedford, Victor Potel, Frances McInerney, Sally Cairns and top-billed MR as Danny Churchill, Jr., a Yale playboy.

Front and center with Tommy Dorsey and Judy Garland in the grand finale of *Girl Crazy* (1943) (MGM).

His stuffy dad (Henry O'Neill) sends him to an exclusive boys college out West, where, to save it from foreclosure, Rooney teams up with Judy Garland, Tommy Dorsey's orchestra, a young June Allyson and others to stage a big jamboree and also turn the school coed. Mickey sings "Treat Me Rough" with June Allyson and "Could You Use Me?" with Judy Garland. One Rooney–Garland number, along with Nancy Walker and chorus, "Bronco Busters," was cut from the final print. Busby Berkeley choreographed the elaborate "I Got Rhythm" number with Judy and the Dorsey Orchestra.

The first play was filmed in 1932 as a vehicle for the comedy team of Wheeler and Woolsey. This second version was intended for Fred Astaire and Eleanor Powell. It would be remade in 1965 as the Connie Francis musical *When the Boys Meet the Girls*, and much later would be the basis for the "new Gershwin Broadway musical" *Crazy for You*— a mid–1990s Toronto production in which Rooney would star.

67. Thousands Cheer, MGM, 1943

Director: George Sidney; *Screenplay:* Paul Jarrico and Richard Collins from their story "Private Miss Jones."

Cast: Kathryn Grayson (*Kathryn Jones*), Gene Kelly (*Pvt. Eddy Marsh*), Mary Astor (*Hyllary Jones*), John Boles (*Col. Bill Jones*), Ben Blue (*Chuck Polansky*), Frances Rafferty (*Marie Corbino*), Frank Jenks (*Sgt. Koslack*), Frank Sully (*Alan*), Dick Simmons (*Capt. Fred Avery*), Ben Lessy (*Silent Monk*), Wally Cassell (*Jack*), Connie Gilchrist (*Cab Driver*), Sig Arno (*Uncle Algy*), Pierre Watkin (*Alex*), Ray Teal (*Ringmaster*), Harry Strang (*Maj. Haines*), Will Kaufman (*Papa Corbino*), Odette Myrtil (*Mama Corbino*), Bryant Washburn, Sr. (*Lt. Col. Brand*), Lionel Barrymore (*Announcer's Voice*), William Tannen, Eve Whitney, James Warren, Don Taylor, Eileen Coghlan, Florence Turner and MR as the emcee of a USO show featuring most of MGM's contract players, including Judy Garland, Red Skelton, Eleanor Powell, Ann Sothern, Lucille Ball, Virginia O'Brien, Frank Morgan, Lena Horne, June Allyson, Gloria De Haven, Margaret O'Brien, Donna Reed, Marsha Hunt, Marilyn Maxwell, John Conte, Sara Haden and pianist José Iturbi, plus the orchestras of Kay Kyser, Bob Crosby and Benny Carter. The basic plot of this wartime musical flag-waver: Army private Kelly romances concert singer Grayson, daughter of base commander Boles. Rooney and many of MGM's top stars turn up in a spectacular USO show that becomes the heart of the film.

68. Andy Hardy's Blonde Trouble, MGM, 1944

Director: George B. Seitz; *Screenplay:* Harry Ruskin, William Ludwig and Agnes Christine Johnston, based on characters created by Aurania Rouverol.

Cast: Lewis Stone (*Judge Hardy*), Fay Holden (*Mrs. Emily Hardy*), Herbert Marshall (*Dr. M.K. Standish*), Sara Haden (*Aunt Milly*), Bonita Granville (*Kay Wilson*), Jean Porter (*Katey Anderson*), Keye Luke (*Dr. Lee/Wong How*), Lee and Lyn Wilde (*Lee and Lyn Walker*), Marta Linden (*Mrs. Townsend*), Jackie Moran (*Spud*), Tommy Dix (*Mark*), Connie Gilchrist (*Mrs. Gordon*), Emory Parnell (*Conductor*), Sam McDaniel (*Pullman Porter*), Cliff Clark (*Officer Shay*), Emmett Vogan, Eddie Acuff, Frank Faylen, Barbara Bedford, Garry Owen, Frankie Darien and first-billed MR as Andy Hardy, who here falls for young Wainwright College coed Granville. But she seems to be attracted to English professor Marshall, so he turns his attention to comely blonde twins.

With Elizabeth Taylor in *National Velvet* (1944) (MGM).

69. National Velvet, MGM, 1944

Director: Clarence Brown; *Screenplay:* Theodore Reeves and Helen Deutsch, based on the 1935 novel by Enid Bagnold.

Cast: Donald Crisp (*Mr. Herbert Brown*), Elizabeth Taylor (*Velvet Brown*), Anne Revere (*Mrs. Brown*), Angela Lansbury (*Edwina Brown*), Jackie "Butch" Jenkins (*Donald Brown*), Juanita Quigley (*Malvolia Brown*), Arthur Treacher (*Race Patron*),

Reginald Owen (*Farmer Ede*), Norma Varden (*Miss Simms*), Terry Kilburn (*Ted*), Arthur Shields (*Mr. Hallam*), Alec Craig (*Tim*), Eugene Loring (*Ivan Taski*), Dennis Hoey (*Mr. Greenford*), Aubrey Mather, Matthew Boulton, Frederic Worlock, Harry Allen, Billy Bevan, Wally Cassell, Wilbur Mack, Eric Wilton, Olaf Hytten, Stanley Mann, Doris Stone, Al Ferguson, Charles Irwin, Moyna MacGill [veteran British actress who was Angela Lansbury's mother] and top-billed MR as Mi Taylor, an Irish stable boy who helps 12-year-old Velvet Brown (Taylor, in her star-making role) train her horse to be a champion jumper and to ride it in the Grand National.

Reviewing this film on its world premiere Christmas opening at Radio City Music Hall, Bosley Crowther of *The New York Times* called it, "a joy to all right-minded folks. For this fresh and delightful Metro picture, based on Enid Bagnold's novel of some years back, tells by far the most touching story of youngsters and of animals since Lassie was coming home."

MGM had planned to film this as far back as 1938, possibly with Spencer Tracy and actor Leslie Howard's daughter Leslie Ruth as Velvet. The '40s version (originally to have been directed by Mervyn LeRoy) was filmed in late 1943 — making it Rooney's last movie for the duration of the war. Anne Revere, playing Taylor's mother, won the Oscar as Best Supporting Actress, with other nominations going to director Clarence Brown, cinematographer Leonard Smith and art directors Cedric Gibbons and Urie McCleary.

70. Ziegfeld Follies of 1946, MGM, 1946

Director: Vincente Minnelli.

An all-star musical (filmed in 1944, and initially premiering in Boston in the summer of 1945) in which MR had at least two numbers with Judy Garland: "Will You Love Me in Technicolor as You Do in Black and White?" and "As Long as I Have My Art." Curiously for a star of his caliber, then the studio's number one attraction, both of his songs, and his entire part, ended on the cutting room floor.

71. Love Laughs at Andy Hardy, MGM, 1946

Director: Willis Goldbeck; *Screenplay:* Harry Ruskin and William Ludwig, from a story by Howard Dimsdale.

Cast: Lewis Stone (*Judge Hardy*), Fay Holden (*Mrs. Emily Hardy*), Sara Haden (*Aunt Milly*), Bonita Granville (*Kay Wilson*), Lina Romay (*Isobel Gonzales*), Dorothy Ford (*Coffy Smith*), Hal Hackett (*Duke Johnson*), Dick Simmons (*Dane Kittridge*), Clinton Sundberg (*Haberdashery Clerk*), Addison Richards (*Mr. Benedict*), Charles Peck (*Tommy Gilchrist*), Geraldine Wall (*Miss Geeves*), Eddie Dunn (*Sergeant*), Lee Phelps, Eddy Chandler, Lucien Littlefield, Dick Paxton, Matt Moore, Boyd Davis, Si Jenks, Holmes Herbert, Howard Mitchell, Syd Saylor, Jane Green and top-billed MR as Andy Hardy (in the last entry in the original Hardy series), returning from World War II service to resume his schooling and a romance with Kay Wilson (Granville). When she tells him of her pending marriage to someone else, he decides to leave college — until he spots a new girl (Romay). He stays on to romance her and to get his law degree.

June Allyson originally was to have played the part taken by Granville, when initial production was to have been before Rooney went into the Army. By the time he returned, Allyson was too big a star in her own right.

72. Killer McCoy, MGM, 1947

Director: Roy Rowland; *Screenplay:* Frederick Hazlitt, from a story by Thomas Lennon, George Bruce and George Oppenheimer.

   Cast: Brian Donlevy (*Jim Carrson*), Ann Blyth (*Sheila Carrson*), James Dunn (*Brian McCoy*), Tom Tully (*Cecil Y. Walsh*), Sam Levene (*Happy*), Walter Sande (*Bill Thorne*), Mickey Knox (*Johnny Martin*), James Bell (*Father Ryan*), Gloria Holden (*Mrs. McCoy*), Eve Marsh (*Mrs. Martin*), June Storey (*Waitress*), Bob Steele (*Sailor Graves*), Douglas Croft (*Danny Burns*), David Clarke (*Pete Mariola*), William Tannen, Milburn Stone, Ray Teal, Phyllis Kennedy, Shelley Winters, Wally Cassell, George Chandler, Joseph Crehan, Eugene Borden, Frank Marlowe, John A. Butler and top-billed MR as Tommy McCoy, a young New York City tough who turns boxer. He accidentally kills his pal and mentor in the ring, and then learns that his reprobate one-time vaudevillian dad (Dunn) had secretly sold his boxing contract to gangster Donlevy, whom he ends up reforming.

   Shelley Winters had one of her early screen roles in a bit. This film with a newly mature postwar Rooney was a remake of the 1938 *The Crowd Roars*, which starred Robert Taylor. According to *The Hollywood Reporter*, Elizabeth Taylor was to have played the part taken by Ann Blyth. The "Swanee River" production number in the film was choreographed by Stanley Donen.

73. Summer Holiday, MGM, 1948

Director: Rouben Mamoulian; *Screenplay:* Frances Goodrich and Albert Hackett, adapted by Irving Brecher and Jean Holloway from the 1933 play *Ah, Wilderness* by Eugene O'Neill.

   Cast: Gloria DeHaven (*Muriel McComber*), Walter Huston (*Nat Miller*), Frank Morgan (*Uncle Sid Miller*), Jackie "Butch" Jenkins (*Tommy Miller*), Marilyn Maxwell (*Belle*), Agnes Moorehead (*Cousin Lily*), Selena Royle (*Essie Miller*), Michael Kirby (*Arthur Miller*), Shirley Johns (*Mildred Miller*), Howard Freeman (*Mr. Peabody*), John Alexander (*Dave McComber*), Anne Francis (*Elsie Rand*), Virginia Brissac (*Miss Hawley*), Hal Hackett (*Vint*), Ruth Brady (*Crystal*), Emory Parnell (*Bartender*), Wally Cassell (*Salesman*), Walter Soderling (*Mr. Lipscott*), Don Gardner (*Gilbert Ralston*), Jack Baxley (*Gus*), Ann Kimbell (*Katherine*), and top-billed MR, this time as older brother Richard Miller (he had been younger brother Tommy in the earlier, non-musical version of the nostalgic O'Neill play in 1935). With DeHaven, he sings a passel of original songs by Harry Warren and Ralph Blane, including "Our Home Town" and "The Stanley Steamer." Years before, Huston and Rooney played father and son in one of the latter's earliest features, *The Beast of the City*, also for MGM.

   "*Summer Holiday* has been stripped down [from *Ah, Wilderness!*] to a vehicle for Mickey Rooney's use — all of which sounds, for Mr. O'Neill's drama, like a fate somewhat worse than death," Bosley Crowther said in *The New York Times*. "In a sense it is, too, for this musical is plainly lacking the poignancy and the delicate charm of the original [and] Mr. Rooney is given to clowning in his familiarly broad and impish way."

74. Words and Music, MGM, 1948

Director: Norman Taurog; *Screenplay:* Fred Finklehoffe, from an original story by Guy Bolton and Jean Holloway.

Cast: Perry Como (*Eddie Lorrison Anders/Himself*), Ann Sothern (*Joyce Harmon*), Tom Drake (*Richard Rodgers*), Betty Garrett (*Peggy Lorgan McNeill*), Janet Leigh (*Dorothy Feiner*), Marshall Thompson (*Herbert Fields*), Jeanette Nolan (*Mrs. Hart*), Richard Quine (*Ben Feiner, Jr.*), Clinton Sundberg (*Shoe Clerk*), Harry Antrim (*Dr. Rodgers*), Ilka Gruning (*Mrs. Rodgers*), Helen Spring (*Mrs. Feiner*), Emory Parnell (*Mr. Feiner*), Edward Earle (*James Fernby Kelly*), Dorothy Abbott, Allyn Ann McLerie, John A. Butler, William Fawcett, Irving Bacon, Marietta Canty, George Meeker, William "Bill" Phillips, Stanley Blystone, George Spaulding, Russ Clark and top-billed MR wrapping up his longtime MGM contract as lyricist Lorenz Hart to Drake's Richard Rodgers. This is a romanticized, star-studded musical biography without any nod to reality other than stringing together some of their best known songs.

Guest performers include Gene Kelly and Vera-Ellen (performing the "Slaughter on 10th Avenue" ballet), Judy Garland, June Allyson, Mel Torme, Lena Horne, Cyd Charisse, Dee Tunnell and the Blackburn Twins.

Rooney sings "Manhattan" with Drake and Thompson, "Spring Is Here" solo and, curiously but entertainingly, he (as Hart) duets with Judy (as Judy) on "I Wish I Were in Love Again." (Had Hart and Garland actually performed together, he'd have been 42; she 14.) Also unrealistic is having Perry Como play a role as a fictional buddy of two songwriters and then turn up at the finale as Perry Como to belt out "With a Song in My Heart."

75. The Big Wheel, United Artists, 1949

Director: Edward Ludwig; *Screenplay:* Robert Smith.

Cast: Thomas Mitchell (*Arthur "Red" Stanley*), Mary Hatcher (*Louise Riley*), Michael O'Shea (*Vic Sullivan*), Spring Byington (*Mary Coy*), Hattie McDaniel (*Minnie*), Lina Romay (*Dolores Raymond*), Steve Brodie (*Happy Lee*), Allen Jenkins (*George*), Richard Lane (*Reno Riley*), Monte Blue (*Deacon Jones*), Jack Colin, George Fisher, Eddie Kane, Donald Kerr, Denver Pyle and top-billed MR as Billy Coy, son of a champion auto racing driver. He tries to follow in the latter's tracks, beginning with hot rods and midgets and working his way up to the Indianapolis Classic.

The film's producer (for Rooney's company) was former heavyweight champ Jack Dempsey. Spring Byington once again was playing MR's mom (replacing the originally cast Fay Bainter) a dozen years after the original Andy Hardy movie.

76. Quicksand, United Artists, 1950

Director: Irving Pichel; *Screenplay:* Robert Smith.

Cast: Jeanne Cagney (*Vera Novak*), Peter Lorre (*Nick Dramoshag*), Barbara Bates (*Helen Calder*), Taylor Holmes (*Lawyer Harvey*), Art Smith (*Mackey*), Wally Cassell (*Chuck*), Richard Lane (*Lt. Nelson*), Minerva Urecal (*Landlady*), Patsy O'Connor (*Millie*), John Gallaudet (*Moriarty*), Jimmy Dodd (*Buzz Larson*), Lester Dorr (*Baldy*), Kitty O'Neil (*Madame Zaronga*), Ray Teal (*Motorcycle Cop*), Sidney Marion (*Shorty McCabe*), Frank Marlowe (*Watchman*), Alvin Hammer (*Auditor*), Jack Elam (*Bar Customer*), Red Nichols and His Five Pennies (*Themselves*) and top-billed MR as Dan Brady, a skirt-chasing auto mechanic who commits a series of crimes to cover his initial mistake of borrowing 20 bucks from the boss' till.

This truly low-budget film, Rooney's second in a row for his own independent production company, reportedly had Fritz Lang scheduled as director, and Ava Gardner and Jean Wallace in the roles taken ultimately by Jeanne Cagney (James' sister) and Barbara Bates.

77. He's a Cockeyed Wonder, Columbia Pictures, 1950

Director: Peter Godfrey; *Screenplay:* Jack Henley.

Cast: Terry Moore (*Judy Sears*), William Demarest (*Bob Sears*), Charles Arnt (*J.B. Caldwell*), Ross Ford (*Ralph Caldwell*), Ned Glass (*Sam Phillips*), Mike Mazurki (*"Lunk" Boxwell*), Douglas Fowley (*"Crabs" Freeley*), William "Bill" Phillips (*"Pick" Reedley*), Ruth Warren (*Jenny Morrison*), Eddie Waller (*Pops Dunlap*), Lola Albright (*Actress in Movie at Drive-in*), Richard Quine (*Actor in Movie at Drive-in*), Frank Ferguson (*Sheriff Oliver*), Dick Wessel, Alyn Lockwood, Olin Howlin, Tom Daly, Earle Hodgins and top-billed MR in this low-budget comedy as Freddie Frisby, a magician's nephew and hapless orange sorter in a packing company. To impress girlfriend Moore, he uses tricks to capture a gang of bungling thieves.

The *New York Herald-Tribune*'s critic said: "The Hardy series died a natural death several years ago, with the generally accepted epitaph that enough is enough. It is painfully surprising, therefore, to see Mickey Rooney back at the same old stand in *He's a Cockeyed Wonder*. The name has been changed, this time it's Freddie Frisby, and there's no Hardy clan, but all of Andy's mannerisms are on tap, including the exuberant mugging and the Hardy facility for getting in and out of contrived troubles."

78. The Fireball, 20th Century–Fox, 1950

Director: Tay Garnett; *Screenplay:* Horace McCoy, from an original story by Garnett and McCoy.

Cast: Pat O'Brien (*Father O'Hara*), Beverly Tyler (*Mary Reeves*), James Brown (*Allen*), Ralph Dumke (*Bruno Crustal*), Milburn Stone (*Jeff Davis*), Kenneth Begley (*Track Announcer*), Marilyn Monroe (*Polly*), Sam Flint (*Dr. Barton*), Glenn Corbett (*Mack Miller*), John Hedloe (*Ullman*) and top-billed MR as Johnny Casar, an embattled (if, at 30, a tad overage) orphan who, with the aid of amiable priest O'Brien, becomes a professional roller derby champ. Marilyn Monroe made one of her early pre-stardom appearances in this programmer, which initially was to have been called *Dark Challenge*.

"Rooney does a fine job in a part that appears to fit his proportions and style inside and out," critic James Barstow, Jr., wrote in the *New York Herald Tribune*. "His half pint who hates the world until he finds his niche on a roller rink and then becomes overbearingly egotistical comes through with pungent conviction."

79. My Outlaw Brother, Eagle-Lion Films, 1951

Director: Elliott Nugent; *Screenplay:* Gene Fowler, Jr., based on the story "South of the Border" by Max Brand.

Cast: Wanda Hendrix (*Señorita Carmel Alvarado*), Robert Preston (*Joe Walter*), Robert Stack (*Patrick O'Moore [El Tigre]*), Carlos Múzquiz (*Col. Sanchez*), José Torvey (*Ortiz*), Fernando Wagner (*Burger*), Hilda Moreno (*Señora Alvarado*), Elliott Nugent (*Ranger Captain*), Felipe de Flores, Guillermo Callas, Enrique Cansino, Margarito Luna, José Velasquez and top-billed MR as Denny O'Moore

With Glenn Corbett (left), Marilyn Monroe, and James Brown, in *The Fireball* (1950).

in this second-rate made-in-Mexico oater, about a tenderfoot who goes West to visit his brother Stack, teaming up along the way with Preston, a ranger. Ultimately he learns that Stack is really an outlaw.

80. The Strip, MGM, 1951

Director: Leslie Kardos; *Screenplay:* Allen Rivkin.

   Cast: Sally Forrest (*Jane Tafford*), James Craig (*Delwyn "Sonny" Johnson*), William Demarest (*Fluff*), Kay Brown (*Edna*), Tommy Rettig (*Artie*), Tom Powers (*Detective Bonnabel*), Jonathan Cott (*Behr*), Tommy Farrell (*Boynton*), Myrna Dell (*Paulette Ardrey*), Jacqueline Fontaine (*Frieda*), Robert Foulk (*Deputy*), John McGuire, Russell Trent, Fred Graham, Don Haggerty, William Tannen, Sherry Hall, John Maxwell, Tom Quinn, Jeff Richards, Joyce Jameson, Art Lewis, Earle Hodgins, Lester Dorr, Roger Moore, guest stars Louis Armstrong, Vic Damone, Monica Lewis and Jack Teagarden, and top-billed MR as nightclub drummer Stanley Maxton, a Korean War vet who gets mixed up with big-time Hollywood bookmaker Craig and falls for the latter's girlfriend Forrest, a dancer and cigarette girl at the club. In this minor league MGM crime musical, Armstrong introduced the Oscar-nominated song "A Kiss to Build a Dream On," written by Bert Kalmar, Harry Ruby and Oscar Hammerstein II.

81. Sound Off, Columbia Pictures, 1952

Director: Richard Quine; *Screenplay:* Blake Edwards and Quine.

Cast: Anne James (*Lt. Colleen Rafferty*), Sammy White (*Joe Kirby*), John Archer (*Maj. Paul Whiteside*), Gordon Jones (*Sgt. Crockett*), Wally Cassell (*Tony Baccigalupi*), Arthur Space (*Barney Fisher*), Pat Williams (*Vonnie Vanderveer*), Marshall Reed (*Capt. Karger*), Helen Ford (*Mrs. Rafferty*), Mary Lou Greer (*Evelyn Ames*), Boyd "Red" Morgan (*MP*) and top-billed MR as Mike Donnelly in this light-hearted military comedy. He's a rough-and-tumble entertainer who suddenly finds himself in the Army, where he gets into a series of comic mishaps.

This was the first of a number of films MR did with fellow MGM actor-turned-director Richard Quine, who in turn united with former actor-turned-screenwriter Blake Edwards—who went on to become a major director on his own.

82. All Ashore, Columbia Pictures, 1953

Director: Richard Quine; *Screenplay:* Blake Edwards and Quine, from a story by Robert Wells and Edwards.

Cast: Dick Haymes (*Joe Carter*), Peggy Ryan (*Gay Night*), Ray McDonald (*Skip Edwards*), Barbara Bates (*Jane Stanton*), Jody Lawrance (*Nancy Flynn*), Fay Roope (*Commodore Stanton*), Jean Willes (*Rose*), Rica Owen (*Dotty*), Patricia Walker (*Susie*), Eddie Parker (*Sheriff Billings*), Dick Crockett (*Guard*), Ben Welden (*Bartender*), Frank Kreig (*Arthur Barnaby*), Gloria Pall (*Lucretia*), Joan Shawlee (*Hedy*) and top-billed MR, clowning as Francis "Moby" Dickerson in this low-rent *On the Town*. "Moby" is on shore leave with mates Haymes (the pop singer) and McDonald (Donald O'Connor–style dancer, married at the time to costar Peggy Ryan, here in her last film) and looking to land Bates, the daughter of a rich businessman.

83. Off Limits (aka Military Policemen), Paramount Pictures, 1953

Director: George Marshall; *Screenplay:* Hal Kanter and Jack Sher.

Cast: Bob Hope (*Wally Hogan*), Marilyn Maxwell (*Connie Curtis*), Eddie Mayehoff (*Karl Danzig*), Stanley Clements (*Bullets Bradley*), Carolyn Jones (*Deborah*), Marvin Miller (*Vic Breck*), John Ridgely (*Lt. Comdr. Parnell*). Joan Taylor (*Helen*), Mary Murphy (*WAC*), Tom Harmon (*Himself*), Jack Dempsey (*Himself*), Art Aragon (*Himself*), Norman Leavitt, Kim Spaulding, Jerry Hausner, Mike Mahoney, Tom Dugan, James Seay and second-billed MR as brash young boxer and Army recruit Herbert Tuttle. In this military comedy, he becomes involved with the equally brash prize fight manager (Hope), inadvertently finding himself in uniform and falling for Rooney's "aunt" Maxwell.

84. A Slight Case of Larceny, MGM, 1953

Director: Don Weis; *Screenplay:* Jerry Davis, from a story by James Poe.

Cast: Eddie Bracken (*Frederick Winthrop Clopp*), Elaine Stewart (*Beverly Ambridge*), Marilyn Erskine (*Mrs. Emily Clopp*), Douglas Fowley (*Mr. White*), Robert Burton (*Police Captain*), Charles Halton (*Willard Maibrunn*), Rudy Lee (*Tommy Clopp*), Mimi Gibson (*Mary Ellen Clopp*), Robert Foulk (*Mr. Largen*), Dabbs Greer (*Sandy*), William "Bill" Phillips (*Eddie*), Henry Slate, Al Jackson, Ida Moore, Mitchell Lewis, Joe Turkel, Walter Ridge, Russ Saunders, Harry Wilson and top-billed MR as Augustus "Geechy" Cheevers. In this "B" comedy, he opens a gas station with his Army buddy and fellow knucklehead Bracken and finds himself in a price war with a rival across the street, ending up tapping an industrial gas pipe under their own station.

85. Drive a Crooked Road, Columbia Pictures, 1954

Director: Richard Quine; *Screenplay:* Blake Edwards, from Quine's adaptation of a story by James Benson Nablo.

Cast: Dianne Foster (*Barbara Mathews*), Kevin McCarthy (*Steve Norris*), Jack Kelly (*Harold Baker*), Harry Landers (*Ralph*), Jerry Paris (*Phil*), Paul Picerni (*Carl*), Mort Mills (*Garage Foreman*), Dick Crockett (*Don*), Peggy Maley (*Marge*), Mike Mahoney, George Paul, John Damler, John Close, Patrick Miller, Diana Dawson, Irene Bolton, Linda Danson, Mel Roberts, John Fontaine, Howard Wright, Jean Engstrom and top-billed MR as Eddie Shannon, a garage mechanic and race driver who is duped into steering the escape car for bank robbers McCarthy and Kelly and their moll Foster.

"As is the way in melodrama," Paul V. Buckley wrote in the *New York Herald-Tribune*, "all characters, except the one played by Mickey Rooney, are depicted without much shading ... Mr. Rooney makes a valiant effort to interject conviction into the film but there just wasn't enough to work on." The critic also opined: "The picture is good enough to make one wonder again if it isn't about time someone wrote a really good one for Mr. Rooney, who obviously deserves something besides being continually whirled about on skates or autos or something."

In his autobiography *Life Is Too Short*, Rooney himself gave this one a thumbs-up. "The film got good reviews, and it even won a Redbook Award for best picture of the year."

86. The Atomic Kid, Republic Pictures, 1954

Director: Leslie H. Martinson; *Screenplay:* Blake Edwards, from a story by Benedict Freedman and John Fenton Murray.

Cast: Robert Strauss (*Stan Cooper*), Elaine Davis [Mrs. MR] (*Audrey Nelson*), Bill Goodwin (*Dr. Rodell*), Robert Emmett Keane (*Mr. Reynolds*), Whit Bissell (*Dr. Edgar Pangborn*), Hal March (*Agent Ray*), Fay Roope (*Gen. Lawlor*), Peter Leeds (*Agent Bill*), Joey Forman (*MP in Hospital*), Stanley Adams (*Wildcat Hooper*), Peter Brocco (*Comrade Mosley*), Don Haggerty (*Lieutenant*), Paul Dubov (*Anderson*), Dan Riss, George E. Mather, Robert Nichols, Milton Frome, Don Haggerty, Allan Ray, Joe Rocca, Dick Winslow and top-billed MR playing prospector Barnaby "Blix" Waterberry, a schnook who becomes the radioactive survivor of an A-bomb explosion in this minor league vehicle for Mickey Rooney Productions.

"Five minutes or so are genuinely funny, the rest is a fair, misguided try," *The New York Times*' Howard Thompson wrote. "Nobody is out to compete with H.G. Wells, and The Mick, glued front and center, must be swallowed whole."

87. The Bridges at Toko-Ri, Paramount Pictures, 1955

Director: Mark Robson; *Screenplay:* Valentine Davies, based on the 1953 novel by James Michener.

Cast: William Holden (*Lt. Harry Brubaker, USNR*), Grace Kelly (*Nancy Brubaker*), Fredric March (*Rear Adm. George Tarrant*), Robert Strauss ("*Beer Barrel*"), Charles McGraw (*Cmdr. Wayne Lee*), Earl Holliman (*Nestor Gamidge*), Willis

Bouchey (*Capt. Evans*), Keiko Awaji (*Kimiko*), Dennis Weaver (*Air Intelligence Officer*), Nadine Ashdown (*Cathy Brubaker*), Cheryl Callaway (*Susie Brubaker*), and Charles Tannen, Gene Reynolds, Teru Shimada, James Hyland, Richard Shannon, Robert Kimo, Gene Hardy, Jack Roberts. Paul Kruger, and fourth-billed MR, in his best role in years, as cocky Mike Forney, a Korean War helicopter jockey whose talent is rescuing downed Navy pilots.

88. The Twinkle in God's Eye, Republic Pictures, 1955

Director: George Blair; *Screenplay:* P.J. Wolfson.

    Cast: Coleen Gray (*Laura*), Hugh O'Brian (*Marty Callahan*), Joey Forman (*Ted*), Don "Red" Barry (*Dawson*), Mike "Touch" Connors (*Lou*), Jil Jarmyn (*Millie*), Kem Dibbs (*Johnny*), Anthony Garcen (*Babe*), Ruta Lee (*Dancer*), Raymond Hatton (*Stable Man*), Clem Bevans (*Clem*) and top-billed MR as Rev. William Macklin II, a young traveling parson who attempts to bring religion to a rugged frontier community, despite the intervention of gambling hall owner O'Brian. Rooney also produced the film and wrote the title song, sung by country star Eddy Howard.

89. Francis in the Haunted House, Universal-International, 1956

Director: Charles Lamont; *Screenplay:* Herbert Margolis and William Raynor, based on characters created by David Stern.

    Cast: Virginia Welles (*Lorna MacLeod*), James Flavin (*Chief Martin*), Paul Cavanaugh (*Neil Frazer*), David Janssen (*Lt. Hopkins*), Mary Ellen Kaye (*Lorna Ann*), Ralph Dumke (*Mayor Hargrove*), Richard Deacon (*Jason*), Richard Gaines (*D.A. Reynolds*), Dick Winslow (*Sgt. Arnold*), Timothy Carey (*Hugo*), Charles Horvath (*Malcolm*), Helen Wallace (*Mrs. MacPherson*), Edward Earle (*Howard Grisby*), John Maxwell (*Edward Ryan*), Glen Kramer (*Ephraim Biddle*), Paul Frees (*Voice of Francis*) and top-billed MR taking over for pal Donald O'Connor — who bailed out after starring in the first half-dozen entries in this series involving a talking mule. Bumbler Rooney and Francis track down the killer stalking a medieval castle which has been transplanted stone by stone from Scotland to America. This film at last buried the silly but very profitable series.

90. The Bold and the Brave, RKO Pictures, 1956

Director: Lewis R. Foster; *Screenplay:* Robert Levin.

    Cast: Wendell Corey (*Fairchild*), Don Taylor (*Preacher*), Nicole Maurey (*Fiamma*), John Smith (*Smith*), Race Gentry (*Hendricks*), Ralph Votrian (*Wilbur*), Wright King (*Technician*), Stanley Adams (*Master Sergeant*), Bobs Watson (*Bob*), Tara Summers (*Tina*) and second-billed MR, doing wonders with a stereotypical role in this routine little war movie as Dooley, a happily wed G.I. in Italy who boasts of being a lady-killer and shares with his buddies his dream of opening a New Jersey restaurant. His hilarious dice game where he risks his $30,000 pot under a blanket during an air raid, only to later get killed while on patrol, helped him win a Best Supporting Actor Academy Award nomination. The screenplay also was Oscar-nominated.

91. Magnificent Roughnecks, Allied Artists, 1956

Director: Sherman A. Rose; *Screenplay:* Stephen Kandel.

    Cast: Jack Carson (*Bix Decker*), Nancy Gates (*Jane Rivers*), Jeff Donnell (*Julie*),

Myron Healey (*Werner Jackson*), Willis Bouchey (*Ernie Biggers*), Eric Feldary (*Ramon Serrano*), Alan Wells (*Danny*), Frank Gerstle (*Chuck Evans*), Larry Carr (*Guard*), Matty Fain (*Pepi*), Joe Locke (*Driver*) and second-billed MR as Frank Sommers, who, with fellow roughneck oil driller Carson in South America, vies with wildcatter Healey to get a government contract by bringing in the first producing well in the area.

92. Operation Mad Ball, Columbia Pictures, 1957

Director: Richard Quine; *Screenplay:* Blake Edwards, Jed Harris and Arthur Carter, based on a play by Carter.

 Cast: Jack Lemmon (*Private Hogan*), Kathryn Grant [Mrs. Bing Crosby] (*Lt. Betty Bixby*), Ernie Kovacs [film debut] (*Capt. Paul Locke*), Arthur O'Connell (*Col. Rousch*), Dick York (*Cpl. Bohun*), James Darren (*Private Widowskas*), Roger Smith (*Cpl. Berryman*), William Leslie (*Private Grimes*), L.Q. Jones (*Ozark*), Sheridan Comerate (*Sgt. Wilson*), Jeanne Manet (*Madame LaFour*), Bebe Allen (*Lt. Johnson*), Paul Picerni (*Private Bullard*), Dick Crockett (*Sgt. McCloskey*), Mary LaRoche (*Lt. Schmidt*), David McMahon (*Master Sgt. Pringle*) and fifth-billed MR in a cameo in this very funny military comedy as Yancy Skibo, a bop-talking master sergeant in charge of transportation for the base where wheeler-dealer Lemmon stages an illegal bash for a group of nurses in wartime France. The title song, written by Richard Quine and Fred Karger, was performed on the soundtrack by Sammy Davis, Jr.

93. Baby Face Nelson, Albert Zugsmith/United Artists, 1957

Director: Don Siegel; *Screenplay:* Irving Shulman and Daniel Mainwaring, from a story by Shulman.

 Cast: Carolyn Jones (*Sue*), Sir Cedric Hardwicke (*Doc Saunders*), Leo Gordon (*John Dillinger*), Christopher Dark (*Jerry*), Ted De Corsia (*Rocca*), Anthony Caruso (*John Hamilton*), Jack Elam (*Fatso Nagel*), John Hoyt (*Samuel Parker*), Emile Meyer (*Mac*), Elisha Cook, Jr. (*Van Meter*), Dabbs Greer (*Charles Bonner*), Robert Osterloh (*Johnson*), Dick Crockett (*Powell*), Dan Terranova (*Miller*), Thayer David (*Connelly*), Lisa Davis (*Ann Saper, the Lady in Red*), Gil Perkins (*Duncan*), Murray Alper (*Alex, Bank Guard*), George E. Stone (*Mr. Hall*), Kenneth Patterson (*Ranald Vickman*), Saul Gorss (*Preston*), Paul Baxley (*Aldridge*), Tom Fadden (*Postman Harkins*) and top-billed MR snarling his way through this standard gangster flick as the infamous Prohibition Era killer (who was born Lester Gillis).

 Newsweek's movie critic wrote: "This one offers pocket-size, puckish Mickey Rooney in the unlikeliest role of his career — that of Public Enemy No. 1, vintage 1933. It is as incongruous as Edward G. Robinson playing Pinocchio." Another reviewer found: "Rooney chews up not only the scenery but also the script, cast, and camera."

94. A Nice Little Bank That Should Be Robbed, 20th Century–Fox, 1958

Director: Henry Levin; *Screenplay:* Sydney Boehm, from an article by Evan Wylie.

 Cast: Tom Ewell (*Max Rutgers*), Mickey Shaughnessy (*Harold "Rocky" Baker*), Dina Merrill (*Margie Solitaire*), Madge Kennedy (*Grace Havens*), Frances Bavier (*Mrs. Solitaire*), Richard Deacon (*Mr. Schroeder*), Stanley Clements (*Fitz*), Joe Conley (*Benjy*), Charles Arnt (*Mr. Simms*), George Eldredge (*Bank Examiner*), John

With Carolyn Jones and Anthony Caruso in *Baby Face Nelson* (1957).

Doucette (*Grayson*), Leonard Bremen, Thomas Caldwell, Harry Carter, John Epper, Fred Catania, Tom Greenway and second-billed MR as Gus Harris, a small-time crook in this minor comedy. With hapless pal Ewell, he knocks over a bank, sets up a Saratoga racing stable, loses everything on their nag, pulls another heist, ends up behind bars, and then learns that their horse has become a winner big time.

"Credit the chuckles," *The New York Times* said, "to the free-wheeling script by Sydney Boehm, which appears to be out of Damon Runyon by Aesop."

95. Andy Hardy Comes Home, MGM, 1958

Director: Howard W. Koch; *Screenplay:* Edward Everett Hutshing and Robert Morris.

Cast: Patricia Breslin (*Jane Hardy*), Cecilia Parker (*Marian Hardy*), Fay Holden (*Mrs. Emily Hardy*), Sara Haden (*Aunt Milly*), Teddy Rooney (*Andrew Hardy, Jr.*), Joey Forman ("*Beezy" Anderson*), Jerry Colonna (*Doc*), Don "Red" Barry (*Mr. Fitzgerald*), Vaughn Taylor (*Thomas Chandler*), Frank Ferguson (*Mayor Benson*), William Leslie (*Jack Biley*), Tom Duggan (*Councilman Warren*), Jeanne Baird (*Sally Anderson*), Gina Gillespie (*Cricket*), Pat Cawley (*Betty Wilson*), Almira Sessions, Jimmy Bates, Johnny Weissmuller, Jr., and top-billed MR as Andy Hardy, now all grown up and a West Coast lawyer who returns to his hometown of Carvel after a 12-year absence with his family (son Teddy Rooney plays Andy Jr.) on business

With real-life son Teddy and "reel-life" painting of Lewis Stone as Judge Hardy, *Andy Hardy Comes Home* (1959).

and decides to stay and become a judge like his dad. Cecilia Parker, Fay Holden and Sara Haden are back for one last time as Andy's sister, mom and aunt.

Rooney produced this final Andy Hardy movie, which premiered in New York on Christmas Eve 1958 on the bottom half of a double bill. In its unpublished review (due to a newspaper strike), *The Times* found: "It recalls the golden days of the motion picture when the patrons poured money into the box office to confirm their faith in the happy ending.... The main trouble is that the world itself — and the people who go to the movies — have aged more rapidly in their taste for entertainment."

96. The Last Mile, United Artists, 1959

Director: Howard W. Koch; *Screenplay:* Milton Subotosky and Seton I. Miller, based on the 1930 play by John Wexley.

Cast: Alan Bunce (*The Warden*), Frank Conroy (*Guard O'Flaherty*), Leon Janney (*Guard Callahan*), Frank Overton (*Father O'Connors*), Clifford David (*Convict Richard Walters*), Harry Millard (*Convict Fred Mayor*), John McCurry (*Convict Vince Jackson*), Ford Rainey (*Convict Red Kirby*), Johnny Seven (*Convict Tom D'Amoro*), Michael Constantine (*Convict Ed Werner*), John Vari (*Convict Jimmy Martin*), Don "Red" Barry (*Guard Drake*), Clifton James (*Guard Harris*), Milton Selzer (*Guard Peddie*), George Marcy (*Convict Pete Rodrigues*) and top-billed MR as "Killer" John Mears, who blasts his way off of Death Row. His role was originated on Broadway by Spencer Tracy (along with Clark Gable as a fellow inmate) and by Preston Foster in the first version of the film in 1932.

97. The Big Operator (aka Anatomy of a Syndicate), Albert Zugsmith/ MGM, 1959

Director: Charles Haas; *Screenplay:* Allen Rivkin and Robert Smith, from an original story by Paul Gallico.

Cast: Steve Cochran (*Bill Gibson*), Mamie Van Doren (*Mary Gibson*), Mel Torme *Fred McAfee*), Ray Danton (*Oscar Wetzel*), Jim Backus (*Cliff Heldon*), Ray Anthony [the famed '50s bandleader] (*Slim Clayburn*), Jackie Coogan (*Edward Brannel*), Charles Chaplin, Jr. (*Bill Tragg*), Ben Gage (*Bert Carr*), Billy Daniels (*Tony Webson*), Lawrence Dobkin (*Phil Cernak*), Jay North (*Timmy Gibson*), Leo Gordon (*Danny Sacanzi*), Don "Red" Barry (*Detective Sergeant*), Joey Forman (*Raymond Baily*), Ziva Rodann (*Alice McAfee*), Norman Grabowski (*Lou Green*), Vampira (*Gina*) and top-billed MR (at the head of a truly eclectic cast) as Little Joe Braun, a tyrannical Hoffa-life union boss who

As Killer Mears in *The Last Mile* (1959) (UPI).

terrorizes good guy Cochran — playing against type — when the latter threatens to expose his racket. This was previously filmed in 1942 as *Joe Smith, American*, starring Robert Young (in the role done here by Cochran).

98. Platinum High School (aka Trouble at 16), Albert Zugsmith/MGM, 1960

Director: Charles Haas; *Screenplay:* Robert Smith, from a story by Howard Breslin.

Cast: Terry Moore (*Jennifer Evans*), Dan Duryea (*Maj. Redfern Kelly*), Yvette Mimieux (*Lorna Nibley*), Conway Twitty (*Billy Jack Barnes*), Warren Berlinger (*"Crip" Hastings*), Jimmy Boyd (*Bud Starkweather*), Richard Jaeckel (*Hack Marlow*), Jack Carr (*Joe Nibley*), Harold Lloyd, Jr. (*Charley-Boy Cable*), Christopher Dark (*Vince Perley*), Elisha Cook, Jr. (*Harry Nesbit*), Jimmy Murphy (*Cadet Phillips*), Mason Alan Dinehart (*Dingbat Johnston*), David Landfield (*Drill instructor*) and top-billed MR. This loose remake of the 1955 *Bad Day at Black Rock*, he plays the estranged dad of a young boy, and comes to town to investigate his son's death at an exclusive military school. This film was called *Rich, Young and Deadly* when it was reviewed at the Rialto Theatre in New York's Times Square.

The New York Times' Eugene Archer wrote: "Mickey Rooney, twenty years after his peak period as Andy Hardy, MGM's conception of the all–American boy, is still laboring for the studio with indefatigable professionalism. Unfortunately, he has done more for the studio than MGM has done for him. For Mr. Rooney's vigorous playing is the only merit in this shoddy and obviously inexpensive exploitation melodrama."

99. The Private Lives of Adam and Eve, Albert Zugsmith/Universal-International, 1960

Directors: Albert Zugsmith and Rooney; *Screenplay:* Robert Hill, from a story by George Kennett.

Cast: Mamie Van Doren (*Evie Smith/Eve*), Fay Spain (*Lil Lewis/Lilith*), Mel Torme (*Hal Sanders*), Tuesday Weld (*Vangie Harper*), Martin Milner (*Ad Simms/Adam*), Paul Anka (*Pinkie Parker*), Cecil Kellaway (*Doc Bayles*), Ziva Rodann (*Passiona*), June Wilkinson (*Devil's Familiar*), Theona Bryant, Phillipa Fallon, Barbara Waldon, Toni Covington, Nancy Root, Donna Lynne, Stella Garcia and top-billed MR (the film's co-director) as both Nick Lewis, a chiseling gambler, among a Reno-bound group of bus passengers taking refuge in a church where they share a common dream of the Creation, and a puckish devil in the Garden of Eden in the dream with Milner and Van Doren as Adam and Eve.

The New York *Daily News* observed: "Aside from Mickey Rooney, who sometimes overplays, there is little evidence of talent." (The Catholic Legion of Decency pressured the studio to take the film out of circulation, and it later was drastically reedited.)

100. Breakfast at Tiffany's, Paramount Pictures, 1961

Director: Blake Edwards; *Screenplay:* George Axelrod, based on the 1959 novella by Truman Capote.

Cast: Audrey Hepburn (*Holly Golightly*), George Peppard (*Paul Varjak*), Patricia

With Mamie Van Doren in *The Private Lives of Adam and Eve* (1960).

Neal ("*2E*"), Buddy Ebsen (*Doc Golightly*), Martin Balsam (*O.J. Berman*), Alan Reed (*Sally Tomato*), John McGiver (*Tiffany Salesman*), José-Luis de Villalonga (*Jose da Silva Perreira*), Gil Lamb (*Party Guest*), Stanley Adams (*Rusty Trawler*), Dorothy Whitney (*Mag Wildwood*), Claude Stroud (*Sid Arbuck*) and fifth-billed MR in a cameo as the bucktoothed, myopic Japanese photographer Mr. Yunioshi, who is the upstairs neighbor of madcap call-girl Hepburn.

101. King of the Roaring '20s, Allied Artists, 1961

Director: Joseph M. Newman; *Screenplay:* Jo Swerling, based on the 1959 book *The Big Bankroll: The Life and Times of Arnold Rothstein* by Leo Katcher.

    Cast: David Janssen (*Arnold Rothstein*), Dianne Foster (*Carolyn Green*), Jack Carson ("*Big Tim*" *O'Brien*), Diana Dors (*Madge*), Dan O'Herlihy (*Phil Butler*), Mickey Shaughnessy (*Jim Kelly*), Keenan Wynn (*Tom Fowler*), Joseph Schildkraut (*Abraham Rothstein*), William Demarest (*Henry Hecht*), Murvyn Vye (*Williams*), Regis Toomey (*Bill Baird*), Robert Ellenstein (*Lenny*), Teri Janssen (*Joanie*), Jimmy Baird (*Arnold as a Boy*), Tim Rooney, Viola Harris, Steve Hammer, Howard Wendell and third-billed MR as Johnny Burke, a boyhood friend of notorious real-life '20s gangster-gambler Arnold Rothstein (Janssen) who rats out to the press their childhood-enemy-turned-police-biggie on the take and is rubbed out for his effort. Music score was by, of all people, the venerable Franz Waxman.

102. Everything's Ducky, Columbia Pictures, 1961

Director: Don Taylor; *Screenplay:* John Fenton Murray and Benedict Freedman.

Politically incorrect in *Breakfast at Tiffany's* (1961) (Paramount Pictures).

Cast: Buddy Hackett (*Adm. John Paul Jones*), Jackie Cooper (*Lt. Parnell*), Joanie Sommers (*Nina Lloyd*), Roland Winters (*Capt. Lewis Bollinger*), Elizabeth MacRae (*Susie Penrose*), Gene Blakely (*Lt. Cmdr. Kemp*), Gordon Jones (*Chief Conroy*), Richard Deacon (*Dr. Deckham*), James Milhollin (*George Imhoff*), King Calder (*Frank*), Dick Winslow (*Froehlich*), Alvy Moore (*Jim Lipscott*), Harold J. Kennedy

With daffy feathered friends in *Everything's Ducky* (1961), along with Buddy Hackett (Columbia Pictures).

(*Mr. Johnston*), Jimmy Cross, Robert B. Williams, Ellie Kent, William Hellinger, Ann Morell, George Sawaya and top-billed MR as sailor Beetle McKay. In this silly comedy involving a talking duck that has memorized a top-secret rocket guidance system, Beetle teams with mate Buddy Hackett as Adm. John Paul Jones to get themselves both inadvertently trapped in space orbit with their fowl pal. (Don't ask!) Rooney also sings the title song over the credits.

When this flick opened on the bottom half of a double bill in the "nabes" in and around New York a couple of days before Christmas 1961, *The Times* found it to be "an ostensible farce in which Mickey Rooney is required to play straight man to the comic Buddy Hackett and a talking duck. The alarming title is *Everything's Ducky*, and that should be warning enough for anyone."

With daffy feathered friend in *How to Stuff a Wild Bikini* (1966).

103. Requiem for a Heavyweight, Columbia Pictures, 1962

Director: Ralph Nelson; *Screenplay:* Rod Serling, based on his television play.

   Cast: Anthony Quinn (*Mountain Rivera*), Jackie Gleason (*Maish Rennick*), Julie Harris (*Grace Miller*), Stanley Adams (*Perelli*), Madame Spivy (*Ma Greeny*), Herbie Faye (*Bartender*), Lou Gilbert (*Ring Doctor*), Cassius Clay (*Ring Opponent*), Jack Dempsey (*Himself*), Val Avery, Barney Ross, Willy Pep, Arthur Mercante, Steve Belloise and third-billed MR as, Army, the trainer and "cutman" of washed-up prizefighter Mountain Rivera (Quinn). In this memorable boxing film, Rooney had the role played by Ed Wynn in the 1956 *Playhouse 90* television production.

104. It's a Mad, Mad, Mad, Mad World, Stanley Kramer/United Artists, 1963

Director: Stanley Kramer; *Screenplay.* William and Tania Rose.

   Cast: Spencer Tracy, Milton Berle, Sid Caesar, Buddy Hackett, Ethel Merman, Dick Shawn, Phil Silvers, Terry-Thomas, Jonathan Winters, Edie Adams, Peter Falk, Dorothy Provine, Jimmy Durante, Jack Benny, Eddie "Rochester" Anderson, The Three Stooges, Don Knotts, Carl Reiner, Joe E. Brown, Jim Backus, Art Carney, Andy Devine, Leo Gorcey, Edward Everett Horton, Buster Keaton, Jerry Lewis and dozens of others, and MR, billed sixth in a basically alphabetical list, as a wacky pilot named Dingy Bell. With pal Hackett, he joins the madcap race to locate a hidden cache of stolen money, among strangers who are given a clue to its where-abouts by an injured man (Durante) before he literally kicks the bucket. Tracy, as Police Capt. Culpepper, tails them all in a bemused manner.

105. Secret Invasion, United Artists, 1964

Director: Roger Corman; Screenplay. R. Wright Campbell.

Cast: Stewart Granger (*Maj. Richard Mace*), Raf Vallone (*Roberto Rocca*), Edd Byrnes (*Simon Fell*), Henry Silva (*John Durrell*), Mia Massini (*Mila*), William Campbell (*Jean Saval*), Peter Coe (*Marko*), Nan Morris (*Stephana*), Enzo Fiermonte (*Gen. Quadri*), Helmuth Schneider, Giulio Marchetti, Nicholas Rend, Todd Williams, Richard Johns, Kurt Bricker, Katrina Rozan and third-billed MR as vociferous IRA member Terence Scanlon, part of a team of convict specialists recruited by British officer Granger for a wartime mission in Yugoslavia.

"The picture's plot is not that good, and neither is the direction of Roger Corman," the *New York Post*'s Archer Winsten wrote. "The acting and the film's message are wholly within the boundaries of fast-moving action melodrama of World War II."

106. Twenty-Four Hours to Kill, Associated British, 1965

Director: Peter Bezencenet; *Screenplay:* Peter Yeldham and Peter Welbeck.

Cast: Lex Barker (*Jamie Faulkner*), Walter Slezak (*Malouf*), Michael Medwin (*Tommy Gaskell*), Helga Somerfeld (*Louise Braganza*), Wolfgang Lukaschy (*Kurt Hoffner*), France Anglade (*Franzi Bertram*), Helga Lehner (*Marianne*), Marie Rohm (*Claudine*), Nadia Gamel (*Mimi*), Shakib Khouri (*Andronicus*) and second-billed MR as international flight pilot Norman Jones, who finds his life at risk after double-crossing a gold smuggling syndicate run by Slezak in Beirut.

107. L'Arcidiavolo, Fair Films (Italy), 1966 [released in the U.S. as *The Devil in Love*, Warner Bros., 1968]

Director: Ettore Scala; *Screenplay:* Ruggero Massari and Scala.

Cast: Vittorio Gassman (*Balfagor*), Claudine Auger (*Magdalena*), Gabrielle Ferzetti (*Lorenzo de Medici*), Ettore Manni (*Guard Captain*), Liana Orfei (*Olimpia*), Giorgia Moll (*Aristocrat's Wife*), Annabella Incontrera (*Lucretia*), Luigi Vannucchi (*Prince Cybo*), Helene Chanel (*Clarice*), Paolo Di Credico (*Cardinal Giovanni*) and second-billed MR as Adramalek, the puckish aide to Gassman (and invisible to everyone but his boss), the Devil's emissary sent to Florence to cause discord between the Medicis and the Papal State.

108. Ambush Bay, United Artists, 1966

Director: Ron Winston; *Screenplay:* Marve Feinberg and Ib Melchior.

Cast: Hugh O'Brian (*First Sgt. Steve Corey*), James Mitchum (*Pfc James Grenier*), Tisa Chang (*Miyazaki*), Peter Masterson (*Platoon Sgt. William Maccone*), Harry Lauter (*Cpl. Alvin Ross*), Gregg Amsterdam (*Cpl. Stanley Parrish*), Tony Smith (*Pvt. George George*), Clem Sadler (*Capt. Alonzo Davis*), Amado Abello, Juris Sulit, Max Quismundo, Buff Fernandez, Joaquin Fajardo and second-billed MR as tough gunnery sergeant Ernest Wartell. He is a member of a nine-man Marine patrol in the wartime Philippines on a mission to contact a female spy with information vital for MacArthur's upcoming invasion; he then heroically stays behind to hold off an enemy patrol. (Rooney became ill, left the Philippine location

With Vittorio Gassman in *The Devil in Love* (1968).

filming early, returned to Los Angeles and walked in on a murder-suicide scene
in his bedroom involving his estranged wife and her gigolo friend.)

109. How to Stuff a Wild Bikini, American-International, 1966

Director: William Asher; *Screenplay:* Leo Townsend and Asher.

    Cast: Annette Funicello (*Dee Dee*), Dwayne Hickman (*Ricky*), Brian Donlevy
(*B.D. [Big Daddy]*), Harvey Lembeck (*Eric Von Zipper*), Beverly Adams (*Cassan-
dra*), John Ashley (*Johnny*), Jody McCrea (*Bonehead*), Len Lesser (*North Dakota
Pete*), Irene Tsu (*Native Girl*), Arthur Julian (*Dr. Melamed*), Bobbi Shaw (*Koola
Koku*), Buster Keaton (*Bwana*) and MR in a cameo in *Beach Party* territory as
fast-talking promoter Peachy Keane, searching the beach for the perfect body for
a contest, with the aid of Tahitian witch doctor Keaton and a pelican. Frankie
Avalon even turned up in an uncredited walk-on, as did Elizabeth Montgomery
(in one of her rare feature films, as a favor to her director husband Asher) in a
gag appearance as Bwana's witch daughter.

110. The Extraordinary Seaman, MGM, 1968

Director: John Frankenheimer; *Screenplay:* Philip Rock and Hal Dresner, based on
the 1967 novel by Rock.

    Cast: David Niven (*Lt. Cmdr. Finchhaven*), Faye Dunaway (*Jennifer Winslow*),

Alan Alda (*Lt. jg Morton Kim*), Jack Carter (*Gunner's Mate Orville Toole*), Juano Hernandez (*Ali Shar*), Barry Kelley (*Adm. Barnwell*), Manu Topou (*Seaman I/C Lightfoot Star*), Leonard O. Smith (*Dyak*), Jerry Fujikawa (*Adm. Ahimagoshi*) and third-billed MR as Cook Third Class W.G. Oglethorpe, a sailor in this little seen whimsical comedy (a strange choice for Frankenheimer). Fleeing the Japanese in the Philippines with motley mates Alda and Carter, Oglethorpe comes across a bearded ghost (Niven) from the World War I Royal Navy, doomed to live on shipboard until he vindicates his family honor.

In the U.S., the studio walked away from it. In Great Britain, on its premiere in 1970, *Today's Cinema* called it "a cleverly made curiosity. Not so much produced as manufactured [but] anyone looking forward to David Niven, Faye Dunaway, and Mickey Rooney will be sadly disappointed." And the *Monthly Film Bulletin* reported, "Compressed to 80 minutes, the film takes on the appearance of a pop art collage ... the satire of war works at a fairly simple level of enjoyable buffoonery, made more enjoyable by a pleasant set of characters pleasantly played."

111. Skidoo, Paramount Pictures, 1968

Director: Otto Preminger. *Screenplay:* Doran William Cannon.

Cast: Jackie Gleason (*Tony Banks*), Carol Channing (*Flo Banks*), Frankie Avalon (*Angie*), Fred Clark (*A Tower Guard*), Michael Constantine (*Leech*), Frank Gorshin (*The Man*), John Phillip Law (*Stash*), Peter Lawford (*The Senator*), Burgess

In *Skidoo* (1968) (Sigma Productions).

Meredith (*The Warden*), George Raft (*Capt. Garabaldo*), Cesar Romero (*Hechy*), Groucho Marx (*"God"*), Austin Pendleton (*The Professor*), Alexandra *Hays* (*Darlene Banks*), Arnold Stang (*Harry*), Doro Merande (*The Mayor*), Slim Pickens (*Telephone Operator*), Richard Kiel (*Beany*), Luna (*"God's" Mistress*), Phil Arnold, Robert Donner, Stacy King, Renny Roker, Roman Gabriel, Harry Nilsson, Stone Country and twelfth-billed (alphabetically) MR as "Blue Chips" Packard, a gangster living in luxury in prison, whom syndicate boss Marx calls on ex-mobster Gleason to rub out. Preminger's star-studded but bloated "hippie" comedy is better remembered for its soundtrack (music and lyrics by Harry Nilsson; he actually "sings" the credits, down to gaffers, best boys, the film's copyright date and the IATSE bug) than for its stellar cast.

112. The Comic, Columbia Pictures, 1969

Director: Carl Reiner; *Screenplay:* Aaron Rubin and Reiner.

Cast: Dick Van Dyke (*Billy Bright*), Michele Lee (*Mary Gibson*), Cornel Wilde (*Frank Powers*), Nina Wayne (*Sybil*), Jeannine Riley (*Lorraine*), Pert Kelton (*Mama*), Jeff Donnell (*Nurse*), Steve Allen (*Himself*), Carl Reiner (*Al Shilling*), Barbara Heller (*Ginger*), Gavin MacLeod (*Director*), Jay Novello (*Miguel*), Fritz Feld (*Armand*), Jerome Cowan (*Lawrence*), Ed Peck (*Edwin C. Englehardt*), Pauline Meyers (*Phoebe*), Bill Zuckert (*Warden*), Isabel Sanford (*Woman*) and third-billed MR as Cockeye, the rummy-eyed vaudeville pal of the egocentric Stan Laurel–like onetime star (Van Dyke) in Reiner's heartfelt but unsuccessful look back at the life of a boozing former film great. Original title: *Billy Bright.*

Roger Greenspun wrote in *The New York Times*: "It isn't a good movie but it is often an interesting one, and it is full of lovely people. The loveliest is Mickey Rooney, as a cockeyed comedian, who plays old age as a quality as well as a time of life."

113. 80 Steps to Jonah, Warner Bros., 1969

Director: Gerd Oswald; *Screenplay:* Frederic Lewis Fox, from a story by Fox and Oswald.

Cast: Wayne Newton (*Mark Jonah Winters*), Jo Van Fleet (*Nonna*), Keenan Wynn (*Barney Glover*), Sal Mineo (*Jerry Taggart*), Diana Ewing (*Tracy*), Slim Pickens (*Scott*), R.G. Armstrong (*Mackray*), Brandon Cruz (*Little Joe*), Erin Moran (*Kim*), Teddy Quinn (*Richard*), Butch Patrick (*Brian*), Jackie Kahane (*Himself*), Susan Mathews (*Velma*), Lily Martens (*Nina*), Ira Angustain (*Pepe*), Dennis Cross (*Maxon*), Joe Conley (*Jenkins*), Frank Schuller (*Whitney*), Fred Dale (*Sheriff*) and MR in a cameo as Wilfred Bashford, a drunk whose testimony about a stolen car accident is needed to clear Newton, who has been hiding out as a handyman at a school for blind children. This vehicle for singer Newton was an unsuccessful attempt to make him a film star before he went off to become the king of Las Vegas.

114. The Cockeyed Cowboy of Calico County, Universal Pictures, 1970

Director: Tony Leader; *Screenplay:* Ranald MacDougall.

Cast: Dan Blocker (*Charley*), Nanette Fabray (*Sadie*), Jim Backus (*Staunch*), Wally Cox (*Mr. Bester*), Jack Elam (*Kittrick*), Henry Jones (*Hanson*), Stubby Kaye (*Bartender*), Noah Beery, Jr. (*Eddie*), Marge Champion (*Mrs. Bester*), Don "Red"

In *The Cockeyed Cowboys of Calico County* (1970) (Universal Pictures).

Barry (*Rusty*), Jack Cassidy (*Roger Hand*), Hamilton Camp (*Mr. Fowler*), Byron Foulger (*Reverend Marshall*), Iron Eyes Cody (*Crazy Foot*), James McCallion (*Dr. Henry*) and eighth-billed MR as Indian Tom, a local cowpoke, in this lighthearted Western about a lonely frontier blacksmith (Blocker) who sends for a mail-order bride (Fabray).

115. Hollywood Blue, Sherpix, 1970
Director: Bill Osco.

In this tasteless compilation of erotic shorts and newly filmed hard-core porn, the "redeeming values" are the interpolated interviews with MR (his all-time low in films) and June Wilkinson, talking heads who stay clothed and philosophize on Hollywood's sex life.

116. B.J. Lang Presents, CoBurt Productions/Maron Films, 1971
Director: Yabo Yablonsky; *Screenplay:* Yablonsky, from a story by John Durin.

Cast: Keenan Wynn (*Old Charlie*), Luana Anders (*Carlotta*) and top-billed MR as B.J. Lang, an insane has-been movie director who fantasizes about the past and acts out his productions with a terrified girl in a warehouse of film memorabilia. The barely released flick played for a couple of days at a dingy 42nd Street movie house in the Big Apple and then disappeared. A number of years later, it became available on tape under the title *The Manipulator*.

117. Evil Roy Slade, Universal Pictures, 1972

Director: Jerry Paris; *Screenplay:* Garry Marshall and Jerry Belson.

   Cast: John Astin (*Evil Roy Slade*), Dick Shawn (*Bing Bell*), Henry Gibson (*Clifford Stool*), Dom DeLuise (*Logan Delp*), Edie Adams (*Flossie*), Pam Austin (*Betsy Potter*), Milton Berle (*Harry Fern*), Luana Anders (*Alice Fern*), Robert Liberman (*Preacher*), Milton Frome (*Foss the Telegrapher*), Ed Cambridge (*Smith*), Arthur Batanides (*Lee*), Larry Hankin (*Snake*), Connie Sawyer (*Aggie Potter*), Pat Morita (*Turhan*), Billy Sands (*Randolph Sweet*), Leonard Barr (*Crippled Man*), Penny Marshall (*Bank Teller*), John Ritter (*Minister*), Jerry Paris (*Souvenir Salesman*), Pat Buttram (*Narrator*) and top-billed MR as railroad president Nelson Stool in this made-for-TV comedy Western, the nemesis of rotten outlaw Astin, whose villainy knows no bounds.

118. Richard, Bertrand Castelli/Aurora City Group, 1972

Director: Loress Yerby and Harry Hurwitz; *Screenplay:* Yerby and Hurwitz.

   Cast: Richard M. Dixon [James LaRoe] (*Richard*), Dan Resin (*Young Richard*), Lynn Lipton (*Young Pat*), John Carradine (*Plastic Surgeon*), Paul Ford, Vivian Blaine, Kevin McCarthy (*Washington Doctors*), Hazen Gifford (*Advisor*), Hank Garrett (*Advisor*), Paul Forrest (*Advisor*) and seventh-billed MR as Richard Nixon's guardian angel in this satirical study of Nixon's life from boyhood through the presidency. Nixon impersonator Richard M. Dixon has the title role.

119. Pulp, United Artists, 1972

Director: Mike Hodges; *Screenplay:* Hodges.

   Cast: Michael Caine (*Mickey King*), Lizabeth Scott (*Princess Betty Cippola*), Lionel Stander (*Ben Dinuccio*), Dennis Price (*Mysterious Englishman*), Nadia Cassini (*Liz Adams*), Al Lettieri (*Prof. Miller*), Leopoldo Trieste (*Marcovic*), Amerigo Tot (*Sotgio*), Robert *Sacchi* (*Jim Norman*) and second-billed MR in his best role in years as fictional '30s Hollywood star Preston Gilbert, famed for his gangster roles, who hires a hack writer (Caine) to "ghost" his revealing memoirs. *Time* magazine wrote of Rooney's work in the film: "The performance, like the movie itself, deserves to become some crazy kind of minor classic."

120. The Godmothers, Michael Viola Productions, 1973

Director: William Grefe; *Screenplay:* Mickey Rooney, from a story by Woody Kling and Robert Hilliard, based on an idea by Jerry Lester.

   Cast: Frank Fontaine (*Don Palermo*), Jerry Lester (*Ricky Mastrasso*), Joe E. Ross (*Gino*), Billy Barty (*The Hawk*), Danny Aiello (*The Shark*), Lou Marsh, Tony Adams, Muriel Jones, Bob Gordon and top-billed MR who, with fellow hood Lester, he goes on the lam in drag—*a la* Tony Curtis and Jack Lemmon in Billy Wilder's *Some Like It Hot*—after angering godfather Fontaine in this gangster spoof, filmed virtually in the star's backyard in Fort Lauderdale. Rooney wrote the screenplay and the music.

   Of this "wild romp about some witless wonders of the underworld" (as Rooney promoted it), the *Miami Herald* film critic found, "It's a slapstick story—if it can

As Richard Nixon's guardian angel in *Richard* (1972) (with Nixon impersonator Richard M. Dixon).

Opposite, top: Rooney (right) with Jerry Lester (center) in *The Godmothers* (1973). *Bottom:* Producer Michael Viola (standing left) and director William Grefe — both well-armed — minding the cast, including Joe E. Ross (standing right) and (front row, from left) Jerry Lester, Rooney, Frank Fontaine, Socrates Ballis and Billy Barty.

be called a story — [in which] Rooney and Lester play a pair of inept hoods who get into scrapes trying to take over the underworld leadership from Don Palermo while escaping the romantic clutches of his hugely homely daughter.... The bulk of the movie, filmed in Fort Lauderdale, is devoted to endless sight gags and one-liners, usually found in the repertoire of television and nightclub comics....' There's no blood in this picture,' Hawk (3'6" Billy Barty) says, 'but it took a lot of guts.' He's right."

121. As de Corazon (Ace of Hearts), Mundial Films, S.A., 1974

Director: Tulio De Micheli; *Screenplay:* Santiago Moncada.

   Cast: Chris Robinson (*Dean Lewis*), Pilar Velazquez (*Jill*), Teresa Gimpera (*Shirley*), Carlos Ballesteros (*Freddy*), Angel Menendez (*Wendy*), Julian Ugarte (*Still*), Eduardo Fajardo (*Edward*), Paul Givonetti (*Charly*), Donald Loshe (*Duke*) and "special guest" MR as Papa Joe, a poker-playing gangster, in this Spanish-Italian co-production about big business intrigue that revolves around the turn of a card. Chris Robinson, Rooney's pal and business partner, has the starring role.

122. That's Entertainment, MGM, 1974

Director: Jack Haley, Jr.

   MR is one of 11 on-camera stars narrating scenes from MGM's best between 1929 and 1958, and talking about the movies he did with Judy Garland.

123. Journey Back to Oz, Filmation, 1974

Director: Hal Sutherland; *Screenplay:* Fred Ladd and Norm Prescott.

   MR provides the voice of the Scarecrow in this animated feature (made in 1971) about Dorothy and Toto's return visit to Oz. Other voices include Liza Minnelli as Dorothy, Milton Berle as the Cowardly Lion, Danny Thomas as the Tinman, Margaret Hamilton as Aunt Em, Paul Ford as Uncle Henry, Rise Stevens as Glinda, the Good Witch, Ethel Merman as Mombi, the Wicked Witch, and Herschel Bernardi, Jack E. Leonard, Mel Blanc and, Larry Storch. Original songs written by Sammy Cahn and James Van Heusen.

124. Thunder County (aka It Snows in the Everglades), Trans-International Films, 1974

Director: Chris Robinson; *Screenplay:* K. Gordon Murray.

   Cast: Chris Robinson (*Victor Di Giorgio/Paul Schumaker*), Ted Cassidy (*Renzo Gambetti*), Carol Lawson (*Adele*), Onya Mark (*Sally*), Dee Dee Bradley (*Lizzie*), Phyllis Robinson (*Carla*), Buddy DeSaro (*Bo Kranker*), Bob Shields (*Siciliano*), Bob Leslie (*Buggy*) and third-billed MR as a scummy bartender in a bayou country roadhouse, a rendezvous for drug dealers on the run from the Feds. It's invaded by a bunch of women who have crashed out of the nearby prison and kidnap him for his outboard motorboat. This low-budget exploitation film is available on tape as *Convict Women*.

125. Bon Baisers de Hong Kong (From Hong Kong with Love), Films Christian Fechner/Renn Productions, 1975

Director: Yves Chiffre; *Screenplay:* Fechner and Chiffre.

In *Thunder County* (1974).

Cast: Les Charlots (*Undercover Men*), Huguette Funfrock (*Queen*), David Tomlinson (*Protocol Chief*), Clifton James (*Bailey*), Jean Manson (*Singer*) and second-billed MR as a mad millionaire who has snatched Britain's queen from Buckingham Palace. This French-made James Bond send-up is a vehicle for the popular French comedy foursome Les Charlots. As the mad kidnapper, *Variety* noted, "a puffy Mickey Rooney manages to kid himself and not fall into the trap of trying to repeat his early élan."

126. Rachel's Man, SJ International/Hemdale, 1975

Director: Moshe Mizrahi; *Screenplay:* Rachel Fabien and Mizrahi.

Cast: Rita Tushingham (*Leah*), Leonard Whiting (*Jacob*), Michal Bat-Adam (*Rachel*), Rachel Levi (*Laban's Wife*), Avner Hiskiyahu (*Isaac*), Dahlia Cohen *Zilpah*), Sari Shapira (*Bilha*), Yair Reuben (*Esau*), Yossi Pollack (*Giant Smith*), Yossi Graber (*Godhead*), Moshe Ish-Cassit (*Angel*), Robert Stevens (*Storyteller*) and top-billed MR, over-the-top in an unlikely performance —channeling Zero Mostel — as Laban, father of Rachel (Bat-Adam) and Lea (Tushingham) and the uncle of Jacob (Whiting) and Esau (Reuben) in this biblical drama filmed in Israel. Britain's *Monthly Film Bulletin* noted: "Fortunately, Mickey Rooney is given some lines to say, and the zest with which he plays them gives much-needed life to a film which generally proceeds in a very poker-faced fashion."

127. Find the Lady, Quadrant Films, 1976

Director: John Trent; *Screenplay:* David Main and Trent.

Cast: Lawrence Dane (*Det. Sgt. Roscoe Brown*), John Candy (*Officer Kopek*), Dick Emery (*Leo the Hood*), Peter Cook (*J.K. Lewenhak*), Alexandra Bastedo (*Victoria*), Richard Monette (*Bruce La Rousse*), Bob Vinci (*Frescobaldi*), Ed McNamara (*Capt. Kaminsky*), Tim Henry (*Rick*), Rummy Bishop (*Charlie "The Wheel" Murphy*), Gino Marrocco (*Mario*), Lou Pitoscia (*Luigi*), Robert McHeady (*Sgt. Reilly*), Laurie Seto (*Officer Flanagan*), Delroy Lindo (*Sam*), Elizabeth Murphy (*Ruby the Stripper*), Michael Kirby, Hugh Webster, Candy Kane, Anne Marie Sten, John Bethune, Dedena Morello, Gloria Sauve, Guy Big and third-billed MR as an inept, gun-happy hood nicknamed Trigger (just three weeks on his own after apprenticing with "Bugsy Spiegel"). With fellow torpedo Emery, he is hired by dastardly Cook to snatch his pretty (but tone deaf) opera wannabe niece. This Canadian-made gangster comedy was the second in a Canadian series of Abbott and Costello–like flicks involving Dane and Candy as bumbling cops.

128. The Domino Principle, ITC/Avco-Embassy, 1977

Director: Stanley Kramer; *Screenplay:* Adam Kennedy, based on his 1975 novel.

Cast: Gene Hackman (*Roy Tucker*), Candice Bergen (*Ellie Tucker*), Richard Widmark (*Tagge*), Edward Albert (*Ross Pine*), Eli Wallach (*Gen. Tom Reser*), Ken Swofford (*Ditcher*), Neva Patterson (*Gaddis*), Jay Novello (*Capt. Ruiz*), Claire Brennan (*Ruby*), Ted Gehrig (*Schnaible*), Joseph Perry (*Bowcamp*), Majel Barrett (*Mrs. Schnaible*), James Gavin (*Lenny*), George Fisher (*Henemeyer*), Denver Mattson (*Murdock*), Bob Herron (*Brookshire*), Charles Horvath (*Harley*), Wayne King, John Hudkins, Patricia Luke, George Sawaya and fourth-billed MR as Spiventa, the San Quentin cellmate of convict and Vietnam marksman Hackman, sprung with him to take part in a highly secret job for a mysterious organization in this somewhat wan political thriller.

129. Pete's Dragon, Buena Vista, 1977

Director: Don Chaffey; *Screenplay:* Malcolm Marmerstein, from a story by Seton I. Miller and S.S. Field.

Cast: Helen Reddy (*Nora*), Jim Dale (*Dr. Terminus*), Red Buttons (*Hoagy*), Shelley Winters (*Lena Gogan*), Sean Marshall (*Pete*), Charlie Callas (*Voice of Elliott*), Jim Backus (*Mayor*), Jeff Conaway (*Willie*), Jane Kean (*Miss Taylor*), Charles Tyner (*Merle*), Walter Barnes (*Captain*) and third-billed MR as a grizzled lighthouse keeper named Lampie in Disney's live action–animated fantasy about young orphan Marshall's adventures with an occasionally visible dragon called Elliot.

130. The Magic of Lassie, Lassie Productions/International Picture Show, 1978

Director: Don Chaffey; *Screenplay:* Jean Holloway, and Robert B. and Richard M. Sherman.

Cast: James Stewart (*Clovis Mitchell*), Pernell Roberts (*Jamison*), Stephanie Zimbalist (*Kelly*), Alice Faye (*Alice*), Michael Sharrett (*Chris*), Gene Evans (*Sheriff Andrews*), Mike Mazurki (*Apollo*), Robert Lussier (*Finch*), Lane Davies (*Allan Fogerty*), The Mike Curb Congregation, Lassie and second-billed MR as Gus, a down-at-the-heels wrestling manager whose life intersects with Lassie's. Bonita Granville, who produced this film with her husband Jack Wrather (they owned the Lassie franchise, as well as the Lone Ranger one), found herself reunited with

With Bonita Granville Wrather in 1977 while filming *The Magic of Lassie*, which she produced, and as they were as costars of *Love Laughs at Andy Hardy* three decades earlier (UPI).

Mickey — puppy love sweethearts back in the Andy Hardy days. This film also marked the comeback after many years for Alice Faye (playing a waitress and singing a song called "A Rose Is Not a Rose," written by Richard M. and Robert B. Sherman). It was her last time on the screen. It was also James Stewart's last starring role.

131. The Black Stallion, Omni Zoetrope/United Artists, 1979

Director: Carroll Ballard; *Screenplay:* Melissa Mathison, Jeanne Rosenberg and William D. Wittliff, based on the 1941 novel by Walter Farley.

Cast: Kelly Reno (*Alec Ramsey*), Teri Garr (*Alec's Mother*), Clarence Muse (*Snoe*), Hoyt Axton (*Alec's Father*), Michael Higgins (*Jim Neville*), Ed McNamara (*Jake*), Doghmi Larbi (*Arab*), John Burton (*First Jockey*), John Buchanan (*Second Jockey*), Kristen Vigard (*Becky*), Fausto Tozzi (*Fishing Boat Captain*), John Karlson (*Archae-ologist*), Leopoldo Trieste (*Priest*), Marne Maitland (*Captain of "The Drake"*); Cass Olé (as The Black/horse) and second-billed MR in a latter day, Oscar-nominated career highlight as Henry Dailey, a onetime jockey who takes in a runaway (11-year-old Reno) and his horse and teaches the youngster to ride. Francis Ford Coppola executive-produced the film.

"Splendidly acted — Mickey Rooney underplays his palpably relished role and at all times defers to Kelly Reno," reported Great Britain's *Monthly Film Bulletin*.

In 1990, Rooney would repeat the role of Henry Dailey in the Canadian-made

With Kelly Reno in *The Black Stallion* (1978) (United Artists Corporation).

TV series *The Adventures of Black Stallion*. He did not, however, appear in the original film's 1983 sequel or the 2003 prequel.

132. Donovan's Kid, Buena Vista, 1979

Director: Bernard McEveety; *Screenplay:* Harry Spaulding, from a story by Peter S. Fischer.

Cast: Darren McGavin (*Timothy Donovan*), Shelley Fabares (*Grace Donovan*), Murray Hamilton (*Henry Carpenter*), Michael Conrad (*Silas Rumford*), Ross Martin (*Mayor Stokes*), Katy Kurtzman (*Jamie Carpenter*), Brenda Scott (*Charity Donovan*), Larry D. Mann (*Larson*), John Crawford (*Thunder City Sheriff*), Martin Kove (*Kelso*), H.B. Haggerty (*Sharkey Lynch*), James Almanzar, Alvy Moore, David Cass, Don "Red" Barry, Larry Pennell, James Chandler, Joe Higgins, Dick Winslow, Warde Donovan, Ralph Manza and second-billed MR as Old Bailey, sidekick to con man McGavin in this lighthearted Disney made-for-television turn-of-the-century Western.

133. Arabian Adventure, Columbia Pictures/EMI, 1979

Director: Kevin Connor; *Screenplay:* Brian Hayles.

Cast: Christopher Lee (*Alquazar*), Milo O'Shea (*Khasim*), Oliver Tobias (*Prince Hasan*), Emma Samms (*Princess Zuleira*), Puneet Sira (*Majeed*), John Wyman (*Bahloul*), John Ratzenberger (*Ahmed*), Shane Rimmer (*Abu*), Hal Galill (*Asaf*), Peter Cushing (*Wazir Al Wuzara*), Capucine (*Vahishta*), Elizabeth Welch

In *Arabian Adventure* (1980).

(*Beggarwoman*), Milton Reid (*Genie*), Jacob Witkin (*Omar the Goldsmith*), Suzanne Danielle, Athar Malik, Andrew Bradford, Tim Peerce, and twelfth-billed MR as Daad El Shar, "guardian of the rose" and keeper of three fire-breathing dragons. A lighthearted Arabian Nights fantasy, the film pits evil sorcerer Lee against heroic prince Tobias to save the latter's beloved Samms from him.

John Pym, critic for Great Britain's *Monthly Film Bulletin*, wrote, "Alan Hume's crisp photography complements an improved standard of effects and model work: the shaky dinosaurs of the past have been replaced by a trio of mechanical monsters, manipulated by the scurrying, gibbering Mickey Rooney, and help make up for the tendentious motions of good and evil floated by Brian Hayles' clotted script."

134. My Kidnapper, My Love, Roger Gimbel Productions/EMI Television, 1980

Director: Sam Wanamaker; *Screenplay:* Louis Elias, based on the novel 1974 *The Dark Side of Love* by Oscar Saul.

Cast: James Stacy (*Denny*), Glynnis O'Connor (*GeeGee/Arlette Fairlain*), J.D. Cannon (*Lt. Kringler*), Jan Sterling (*Letty Fairlain*), Richard Venture (*Arthur Fairlain*), Ellen Geer (*Paula Stanley*), Lonny Stevens (*The King of Spades*), Darryl Young (*Willie*), Louis Elias (*Lowell*), Nick Kreiger (*Admiral*), Christopher Needles (*Perdy*), Lionel Ferbis, Jr. (*Deacon*), and sixth-billed MR as a small-time crook known as "The Maker." He talks his brother Stacy, a crippled New Orleans newsstand vendor (the actor had lost his left arm and his left leg six years earlier in a motorcycle accident), into kidnapping a wealthy, emotionally disturbed runaway as part of a get-rich-quick scheme in this made-for-television movie.

Variety's critic wrote: "Rooney continues to best himself, and in this role creates an extraordinary portrait of someone determined to make it, but frightened he won't."

135. Leave 'Em Laughing, Charles Fries Productions, 1981

Director: Jackie Cooper; *Screenplay:* Cynthia Mandelberg and Peggy Chantler Dick, based on the life story of Jack Thum.

Cast: Anne Jackson (*Shirlee Thum*), Allen Goorwitz [Garfield] (*Dr. Abrahms*), Elisha Cook (*Jetter*), Red Buttons (*Roland Green*), William Windom (*Smiley Jenkins*), Michael LeClair (*Tommy*), Adrianne Kingman (*Alice*), Carol Ann Susi (*Gina*), De'voreaux White (*Ralph*), Bruce French (*McClain*), Gary Miller, Jan Stratton, Candy Morley, Richard Paxton and top-billed MR in this TV biopic about Jack Thum, a failed Chicago clown who, along with devoted wife Jackson, become surrogate parents to 37 orphaned and rejected children.

136. The Fox and the Hound, Buena Vista, 1981

Director: Art Stevens, Ted Berman and Richard Rich.

Disney's animated version of the children's classic by Daniel P. Mannix, featuring MR as the voice of Tod, the fox. Others supplying voices are Kurt Russell, Pearl Bailey, Jack Albertson, Sandy Duncan, Jeanette Nolan, John McIntire, Pat Buttram, John Fiedler and Paul Winchell.

At left with director and boyhood pal Jackie Cooper on the set of *Leave 'Em Laughing* (1981); and as they were in 1935 when filming *The Devil Is a Sissy* (CBS-TV) (Cooper is at the right in both photographs).

137. L'Empereur du Pérou (The Emperor of Peru), Cine-Pacific/ Babylone Films, 1981

Director: Fernando Arrabal; *Screenplay:* Roger Lemelin and Arrabal.

Cast: Jonathan Starr (*Toby*), Anick (*Liz*), Ky Huot Uk (*Hoang*), Jean-Louis Roux (*Uncle Alex*), Monique Mercure (*Aunt Elsa*), Valda Dalton (*Flora*), Guy Hoffman (*Mayor*), John Stanzel (*Jonathan*), Vastra Vrana (*Policeman*), Jean-Pierre Saulnier (*Fireman*), Marie-Josée Morin (*Immigration Officer*), Georges Taborky (*Hoang's father*), Kim Ny Ith (*Hoang's Mother*) and top-billed MR as a former locomotive engineer living in a wagon near an abandoned railway station. He befriends a homeless young brother and sister and a Cambodian orphan they have adopted, in this fanciful Canadian-French co-production, later released on videotape as *Odyssey of the Pacific*.

138. Bill, Alan Landsburg Productions, 1981

Director: Anthony Page; *Screenplay:* Corey Blechman, based on the story of Bill Sackter by Barry Morrow.

Cast: Dennis Quaid (*Barry Morrow*), Largo Woodruff (*Bev Morrow*), Anna Maria Horsford (*Ms. Marge Keating*), Harry Goz (*Dr. Tom Walz*), Kathleen Maguire (*Mrs. Florence Archer*), William J. Daparto (*Ray*), Raymond Serra (*Harry*), Jenny

Dweir (*Amy Hill*), George Hamlin (*Robert Morrow*), Katherine Balfour (*Mrs. Morrow*), Harriet Rogers (*Bill's Landlady*) and top-billed MR in a memorable, Best Actor Emmy-winning role. He plays Bill Sackter, a mentally retarded adult who, with the help of newfound friend Barry Morrow (Quaid), tackles life outside of the institution where he spent 44 years. A made-for-television movie.

"The acting centerpiece is clearly Mickey Rooney. The role of Bill offers the kind of opportunity that could degenerate into a 'bravura' performance," John J. O'Connor said in *The New York Times*. Mr. Rooney has chosen, wisely, to take the road of restraint. As a superb clown, he can look profoundly sad in repose, his eyes going darkly blank. Then, on the slightest pretext, he can switch to a smile that embodies something approaching an all-trusting delight. Between the two extremes, Bill comes firmly into dramatic shape without the need for extra theatrical gimmicks.

139. Bill: On His Own, Alan Landsburg Productions, 1983

Director: Anthony Page; *Screenplay:* Barry Morrow.

Cast: Helen Hunt (*Jenny Wells*), Edie McClurg (*Angela*), Tracey Walter (*Kenny*), Teresa Wright (*Mae Driscoll*), Harry Goz (*Dr. Tom Walz*), Paul Lieber (*Rabbi Jeff Portman*), Dennis Quaid (*Barry Morrow*), Largo Woodruff (*Bev Morrow*), Terry Evans (*Dog*), Marianna Clore Blasé (*Mrs. Noble*), Jeremy Michael Hayes (*Clay*), Sharon Menzel (*Shirley Crandall*), Marina Astudillo (*Dr. Edith Franklin*), Sebastian Beeton (*Jamie Turner*) and top-billed MR repeating his television role as Bill Sackter (another Emmy nomination). He interacts with new friends in a group home run by Wright and mourns the loss of friend and mentor Barry Morrow (Quaid), who is moving far away for a new job.

140. It Came Upon a Midnight Clear, Columbia Pictures Television, 1984

Director: Peter H. Hunt; *Screenplay:* Frank Cardea and George Schenk.

Cast: Scott Grimes (*Robbie Westin*), Barrie Youngfellow (*Kate Westin*), George Gaynes (*Archangel*), Lloyd Nolan (*Monsignor Donoghue*), Christina Pickles (*Chris*), Elisha Cook, Jr. (*Mr. Bibbs*), Hamilton Camp (*Meek Angel*), William Griffis (*Wiley Boggs*), Gary Bayer (*Rick Westin*), Nicholas Hormann (*Mr. Jones*), Wynn Irwin (*Santini*), Babette Tweed (*Joanie*), Annie Potts (*Cindy Mills*), Alyson Kirk (*Missy Westin*), Lurene Tuttle (*Mrs. Hunt*), George Pentecost, Buddy Douglas, Billy Curtis, Jerry Maren, Gary Imhoff, Benny Baker, Paddi Edwards, Eve Smith, Michael Laskin, Jan Chamberlin [Mrs. MR] (*Music Teacher*) and top-billed MR as Mike Halligan, a retired New York City cop living with his family in California. He decides to show his grandson (Grimes) his first snow with a real White Christmas in New York — and on the trip back East he dies. But Mike makes a deal with a Heavenly Angel to return to Earth for a week, until Christmas, to show the boy its glories. A made-for-TV movie.

141. The Care Bears Movie, Goldwyn Pictures, 1985

Director: Arna Selznick; *Screenplay:* Peter Sauder.

Treacly made-in-Canada animated film for tots under the age of four, based on Care Bear Toys characters, with MR as the voice of Mr. Cherrywood, reading children at his orphanage a bedtime story about an ethereal place called Care-A-Lot. Other voices include Georgia Engel, Harry Dean Stanton, Jackie Burroughs, Eva

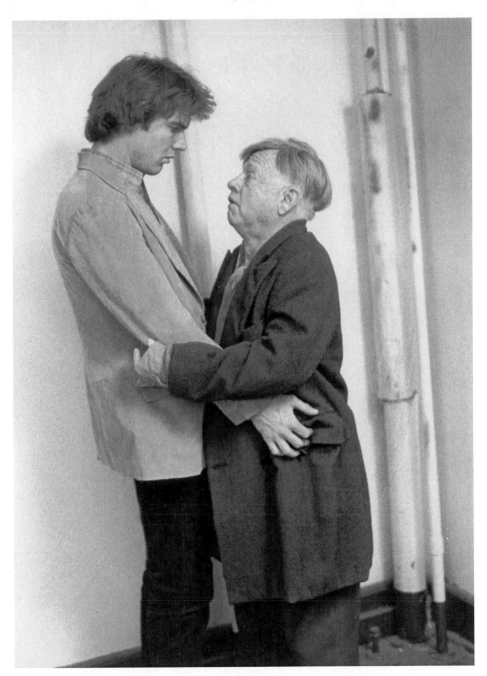

In his Emmy-winning role as Bill Sackter — with Dennis Quaid — in *Bill* (1981) (CBS-TV).

Almos, Patricia Black, Jayne Eastwood, Janet-Laine Green, Melleny Brown, Bob Dermer, Sunny Bensen Thrasher, Anni Evans, Brian George and Susan Roman.

142. Return of Mickey Spillane's Mike Hammer, Columbia Pictures Television, 1986

Director: Ray Danton, *Screenplay:* Janis Hendler, James M. Miller and Larry Brody, based on characters created by Mickey Spillane.

Cast: Stacy Keach (*Mike Hammer*), Don Stroud (*Capt. Pat Chambers*), Lindsay Bloom (*Velda*), Kent Williams (*Lawrence D. Barrington*), Vince Edwards (*Inspector Frank Walker*), Lauren Hutton (*Joanna Lake*), John Karlen (*Simon Chapel*), Frank McRae (*Herschel Dean*), Leo Penn (*Leo Hawkins*), Mike Preston (*Dak*), Stephen Macht (*Nick Anton*), Bruce Boxleitner, Dabney Coleman, Dionne Warwick (*Themselves*), Tom Everett (*Orville Tate*), Emily Chance (*Megan Lake*), Lee Benton (*Jenny*), David Chow (*Prof. Lai*), Peter Iacanagelo (*Norwood Fitz*), Hunter von Leer (*Sneakers Man*), Danny Goldman (*Ozzie the Answer*) and MR in a cameo in this made-for-TV flick, as a gabby movie agent named Jack Bergan.

143. Little Spies, Walt Disney Television, 1986

Director: Greg Beeman; *Screenplay:* Stephen Bons and Stephen Greenfield, from an original story by Bons, Greenfield and John Greg Pain.

Cast: Robert Costanzo (*Bernie*), Peter S. Smith (*Jason*), Candace Cameron (*Julie*), Adam Carl (*Jason*), Sean Hall (*Clarence*), Jason Harvey (*Clint Westwood*), Sarah Jo Martin (*Kristi*), Scott Nemes (*Wendell*), James Tolkan (*The Kennel Master*), Jamie Abbott (*Sponge*), Kevin King Cooper (*Spud*), Laura Jacoby (*Blister*), Eric Walker (*Scratch*), Robin Pearson Rose (*Jason's Mother*), Alan Haufrecht (*Jason's Father*), Art La Fleur (*Sgt. Westwood*) and top-billed MR as neighborhood recluse Jimmy the Hermit, a World War II hero. The neighborhood kids recruit him —*à la* the old Mickey McGuire shorts— to mastermind a raid on a puppy kennel to rescue their adopted dog from the clutches of evil kennel owner Tolkan. A lighthearted Disney made-for-TV entertainment.

144. Lightning — The White Stallion, Cannon Films, 1986

Director: William A. Levey; *Screenplay:* Peter Welbeck.

Cast: Susan George (*Madame René*), Isabel Garcia Lorca (*Stephanie Ward*), Billy Wesley (*Lucas Mitchell*), Martin Charles Warner (*Emmett*), Françoise Pascal (*Marie Ward Leeman*), Boyd "Red" Morgan (*Harvey Leeman*), Stanley Siegel (*Jim Piper*), Jay Rasumny (*Johnny*), Debra Berger (*Lili Castle*), Murray Langston (*Gorman*), Rick Lundin (*Max*), Justin Lundin (*Wiley*), Charles Pitt (*Judge*), Sheila Colligan, Karen Davis, Claudia Stenke, Rob Gage, Jennifer Young, Shannon McLeod, John Warren James and top-billed MR as Barney Ingram, a millionaire gambler and horse breeder. He joins up with a teenage girl who is losing her eyesight (Lorca) to retrieve a prize white stallion that has been stolen — and, in a bow to the long ago *National Velvet*, he teaches her to become a first-class rider.

Variety, reviewing this at the 1986 Cannes Film Festival, noted: "As Ingram, Rooney is trotted out for some mugging, and he just can't help being endearing."

145. Bluegrass, The Landsburg Company 1988

Director: Simon Wincer; *Screenplay:* Mart Crowley, based on the 1976 novel by Borden Deal.

Striking a Teddy Roosevelt–like pose as horse breeder Barney Ingram in *Lightning—The White Stallion* (1986).

Cast: Cheryl Ladd (*Maude Sage Breen*), Brian Kerwin (*Dancy Cutler*), Anthony Andrews (*Michael Fitzgerald*), Shawnee Smith (*Alice Gibbs*), Diane Ladd (*Verna Howland*), Kieran Mulroney (*Merlin Honeycutt*), Wayne Rogers (*Judge Lowell Shipleigh*), Arthur Rosenberg (*Murray Steiner*), Judith-Marie Bergan (*Irene Shipleigh*), Jerry Hardin (*Brock Walters*), Will Cascio (*White Dahl*), Charles David Cooper (*Wilson Goodbody*), Othello Pumphrey (*Bulldog Lewis*), Jack Milton Caldwell, Jack Stubblefield Johnson, Paula Irvine, Duane Wheatley, Chuck Stephenson and seventh-billed MR as an eccentric businessman named John Paul Jones with a keen eye for horse flesh. A romantic made-for-TV drama, *Bluegrass* focusing on Cheryl Ladd's struggles to achieve success and acceptance among Kentucky's horsey set, and in a quandary about which suitor she should choose.

146. Erik the Viking, Orion Pictures, 1989

Director: Terry Jones; *Screenplay:* Jones, from his 1983 book *The Saga of Erik the Viking*.

    Cast: Tim Robbins (*Erik*), Eartha Kitt (*Freya*), Terry Jones (*King Arnulf*), Imogen Stubbs (*Princess Aud*), John Cleese (*Halfdan the Black*), Tsutomo Sekine (*Slavemaster*), Antony Sher (*Loki*), Gary Cady (*Keitel Blacksmith*), John Gordon Sinclair (*Ivan the Boneless*), Samantha Bond (*Helga*), Tim McInnerny (*Sven the Berserk*), Richard Ridings (*Thorfinn Skullsplitter*), Freddie Jones (*Harald the Missionary*), Jim Broadbent (*Ernest the Viking*), Charles McKeown (*Sven's Dad*), Danny Schiller (*Snorri the Miserable*), Jim Carter (*Jennifer the Viking*), Sian Thomas (*Thorhild the Sarcastic*), Angela Connolly (*Thorkatla the Indiscreet*), Cyril Shaps (*Gisli the Chiseller*) and second billed MR, hamming it up as the grandfather of Robbins' heroic title character (who is not much into pillaging and raping) in this Monty Pythonesque romp.

    In his "thumbs down" review, Roger Ebert wrote in *The Chicago Sun-Times*: "Every once in a while a movie comes along that makes me feel like a human dialysis machine. The film goes into my mind, which removes its impurities, and then it evaporates into thin air. *Erik the Viking* is a movie like that, an utterly worthless exercise in waste and wretched excess, uninformed by the slightest spark of humor, wit or coherence."

147. Home for Christmas, New World Pictures, 1990

Director: Peter McCubbin; *Screenplay:* Peter Ferri and McCubbin.

    Cast: Simon Richards (*Reg Spencer*), Lesley Kelly (*Barb Spencer*), Chantellese Kent (*Amanda*), Noah Plener (*Justin Spencer*), Joel Kaiser (*Sam Whitney*), Susan Hamann (*Marla Whitney*), Ken McKenzie (*Archie Whitney*), Hersh Kalles (*Courtney Whitney*), Karen Inwood (*Jessica*), Ken Innes, Peter Ferri, Paul Babiak, John Tench, Alberta Davidson, Austin Schatz, Victoria Shaffleburg, Scott Wickware, Richard Williamson and top-billed MR is a tenderhearted petty thief named Elmer who befriends a six-year-old girl (Kent) wishing for a grandfather for Christmas. He magically learns that her father is the son he never met. A Canadian made-for-TV movie.

148. My Heroes Have Always Been Cowboys, Samuel Goldwyn Company, 1991

Director: Stuart Rosenberg; *Screenplay:* Joel Don Humphreys.

Cast: Scott Glenn (*H.D. Dalton*), Kate Capshaw (*Jolie Meadows*), Ben Johnson (*Jesse Dalton*), Tess Harper (*Cheryl Hornby*), Balthazar Getty (*Jud Meadows*), Clarence Williams III (*Virgil*), Gary Busey (*Clint Hornby*), Dub Taylor (*Gimme Cap*), Clu Gulager (*Dark Glasses*), Dennis Fimple (*Straw Hat*), Megan Parlen (*Becky Meadows*), Jan Hoag (*Retirement Home Nurse*) and, in a cameo, seventh-billed MR as an elderly man named Junior, who spends his days watching religious programming on TV in the room he shares in a nursing home with the father (Johnson) who has been dumped by aging rodeo rider Glenn and his greedy sister Harper and brother-in-law Busey.

The *New York Post* pointed out that "the cast is fine, though Mickey Rooney, in an excellent stint, is allowed to disappear after two early scenes." In *The Chicago Sun-Times*, Roger Ebert wrote: "It was fun to see Mickey Rooney, although he should have turned the energy down a notch."

149. The Gambler Returns: The Luck of the Draw, Ken Kragen Productions, 1991

Director: Dick Lowry; *Screenplay:* Jed Rosebrook and Joe Byrne, based on the song "The Gambler" by Don Schlitz and characters created by Jim Byrnes and Cort Cassady.

Cast: Kenny Rogers (*Brady Hawkes*), Rick Rossovich (*Ethan Cassidy*), Reba McEntire (*Burgundy Jones*), Claude Akins (*Teddy Roosevelt*), Dion Anderson (*Diamond Jim Brady*), Paul Brinegar (*Cookie*), Jere Burns (*Cade Dalton*), James Drury (*Jim*), Linda Evans (*Kate Muldoon*), Patrick Macnee (*Sir Colin Douglas*), Doug McClure (*Doug*), Park Overall (*Melody O'Rourke*), Christopher Rich (*Lute Cantrell*), Brad Sullivan (*Judge Roy Bean*), Dub Taylor (*Gas Station Attendant*), Sheryl Lee Ralph (*Miss Rosalee*), Zelda Rubinstein (*Butterfingers O'Malley*), Ray McKinnon (*Lee Bob*), Barbara March (*Prairie Kate*), Teri Copley (*Daisy McKee*), Kent Broadhurst (*Sailor Johnson*), Mary Cadorette (*Edwina*), Debra Christofferson (*Paula Thomas*), Ann Gillespie (*Eula Boatwright*), Kelly Junkerman (*Smiling Charlie Adams*) and MR as D.W. (as in Griffith), an early film director making a fictional Western. A fanciful tale in the TV-movie series about gambler Brady Hawkes (Rogers), somehow managing to ride his way through 40 or so years, meeting along the way real figures (Teddy Roosevelt, Diamond Jim Brady and Judge Roy Bean), plus some of the top television cowboys like Wyatt Earp (Hugh O'Brian), Bat Masterson (Gene Barry), The Westerner (Brian Keith), Cheyenne (Clint Walker), Bart Maverick (Jack Kelly), Lucas and Mark McCain from *The Rifleman* (Chuck Connors and Johnny Crawford) and Caine from *Kung Fu* (David Carradine).

150. Silent Night, Deadly Night 5: The Toy Maker. Still Silent Films/ International Video Entertainment (IVE), 1991

Director: Martin Kitrosser; *Screenplay:* Brian Yuzna and Kitrosser.

Cast: Jane Higginson (*Sarah Quinn*), Tracy Fraim (*Noah Adams*), Brian Bremer (*Pino*), William Thorne (*Derek Quinn*), Neith Hunter (*Kim*), Amy L. Taylor (*Meredith*), Eric Welch (*Buck*), Van Quattro (*Tom Quinn*), Clint Howard (*Ricky*), Gerry Black (*Harold*), Conan Yuzna (*Lonnie*), Jennifer Pusheck (*Elf*), Catherine Schreiber (*Mother*), Billy Oscar (*Dad*), Thornton Simmons, Cathy Yuzna, Zoe Yuzna, Gary Schmoeller, Jan Linder and twelfth-billed MR as sinister toymaker

Joe Petto (read Gepetto), who is assisted by his eerie teenage son Bremer (as Pino—as in Pinocchio). The limp final entry in the popular '80s slasher series, it went directly to video.

151. Maximum Force, PM Entertainment Group, 1992

Director: Joseph Merhi; *Screenplay:* John Weidner and Ken Lampaugh.

Cast: Sam J. Jones (*Michael Crew*), Sherrie Rose (*Cody Randel*), Jason Lively (*Rick Carver*), Richard Lynch (*Max Tanebe*), Jeff Langton (*Ivan*), John Saxon (*Capt. Fuller*), Victoria Hawley (*Julie*), Sonny Landham (*Pimp*), Pam Dixon (*Sheila Stone*), Michael Delano (*Benny*), Talbot Simons, Jeffrey Anderson-Gunter, Ken Davittan, Addison Randall, Victor Quintero, Ken McLeo, Joe Witherall and seventh-billed MR in a "special guest appearance" as the corrupt chief of police. Along with vicious crime lord Lynch, he becomes the "take down" target of three renegade cops. Direct to video.

152. Sweet Justice, Triboro Entertainment Group, 1992

Director: Allen Plone; *Screenplay:* Jim Tabilio and Plone.

Cast: Marc Singer (*Steve Colton*), Finn Carter (*Sonny Justice*), Frank Gorshin (*Billy Joe Rivas*), Gregg Brazzel (*Eric*), Catherine Hickland (*Chris Barnes*), Kathleen Kinmont (*Heather*), Patricia Tallman (*Josie*), Marjean Holden (*M.J.*), Michelle McCormick (*Kim*), Cheryl Paris (*Suzanne*), C.E. Grimes (*Gonzo*), Michael Canavan (*Eric's Trainer*), Charles Young (*Jake*), Taylor Alderson (*Secretary*), Kenneth R. Brown (*Minister*), Branscombe Richmond (*Biker*), J. Stuart Haldan, Marvin Elkins, Rich Locaaso, Sara B. O'Bryan, James Alex, Scott Leva, Chuck Hicks, Donna Bennett, Tony Rich, Doe Kistler and fourth-billed MR in a "special guest appearance" as Zeke, a local who gets involved with a female biking martial fighting squad (all kick-boxing former commandos in a special unit in Vietnam). After the sister of one of them is brutally murdered, they take on a corrupt small town of bad guys. Direct to video.

153. Little Nemo: Adventures in Slumberland, Hemdale Releasing, 1992

Director: William T. Hurtz and Masami Hata; *Screenplay:* Chris Columbus and Richard Outten, from the story by Jean Moebius Giraud and Yutaka Fujioka.

Animated film with the voices of Gabriel Damon (*Nemo*), Rene Auberjonois (*Prof. Genius*), Danny Mann (*Icarus*), Laura Mooney (*Princess Camille*), Bernard Erhard (*King Morpheus*), William E. Martin (*Nightmare King*), Alan Oppenheimer (*Oomp*), Michael Bell (*Oompy*), Sidney Miller (*Oompe*), Neil Ross (*Oompa*), John Stephenson (*Oompo*), Jennifer Darling (*Nemo's Mother*), Greg Burson (*Nemo's Father*), Nancy Cartwright (*Page*), Kathleen Freeman (*Dance Teacher*), June Foray (*Librarian*), Bert Kramer (*Goblin*) and second-billed MR as Flip, cigar-chomping con artist of Slumberland. This feature-length animated film is based on cartoonist Winsor McCay's turn-of-the-century comic strip about an imaginative boy and his assorted adventures. (*Little Nemo* had no relationship to the later, more famous *Finding Nemo*, just as Rooney's earlier *Black Stallion* had no relationship to his later *White Stallion*.)

154. The Legend of Wolf Mountain, Majestic Entertainment, 1993

Director: Craig Clyde; *Screenplay:* James Hennessy and Clyde.

Cast: Bo Hopkins (*Ranger Steven Haynes*), Robert Z'Dar (*Jocko Painter*), David Shark (*Dewayne Bixby*), Don Shanks (*Simcoe*), Vivian Schilling (*Kathy Haynes*), Nicole Lund (*Kerrie Haynes*), Natalie Lund (*Maggie Haynes*), Jonathan Best (*John Page*), Matthew Lewis (*Casey James*), Frank Magner (*Sheriff Page*), Frank Garrish (*Deputy*), Barta Heiner (*Principal*), Curt Jackson (*Henry*), Star Roman (*Mrs. James*), Lance August (*Kathy's Boyfriend*), Pedaire S. Addie (*Scotty*) and special-billed MR in a cameo as Pete Jensen, a local rancher. A children's adventure, *The Legend of Wolf Mountain* is about life lessons learned by a bunch of kids and a couple of inept prison escapees in Wolf Mountain National Park, filled with universal messages about environmental issues, spirituality of Native Americans, camaraderie among youth and the generational gap with their parents. This had a few regional playdates and then went to video.

155. La Vida Lactea (The Milky Life), Cartel Films (Spain), 1993

Director: Juan Esterlich; *Screenplay:* Chris Doherty and Esterlich.

Cast: Marianne Sagebrecht (*Aloha*), William Hootkins (*Julian Reilly*), May Hatherley (*Victoria*), Emma Suarez (*Bianca*), Michel McKaine (*Marilyn*), Thomas Heinze (*Steven*), Carlos Oda (*Kunyo*), Féodor Atkine (*Bruno*), Angie Gray (*Mimi*), Jack Taylor (*Logan*), Juan Luis Bunuel (*Dr. Davis*) and top-billed MR as shaven-headed Barry Reilly, an 80-year-old millionaire who lives in a huge castle in California with his sponging family, prances around basically wearing nothing but a huge diaper, talks baby talk and suckles at the breast of a wet nurse.

Variety observed: "Rooney gives it the old college try, but this was a role he wasn't born to play." This truly bizarre vehicle was a Spanish-German-French production in English.

156. Revenge of the Red Baron, Concord Films/New Horizons, 1994

Director: Robert Gordon; *Screenplay:* Michael James McDonald.

Cast: Toby Maguire (*Jimmy Spencer*), Cliff De Young (*Richard Spencer*), Laraine Newman (*Carol Spencer*), Ronnie Schell (*Lou*), Don Stark (*Detective Lewis*), Joe Balogh (*Cop*), Gerry Gibson (*Dr. Weintraub*), Kristen Horton (*Nurse Sally Cimi*), Michael James McDonald (*Psychiatrist*), Patrick Bristow (*Guard*), John McDonnell (*Voice of the Red Baron*) and top-billed MR as the wheelchair-bound, nearly senile 93-year-old grandpa, a World War I flying ace. He bonds with grandson Maguire through a lethal toy version of Red Baron with a model German tri-plane, returning to take revenge on the man who shot him down (in the 1971 film *Von Richtofen and Brown* by Roger Corman, who here is executive producer).

157. That's Entertainment III, MGM, 1994

Directors and writers: Bud Friedgen and Michael J. Sheridan.

As MR had in the original musical tribute to MGM two decades earlier, he wanders around the old Andy Hardy house in the fictional Carvel and around the schoolhouse for child stars, while reminiscing about Judy Garland. Other on-camera hosts: June Allyson, Cyd Charisse, Lena Horne, Howard Keel, Gene Kelly, Ann Miller, Debbie Reynolds and Esther Williams.

158. Making Waves (aka Angels Without Wings), 1994.

Writer and Director: George Saunders.

Cast: George Saunders, Nicola Kelly, April Breneman, Betsy Morrow, Eden Young, Jack Adams, Eden Young and fourth-billed MR as a cigar-chomping head angel, what one critic described as "an angelic drill sergeant," who sends a naked New Age guardian (Kelly) earthbound to help straighten out a yachting group of debauched people (including director-writer-poetry-spouting star Saunders). Direct to video.

159. Outlaws: The Legend of O.B. Taggart, Curb Entertainment/ Harstad-Lund Productions, 1994

Director: Rupert Hitzig; *Screenplay:* Mickey Rooney.

Cast: Ben Johnson (*Jack Parris*), Randy Travis (*Phoenix Taggart*), Larry Gatlin (*Gale Taggart*), Ned Beatty (*Sam Lawrence*), Ernest Borgnine (*Sheriff Lawton*), Gloria De Haven (*Molly Plenty*), Nicholas Guest (*Slocum Taggart*), Brandon Maggart (*Bartender Smiley*), Billy Barty (*Piggy Benson*), Natalie Rose (*Rachel Saxby*), Nicole Lund (*Jenny Lawrence*), Ellen Blake (*Luanne Lawrence*), Marietta Maxime (*Loretta*), Sonia Fernandez (*Consuela*), Lisa Bonnano (*Nikki*), Richard Lee-Sung (*The Irishman*) and special-billed MR (top-billed in closing credits) as ratty Western bank robber O.B., who returns home after serving time in prison to find his family in turmoil, still searching for the stolen money which had been stashed by an old pal.

Travis and Gatlin (Rooney's "son" on Broadway in *The Will Rogers Follies*) play two of Taggart's greedy sons and perform a couple of songs on the soundtrack. Jan Chamberlin Rooney also sings a traditional hymn on the soundtrack.

160. Brothers' Destiny (aka The Road Home), Republic Pictures, 1995.

Director: Dean Hamilton; *Screenplay:* Keith O'Leary.

Cast: Kris Kristofferson (*Davis*), Charles Martin Smith (*Lionel Merriman*), Dee Wallace Stone (*Mrs. Lucille Bagtian*), Danny Aiello (*Duke*), Will Estes (*Michael Murphy*), Keegan MacIntosh (*John Murphy*), Robert Prosky (*Father Tierney*), Vincent Schiavelli (*Davisport*), Rick Aiello (*Yale Preacher*), Sheila Patterson (*Sister Elizabeth*), Robin Dunne (*Clay Berry*), Jaimz Woolvett (*Tully*), Dom McKay (*Henry Jackson*), John Novak (*Daniel Murphy*), Stellina Rusich (*Eleanor Murphy*), Alan Robertson (*Geoffrey*), Peter Fleming (*Dr. Hale*) and fourth-billed MR in a throwaway "special guest appearance" as Father Flanagan (of the Boys Town where Rooney found himself as a kid five decades earlier). He takes in a pair of Depression Era orphans from New York (Estes and MacIntosh) who have hit the road to Omaha with the help of a band of friendly hobos led by Aiello, trying to stay together as a family despite efforts to break them up.

161. Animals, Mondo Films, 1997

Director: Michael Di Jiacomo; *Screenplay:* Di Jiacomo.

Cast Tim Roth (*Henry Berst*), Mili Avital (*Fatima Chue*), Rod Steiger (*Fontima*), John Turturro (*Tuxedo Man*), Jacques Herlin (*Laurent*), Lothaire Bluteau (*Young Laurent*), O-Lan Jones (*Essie*), Christopher Fennell (*Sweet Potata*), Barbara Bain (*Mother*), Raoul Delfosse (*Felipe*), Francis Bouc (*Henri*), Gianin Loffler (*Young Henry*), Johnny Cenicola (*Angel*), Joanne Pankow (*Beatrice Lincoln*), Mike Starr (*Young Felipe*) and fourth-billed MR as an eccentric, tuba-playing toll keeper in the Utah desert between two ghost towns. Mickey Rooney appears in a ten-minute black-and-white prologue to this imaginative but quite confusing allegorical fable focusing mainly on a world-weary New York cabbie (Roth) who, after being robbed, picks up an out-of-town fare (three members of a film crew) and hits the road. Direct to video.

162. Killing Midnight, Stony Brook Entertainment, 1997

Director: Alexander J. Dorsey; *Screenplay:* Arthur C. Cross and Dorsey.

Cast: Joe A. Dorsey (*Anthony Chambers*), Ryan Alosio (*William Rhodes*), Karen Mistal (*Gina*), Ray Clemente Rodriguez (*Detective Sanchez*), Wendy Schenker (*Toni Rossano*), Alexander J. Dorsey, Patricia D. Wagstaff, David Wagstaff IV, Allan Galvin, Tim Camicceri, Arthur C. Cross, Sherri Rosenberg, Hilary Hayes and sixth-billed MR as Prof. Mort Sang, a noted criminologist (he manages to turn up dressed as Santa, but don't ask). Sang is called upon by a suspense novelist (Alosio) with a severe case of writer's block in search of material to inspire him. Direct to video.

163. Boys Will Be Boys, Crystal Sky Communications, 1997

Director: Dom DeLuise; *Screenplay:* Mark Dubas and Gregory Poppen.

Cast: Julie Haggerty (*Emily Clauswell*), Randy Travis (*Lloyd Clauswell*), Michael DeLuise (*Skip LaRue*), Catherine Oxenberg (*Patsy "B.B." Parter*), Jon Voight (*Lt. Fred Palladino*), Charles Nelson Reilly (*Sidney Rudnick*), Ruth Buzzi (*Mrs. Rudnick*), Carol Arthur [DeLuise] (*Blanche*), Dom DeLuise (*Angry Chef*), James Williams (*Matt Clauswell*), Drew Winget (*Robbie Clauswell*), Glenndon Chatman (*Einstein*), Steven Hartman (*Bugsy*), Brian Wagner (*Eddie*), Skylar Shuster (*Samantha*), Lloyd Batista (*Man in Hallway*), Eileen Saki (*Barbeque Chef*) and third-billed MR as Wellington, eccentric boss of Travis. With wife Haggerty, Travis left two somewhat bratty kids home alone to humiliate a bumbling intruder (Michael DeLuise) in this road company version of the Macauley Culkin kid movies of the early '90s. Director Dom DeLuise gave himself a cameo as an angry chef at Rooney's barbeque, and roles to his wife Carol Arthur and son Michael. Direct to video

164. Babe: Pig in the City, Kennedy Miller Production/Universal Pictures, 1998

Director: George Miller; *Screenplay:* Miller, Judy Morris and Mark Lampell, based on the novel *The Sheep-Pig* by Dick King-Smith.

Cast: James Cromwell (*Arthur Hoggett*), Magda Szubanski (*Esme Hoggett*), Mary Stein (*Landlady*), Julie Godfrey (*Neighbor*). E.G. Dailey (*Voice of Babe the Pig*), Paul Livingston, Babs McMillan, Matt Parkinson, Kim Story, Simon Westaway and the voices of Roscoe Lee Brown (*Narrator*), Glenne Headly (*Zootie*), Steven Wright (*Bob*), Danny Mann (*Ferdinand the Duck*), James Cosmo (*Thelonius*), Nathan Kress, Myles Jeffrey, Stanley Ralph Ross, Russi Taylor, Adam Goldberg, Eddie Barth, Miriam Margolyes and Hugo Weaving. Fourth-billed MR is Fugly Floom in a few nearly wordless scenes as a ringmaster-clown heading a Felliniesque group of performing chimps. This is a wildly imaginative sequel to the 1995 Australian film sleeper about a talking shepherd-wannabe pig, here leaving the country farm with a bunch of animal pals for a faraway storybook city.

165. The Face on the Barroom Floor, 1998

Director: Paul Gibran Begum; *Screenplay:* Begum, based on the turn-of-the-century poem by H. Anton D'Arcy.

Cast: Lincoln Hoppe, Christie Starley, Christy Sumerhays, Bonnie Baker-Story, Anthony Leger, Corey Dangerfield, Melissa Pace, Kim Blazer, Jason Merrell and top-billed MR as an old drunkard who has an abrasive encounter with assorted bar regulars and goes on to relate the story of how he lost his love about 100 years earlier. This vanity production, written, produced and directed by Begum, was filmed in Salt Lake City. Direct to video

166. Michael Kael Contre La World News Company, Le Studio Canal Plus, 1998

Director: Christophe Smith; *Screenplay:* Benoit Delépine.

Cast: Benoit Delépine (*Michael Kael*), Marine Delterme (*Paola Maertens*), Chad Ayers (*William*), Victoria Principal (*Leila Parker*), Elliott Gould (*Coogan*), William Atherton (*James Denit*), Féodor Atkine (*Maj. Sylvain*), Yves Jacques (*Charles Robert*), Alix De Konopka (*Miss Picotte*), Michael Morris (*Robert Kipp*), Luc Bernard (*Steve Walsh*), Paul Van Mulder (*Jean Crevier*), Pat Rick (*Bill Clinton*), Jules-Edouard Moustic, Renée Le Calm, Jacques Bonaffé, Jeff Breslaur, Wayne LeGette and fifth-billed MR as Griffith, a Miami-based news network bigwig. In this French-made political comedy, Griffith has one of his correspondents, Michael Kael (Delépine), an inept reporter stationed in Paris, become involved with creating an international event to get Bill Clinton reelected for an unconstitutional third term.

167. Sinbad: The Battle of the Dark Knights, FM Entertainment 1998

Director: Alan Mehrez; *Screenplay:* Elvis Restaino and Mehrez.

Cast: Richard Grieco (*Sinbad*), Ryan Slater (*Anthony*), Dean Stockwell (*Bophisto*), Elvis Restaino (*Murki Khan*), Anthony De Longis (*Gen. Numbus*), Nikolai Binev (*Pop-Pop*), Lisa Ann Russell (*Princess Salazar*), Dante Basco (*Prince Hong*), Robert Chapin (*Kether*), Zelda Rubinstein (*Older Princess Salazar*), Alan Mehrez (*Sultan*), Maya Bejanska (*Minion*), Eva Kirilova (*Gypsy leader*), Anthony Medwetz (*Young Sinbad*), Kristina Bartlett (*Young Salazar*), Katerina Foreman (*Sultan's Wife*), Ron Hall (*Teric*), Jerry Hyman (*Sala*), Eyad Karadshah (*Mozari*), Andrew Hawkes, Christopher Aber, Steve Bannon, Carolyn Grieco and fourth-billed MR as the grandfather of a young boy (Slater). Mickey Rooney teaches him to use his imagination, and with a magical coin time travels back to the medieval world of Sinbad (Grieco), who is battling an evil knight (Stockwell) trying to rescue a beautiful princess. Filmed in Bulgaria. Direct to video

168. The First of May, Sho Entertainment, 2000

Director: Paul Sirmons; *Screenplay:* Gary Rogers, based on the 1991 book *The Golden Days* by Gail Radley.

Cast: Julie Harris (*Carlotta*), Dan Byrd (*Cory*), Charles Nelson Reilly (*Dinghy the Clown*), Robin O'Dell (*Michelle*), Tom Nowicki (*Dan*), Gerard Christopher (*Zack*), Mikki Scanlon (*Loralie*), Patricia Clay (*Social Worker*), Laurie Coleman (*Waitress*), David E. Conley (*Sgt. David Conley*), Joe DiMaggio (*Himself*) and fourth-billed MR as the crusty boss of the Clyde Beatty-Cole Brothers Circus to which a nursing home resident (Harris) and an 11-year-old who has befriended her (Byrd) run away in this family movie filmed in Orlando, Florida.

169. Phantom of the Megaplex, Grossbart/Barnett Productions, 2000

Director: Blair Tru; *Screenplay:* Stu Kreiger.

Cast: Taylor Handley (*Pete Riley*), Corinne Bohrer (*Julie Riley*), Caitin Wachs (*Karen Riley*), Jacob Smith (*Brian Riley*), Rich Hutchman (*Steven MacGibbon*), Colin Fox (*Wolfgang Nedermeyer*), John Novak (*George*), Ricky Mabe (*Ricky Leary*), Julia Chantrey (*Terri Tortora*), Joanne Boland (*Hilary Horan*), J.J. Stocker (*Mark Jeffries*), Lisa Ng (*Lacy Ling*), Joe Pingue (*Merle the Projectionist*) and "guest star" MR as Movie Mason, an old-time movie fan who befriends a teen (and his pals) working part-time in a new multiplex haunted by a ghost from the old theater it has displaced. An amiable Disney TV movie

170. Lady and the Tramp II: Scamp's Adventure, Disney Television Animation, 2001

Director: Darrell Rooney and Jeannine Rousel; *Screenplay:* Bill Motz and Bob Roth.

Voices of Scott Wolf, Alyssa Milano, Chazz Palminteri, Jeff Bennett, Jodi Benson, Bill Fagerbakke, Bronson Pinchot, Cathy Moriarty, Mary Kay Bergman, Debi Derryberry, Barbara Gordon, Nick Jameson, Tress MacNeille, Michael Gough, Frank Welker, Andrew McDonough, Rob Paulson, Kath Sousie, Melissa Manchester, Susan Egan, April Winchell, Roger Bart, Jess Harnell and seventh-billed MR as Sparky, the junkyard dog, in this very much belated direct-to-video sequel to Disney's animated theatrical film of 1955. Songs by Melissa Manchester and Norman Gimbel.

171. Topa Topa Bluffs, Topa Topa Bluffs Productions, 2002

Director: Eric Simonson; *Screenplay:* Rick Cleveland.

Cast: Robert Knepper (*Frank*), Martin McClendon (*Henry*), Maggie Welsh (*Leslie*), Kayren Ann Butler (*Beth*), Kristen Chenoweth (*Patty*), Evan Gore (*Shane Black*) and fifth-billed MR in a cameo as a grizzled prospector who gets involved with a pair of struggling screenwriting buddies who decide that a weekend backpacking trip would do wonders for their creative juices and nearly end up killing one another. This contemporary black comedy is a nod to *The Treasure of the Sierra Madre*.

172. Paradise, Sunset International Ltd., 2003

Director: Roger Steinmann; *Screenplay:* Steinmann, from the autobiography of Patricia Paradise.

Cast: Dee Wallace-Stone (*Patricia Paradise*), Barbara Carrera (*Katherine Hiller*), Timothy Bottoms (*Francis Hiller/Douglas/Henry/Alan at 40/Patricia's Father*), Theresa Saldana (*Maria*), Lilyan Chauvin (*Nurse*), Martin Kove (*Taxi driver*), Kristian Hans Horn (*Alan at 18*), Jolie Jackunas (*Young Patricia*), Buddy Daniels (*Casino Manager*), Phil Peters (*Attorney*) and second-billed MR (replacing Ray Walston, who died during production) in two roles, as Henry Hiller, the father-in-law of Las Vegas singer-songwriter Patricia Paradise and an earthly (and earthy) angel in her lifelong search for Shangri-La. Rooney and Bottoms (as Patricia's casino owner husband, among other parts) have the roles initially scheduled for Eddie Albert and real-life son Edward Albert, in this rambling film by Swiss moviemaker Steinmann.

173. Strike the Tent, Solar Filmworks, 2003
Director: Blaine Miller; *Screenplay:* Julian Adams.
   Cast: Julian Adams (*Robert Adams*), Wendy Belt Edwards (*Eveline McCord Adams*), Eric Holloway (*Benjamin Young*), Amy Redford (*Sylvia McCord*), Joshua Lindsey (*Nelson McCord*), Weston Adams (*Grandfather Robert*), Tippi Hedren (*Grandmother Eveline*), Lee Majors (*Dr. Jack Lee*), Bob Dorian (*Gov. James Adams*), Elizabeth Nelson Adams (*Mrs. Lownes*), LaChanda Alexander (*Elizabeth*), Fred Griffith (*Rev. Ellison Capers*), Clarke McNair (*Duncan Ray*), Mick Walker (*John Boone*), Randall Carlton, James Guignard, Shaun O'Rourke, Timmy Sherrill, Tracy Wilson and sixth-billed MR as plantation owner David McCord in this Civil War drama based on the lives of writer-star Adams' great-great-grandparents.

174. A Christmas Too Many, 2004
Writer and director: Stephen Wallis
   Cast: Kevan Michaels (*Sonny*), Sam McMurray (*Harry*), Ruta Lee (*Grandma*), Andrew Keegan (*Matt*); Marla Maples (*June*), Austin O'Brien (*Jack*), Melissa Wyler (*Sally*), Clint Howard (*Todd*), Elisabeth Lund (*Julie*), Jan Rooney (*Trudy*), Gary Coleman (*Pizza Guy*) and top-billed MR as Grandpa in this holiday comedy-drama about a dysfunctional family. Produced by Michaels and Keegan. Direct-to-video.

   Mickey Rooney also had cameos roles as himself in the made-for-TV movies *Senior Trip!* (1981) (Scott Baio and the youthful stars, on a class trip to the Big Apple, go backstage to meet him after seeing *Sugar Babies*) and *There Must Be a Pony* (1986) (reuniting him if only briefly with Elizabeth Taylor, who starred).

   Rooney directed, but not appear in, *My True Story* (Columbia Pictures, 1951), starring Helen Walker and Willard Parker. And he co-produced, but did not appear in the Sabu film *Jaguar* (Republic Pictures, 1955).

Mickey Rooney One- and Two-Reelers and Shorts

   (Rooney, as Mickey McGuire, was emcee for a 1930 "Screen Snapshots" Columbia Pictures short which featured Mary Pickford, Douglas Fairbanks, Dolores Del Rio, June Collyer, Ruth Roland, Buck Jones, Alice White, Lloyd Hughes, Mae Murray, Larry Gray, Jack Holt, Matt Moore and Marie Prevost.)

Pirate Party on Catalina Isle, MGM, 1935
Director: Gene Burdette
   A Technicolor two-reeler with a batch of Hollywood star partying, among them MR, Charles "Buddy" Rogers, Virginia Bruce, Marion Davies, Cary Grant, Randolph Scott, Errol Flynn, Lili Damita, Lee Tracy, Chester Morris, Irene Hervey, Leon Errol, Sterling Young, Robert Armstrong, Vince Barnett, Jack Duffy, Blanche Mahaffey, Rue Tyler, Betty Burgess, Johnny Downs and Eddie Peabody.

Cinema Circus, MGM, 1937
Director: Roy Rowland
   A Technicolor two-reeler filmed at the Pan Pacific Auditorium in Los Angeles, with Lee Tracy emceeing a show featuring MR, William S. Hart, Olsen and Johnson, the Ritz Brothers, Boris Karloff, Ben Turpin, Charlie Murphy, Bob Burns, Leo

Carrillo, Alice Faye, Dixie Dunbar, Chester Conklin, Allan Jones, Martha Raye, Bob Burns, Baby LeRoy, Cliff Edwards, James Gleason, Fred Stone and many others.

Hollywood Handicap, MGM, 1938
Director: Buster Keaton

A one-reel musical short set at Santa Anita with a stadium full of celebrities, including MR, Al Jolson, Ruby Keeler, Stuart Erwin, June Collyer, Charles Butterworth, Irene Rich and Gregory Ratoff.

Rodeo Dough, MGM, 1940
Director: Sammy Lee

One-reel sepiatone short revolving around the Palm Springs rodeo with MR along with Gene Autry, Roy Rogers, Johnny Weissmuller, Joe E. Brown, Jackie Cooper, Sally Payne, Mary Treen and Tom Neal.

Andy Hardy's Dilemma, MGM, 1940.
Director: George B. Seitz.

A public service two-reeler (subtitled "A Lesson in Mathematics and Other Things"), this was written and narrated by Carey Wilson and featured MR and the Hardy family plus Roger Moore (not the British actor but Joe Young, brother of the more famous Robert Young). This previously "lost" 19 minute short, with the Judge helping Andy decide between spending $200 to have the jalopy of his dreams fixed when it falls apart or donating the money he scrapes together to a children's charity, resurfaced in 1999 on the Turner Classic Movies channel.

Personalities, MGM 1942

For its "Romance of Celluloid" series of one-reel shorts, narrated by Frank Whitbeck, MGM showcased performers whose careers were just starting (except for MR, seen in screen test footage for his Andy Hardy from the mid–'30s), with Esther Williams, Carole Gallagher and Frances Rafferty each testing for the Sheila Brooks character for *Andy Hardy's Double Life*, and other younger actors promoting current MGM films of the day: Donna Reed, Jean Rogers, Robert Sterling, Van Johnson, Richard Ney, Patricia Dane, Susan Peters and Lucille Norman. Music was by Lennie Hayton, then a young studio music director.

Show Business at War, 20th Century–Fox, 1943

A "March of Time" two-reeler, produced by Louis de Rochemont as a tribute to the contributions to the war effort of the top entertainers of the day. Among them: MR, Tyrone Power, Clark Gable, Hedy Lamarr, Dorothy Lamour, Carole Lombard, Loretta Young, The Ritz Brothers, Jack Benny and Mary Livingstone, Edgar Bergen and Charlie McCarthy, John Garfield, Joe E. Brown, Martha Raye, Rita Hayworth, Fred MacMurray, Deanna Durbin, Rochester, the Ballet Rouse and Al Jolson singing "Mammy."

Out of This World Series, Columbia Pictures, 1948
Director: Ralph Staub

A one-reel entry in the "Screen Snapshots" series, dealing with a summer amateur baseball game between two teams of Hollywood actors playing for charity. MR appears along with Eddie Bracken, Jack Carson, Danny Kaye, John Garfield, Danny Thomas, Jackie Cooper, Keenan Wynn, Peter Lawford, Kay Kyser and Harold (The Great Gildersleeve) Peary.

Spike Jones in Hollywood, Columbia Pictures, 1953

Director: Ralph Staub

A one-reeler in the "Screen Snapshots" series featuring Ken Murray showing bandleader Spike Jones and family around Hollywood of the late '30s/early '40s to see the stars at play, among them MR, Judy Garland, Charlie Chaplin and wife Paulette Goddard, Boris Karloff, Rudy Vallee, Paul Lukas, Ronald Colman and Douglas Fairbanks, Jr.

Mickey Rooney, Then and Now, Columbia Pictures, 1953

Director: Ralph Staub.

A "Screen Snapshots" one-reeler featuring MR commenting on scenes from his films since 1930.

Playtime in Hollywood, Columbia Pictures, 1956

Director: Ralph Staub

A one-reel black-and-white documentary short in the long-running "Screen Snapshots" series, featuring MR along with Joe E. Brown, Jack Carson, Danny Kaye, Burt Lancaster, Groucho Marx, Jane Russell, Frank Sinatra, Barry Sullivan, Danny Thomas, Keenan Wynn and others.

Glamorous Hollywood, Columbia Pictures, 1958

Director: Ralph Staub

A "Screen Snapshots" one-reeler, with MR, Gary Cooper, David Niven, Lauritz Melchior and other celebrities being interviewed by producer-director Staub as they enter a Hollywood charity event.

Mooch Goes to Hollywood, 1971

Director: Richard Erdman; Writer: Jim Backus

55-minute mini-feature dealing with a pooch (played by star dog Benji) who wants to try his paw in Tinseltown. The celebrities he meets include MR, Vincent Price, Phyllis Diller, Edward G. Robinson, Cesar Romero, David Wayne, Marty Allen, Dick Martin, Sam Jaffe, James Darren, Jim Backus, Darren McGavin and Jill St. John. The odd couple of Richard Burton and Zsa Zsa Gabor are narrators, and Lynne Lipton is the voice of Mooch the pooch.

Mickey Rooney also co-directed (with Herbert Glaser) the 1942 "Our Gang" MGM one-reel short *Mighty Lak a Goat*, directing scenes featuring his new wife Ava Gardner (playing a movie cashier) and his dad Joe Yule, Sr.

Television Appearances

Hey Mulligan (aka **The Mickey Rooney Show**). NBC, August 28, 1954–June 4, 1955

MR stars as Mickey Mulligan, an NBC Hollywood studios page with aspirations of being a serious actor. Regis Toomey and Claire Carleton play his parents, a retired cop and a onetime burlesque star; Carla Balenda is his girlfriend Pat, a secretary at NBC; John Hubbard is his boss; and real-life pal and '50s performing partner Joey Forman is his buddy Freddie.

Mickey. ABC, September 16, 1964–January 13, 1965

MR as Mickey Grady, a Coast Guard recruiter in landlocked Omaha who inherits a luxurious beachfront hotel in California (at least getting him closer to the open sea). Emmaline Henry is his supportive wife, Nora; real-life son Tim Rooney and Brian Nash play his two kids; Sammy Tong is his hotel manager; and Alan Reed plays the resident shyster.

A Year at the Top. CBS, August 5, 1977

MR stars as Mickey Durbin in the pilot to the dark-sided Norman Lear series, giving rabid hopefuls a shot at a record career — at a price, since the record company is owned by the Devil and run by his son (Gabe Dell). The subsequent series, beginning several weeks later without MR, had a run of five episodes. (This was the second of two pilots, both with Rooney, revolving around the same concept; the first one, filmed in February 1977, never aired.)

One of the Boys. NBC, January 23–June 2, 1982; August 6–20, 1982

MR plays Oliver Nugent, a retired, energetic 66-year-old who decides to enroll in college and moves in with his grandson Adam Shields (Dana Carvey) and Adam's somewhat crabby, often snide roommate Jonathan Burns (Nathan Lane), Also in the cast: Francine Beers, an irritating divorcée who owns their apartment building and has a crush on Oliver; Scatman Crothers as Benjamin Solomon, a retired entertainer with whom Oliver had occasionally worked; and a young Meg Ryan as pert coed Jane. (The show was taped in New York during Rooney's *Sugar Babies* run.)

Tom Shales, in *The Washington Post*, wrote of the premiere episode: "Commences now another in the nine lives of Mickey Rooney, who is still in phase three of his amazing, daunting career.... [He] is at his pushily lovable best.... Perhaps Rooney is not universally irresistible; it's just that there is no longer any point in trying to resist him. He's safely in the legend class, and his clowning and camaraderie with Scatman Crothers is extremely appealing. This is a Super Bowl of ham, and so a fairly routine comic vehicle is elevated into a rarefied plaything, just right for bouncing on the national lap. Experience does count, after all."

O'Malley. NBC, January 8, 1983

MR is hard-boiled Michael O'Malley, an ex–NYC cop turned cigar-chomping gumshoe, in this failed series pilot. He lives out of an art gallery run by Guy (Peter Coffield), the son of his late crony, and lumbers around in a battered '59 Caddy. Sara Abrell is Guy's secretary; Anne Francis, O'Malley's chic ex-wife; and Jeffrey DeMunn, an indigent down-and-outer.

The Adventures of the Black Stallion. The Family Channel, September 15, 1990–April 23, 1992

MR reprises the role (veteran horse trainer Henry Dailey) that he played in the film *The Black Stallion*, in this Canadian-made series, in which Richard Ian Cox plays the tousled-haired youngster he takes under his wing and coaches on The Black, the beautiful Arabian stallion. Other regulars in the all–Canadian cast: Michele Goodger, Ken Pogue, Jean-Paul Solal, Virginie Demians, Marianne Filali, Ryan Koch and David Taylor

Variety on the premiere episode: "Rather than focusing on the magic of the relationship between boy and horse, pilot is all about boy and trainer, with Rooney dominating the 30-minute seg.... Roly poly, crusty Rooney brings out his practiced scene-stealing techniques, but it's doubtful many youths [the target audience] will want to tune in to the Mickey Rooney show."

Other Television Acting

Chronicled are solely his dramatic acting appearances and the assorted series in which he starred. Not included are appearances on game shows (like *The Hollywood Squares*), talk shows (*The Tonight Show* with Jack Paar, on which Rooney was chastised for turning up in his cups, or *Person to Person* with Edward R. Murrow or chats with David Frost and Dick Cavett), Dean Martin Celebrity Roasts and variety specials (like *The Ed Sullivan Show* and *The Hollywood Palace*).

(Unsold pilot for unnamed series based on the life of Daniel Boone, CBS, 1951)

Celanese Theater. ABC, March 19, 1952

Episode: "Saturday's Children" (adapted by Alan Haskett from the 1927 Maxwell Anderson play), directed by David Alexander, also starring Shirley Standlee, Patricia Bright, Morrison Dowd, June Walker, Doro Merande and Fredd Wayne. *Variety*'s TV critic called this production "a disappointing treatment [with] an ineffectual performance by Mickey Rooney, who was making his video dramatic bow."

Hey, Mulligan (aka **The Mickey Rooney Show**). NBC series, August 28, 1954–June 4,1955, with Joey Forman

Schlitz Playhouse of Stars. CBS, January 4, 1957
Episode: "The Lady Was a Flop," directed by Les Martinson, and adapted by Martin Berkeley from Borden Chase's original story, also starring J. Pat O'Malley, Hayden Rorke, George Pirrone, Jimmy Murphy, Harry Strang, Pierre Lyden, Alan Reynolds and Bill Baldwin.
"Mickey Rooney delivers a top-drawer dramatic performance in this racetrack story, playing an ex-jockey who hangs up his tack after losing his saddlesmith nerve when injured in a fall," *Variety* found. "Rooney outshadows everyone with his sterling performance."

Playhouse 90. CBS, February 14, 1957
Rod Serling's "The Comedian" (adapted from a novel by Ernest Lehman), directed by John Frankenheimer, also starring Edmond O'Brien, Kim Hunter, Mel Torme, Constance Ford and Whit Bissell. *The New York Times'* Jack Gould admired "a remarkable performance by Mickey Rooney."

Producers Showcase. NBC Musical Special, May 11, 1957
In "Mr. Broadway" as George M. Cohan, written by Sam and Bella Spewack, directed by Sidney Lumet, and choreographed by Peter Gennaro, also starring James Dunn, Gloria DeHaven, Eddie Foy, Jr., June Havoc and Roberta Sherwood, with Garry Moore as narrator. *Time* magazine found, "Rooney evoked Rooney. But if the tumultuous Rooney was not the debonair Cohan, he was still a sliver off the same shank and great fun to watch as an outrageously brash song-and-dance man taking a reluctant theater by storm." Album: "Mickey Rooney Sings George M. Cohan" on RCA Victor.

Pinocchio. NBC Musical Special, October 13, 1957
Executive producer, David Susskind; director, Paul Bogart; choreographer, Hanya Holm, also starring Walter Slezak, Fran Allison, Martyn Green, Jerry Colonna, Stubby Kaye, Sondra Lee, Matt Maddox, Mata & Hari (dance team); Musical score: Alec Wilder (music) and William Engvick (lyrics). Original cast recording on Columbia Records.

December Bride. CBS, April 14, 1958
Episode: "The Mickey Rooney Show," with MR being reunited with his "mother" from the first Andy Hardy movie, Spring Byington.

Alcoa Theater. NBC, November 17, 1958
Episode: "Eddie," directed by Jack Smight and written by Alfred Brenner and Ken Hughes. MR, as a small-time gambler, spends the entire time on the phone frantically trying to come up with $1,000 he owes to a hoodlum, realizing he has only a few hours to cough up the cash or be bumped off. (Rooney was Emmy nominated, as were the writers; Smight won an Emmy for directing.)
"Although armed with a far-fetched script," *Variety* reported, "Mickey Rooney developed an interesting, at times exciting one-man performance."

Wagon Train. NBC, October 7, 1959

Episode: "The Greenhorn Story," also starring Ward Bond, Robert Horton, Byron Foulger, Ellen Corby and Daria Massey.

The Mickey Rooney Show. CBS special, January 28, 1960

Produced by Perry Lafferty; Directed by Abe Burrows and Lafferty. Premiere program in a series of weekly specials under the umbrella title "Revlon Review," each hosted by a different star. Guests included Joey Forman, Dick Shawn, Patachou (the French singing comedienne-chanteuse), Bob Crewe and Caroline Strickland.

The *New York Herald Tribune* television critic wrote: "Pint-sized Mickey Rooney last night brought a variety show to home viewers that had freshness, taste and pace. It was a streamlined sixty minutes that moved swiftly and seemed to have something for everyone.... Through it all Rooney handled his hosting chores in a subdued, likable fashion as well as coming up with a strong comedy routine with his long-time partner, Joey Forman."

The Many Sides of Mickey Rooney. CBS special, March 31, 1960

Variety hour, produced and directed by Jack Donohue, with guests Gloria De Haven and Joey Forman. MR sang, danced, played the piano of his own songs ("I Couldn't Be More in Love" and "Night of a Thousand Dreams") and performed a dramatic scene from "Eddie."

Variety reported: "The title dared Rooney to show off his theatrical aptitude, and so the segments celebrated, one at a time, his flair for comedy, mimicry, serious acting, dancing, singing, piano playing, and songwriting. Even on tape it was quite a workout."

Wagon Train. NBC, September 28, 1960

Episode: "Wagons Ho!" also starring Robert Horton, Ellen Corby, Olive Sturgess, Henry Corden, Carlos Romero. MR repeated his role of newsman Sam Evans from "The Greenhorn Story."

G.E. Theater. CBS, December 18, 1960

Episode: "The Money Driver," also starring Jocelyn Brando and Teddy Rooney.

Checkmate. CBS, March 25, 1961

Episode: "The Paper Killer," also starring Dianne Foster, William Schallert, Donna Douglas and Dennis Patrick.

Hennesey. CBS, May 8, 1961

Episode: "Shore Patrol Revisited" (reuniting MR with long-ago MGM pal Jackie Cooper), also starring Ken Berry and Stafford Repp.

The Dick Powell Show. NBC, September 26, 1961

Episode: "Who Killed Julie Greer?" (pilot to the later "Amos Burke" series), directed by Robert Ellis Miller and written by Frank D. Gilroy, also starring Dick

Powell as Burke (later it would be Gene Barry), Lloyd Bridges, Ronald Reagan, Dean Jones, Nick Adams, Jack Carson, Carolyn Jones, Edgar Bergen and Kay Thompson.

The Investigators. CBS, October 26, 1961

Episode: "I Thee Kill," directed by Joseph H. Lewis, also starring James Franciscus, Mary Murphy, James Philbrook, Claire Griswold and Richard Rust.

The Dick Powell Show. NBC, November 7, 1961

Episode: "Somebody's Waiting," directed by Arthur Hiller and written by Adrian Spies, also starring Susan Oliver, Tige Andrews and Warren Oates.

Naked City. ABC, December 13, 1961

Episode: "Ooftus Goofus," directed by Arthur Hiller, written by Jo Pagano, with MR as a crotchety neighborhood supermarket manager and Maureen Stapleton as his long-suffering wife. It also features Graham Jarvis, Joseph Warren, Don Briggs, William Cottrell, Louis Sorin and regulars Paul Burke, Horace McMahon and Harry Bellaver.

Frontier Circus. CBS, March 8, 1962

Episode: "Calamity Circus," also starring Chill Wills, John Derek, Richard Jaeckel and Nico Minardos.

Pete and Gladys. CBS, April 16, 1962

Episode: "The Top Banana" (MR in the title role, playing himself). Also starring Harry Morgan and Cara Williams.

The Dick Powell Show. NBC, September 25, 1962

Episode: "Special Assignment," directed by Don Taylor, also starring Barbara Stanwyck, June Allyson, Dick Powell, Edgar Bergen, Frances Bergen and Lloyd Nolan.

The Dick Powell Show. NBC, January 22, 1963

Episode: "Everybody Loves Sweeney," directed by Don Medford, also starring Joanne Linville, Ross Martin and Jack Albertson, with Frank Sinatra, the guest host following Powell's death several weeks earlier.

Alcoa Premiere. ABC, January 24, 1963

Episode: "Five, Six, Pick Up Sticks" (pilot for an unsold series called *Tempo*), also starring John Forsythe, Barbara Nichols, Geraldine Brooks, John Lupton, Bibi Osterwald and MR as Babe Simms, an alcoholic, much-married drummer who'd had an affair 15 years earlier with a dead bandleader's wife. Fred Astaire was the show's regular host.

The Twilight Zone. CBS, October 25, 1963

Episode: Rod Serling's "The Last Night of a Jockey," directed by Joseph Newman.

Kraft Suspense Theater. NBC, December 19, 1963

Episode: "The Hunt," directed by Robert Altman, also starring James Caan and Bruce Dern.

Arrest and Trial. ABC, January 5, 1964

Episode: "Funny Man with a Monkey," also starring Ben Gazzara, Chuck Connors, Rachel Ames, Bert Freed, Roland Winters, Merry Anders and MR as Hoagy Blair, a nightclub comic accused of killing a doctor for narcotics.

Bob Hope Chrysler Theater. NBC, January 24, 1964

Episode: "The Seven Little Foys," narrated by Bob Hope, who starred in the movie version, and MR repeating his earlier TV role of George M. Cohan. Also starring Eddie Foy, Jr. (as his real-life dad), George Tobias, The Osmond Brothers, Betty Bronson and Elaine Edwards.

Burke's Law. ABC, February 21, 1964

Episode: "Who Killed His Royal Highness?," directed by Robert Ellis Miller and written by Gwen Bagni and Paul Dubov. Also starring Gene Barry, Elizabeth Montgomery, Gale Storm, Bert Parks, Linda Darnell, Telly Savalas, Michael Ansara and Sheldon Leonard.

Rawhide. CBS, March 26, 1964

Episode: "Incident of the Odyssey," directed by Thomas Carr, also starring Eric Fleming, Clint Eastwood, Carole Mathews and Raymond Guth.

Mickey. ABC Series, September 14, 1964–January 13, 1965

Created by Robert Fisher and Arthur Marx and directed by Richard Whorf. (Arthur Marx, the son of Groucho, later wrote a biography of his friend, *The Nine Lives of Mickey Rooney*.)

Combat! ABC, October 13, 1964

Episode: "The Silver Service," directed by Sutton Roley, also starring Jack Hogan, Claudine Longet, Ramon Navarro, Norman Alden, Pierre Jalbert, Joseph Di Reda, King Moody, Pat Patterson and MR as Harry White, described as a dice-cheating schemer who, in this World War II action series, has been fighting the Battle of the Bulge from bar stools.

Bob Hope Chrysler Theater. NBC, October 13, 1965

Episode: "Kicks," directed by Ron Winston and written by Arnold Perl, also starring Jack Weston, Melodie Johnson, Don Gordon, Harold J. Stone, Ron Husmann, Janet MacLachlan, Cliff Norton and MR, "strong as usual," *Variety* wrote, "as the cabbie knocked off he the model [played by newcomer Johnson]."

The Fugitive. ABC, January 18, 1966

Episode: "This'll Kill You," directed by Alex March and written by George Eckstein, also starring David Janssen, Barry Morse, Nita Talbot, Philip Pine and Naomi Stevens.

The Lucy Show. CBS, January 24, 1966

Episode: "Lucy Meets Mickey Rooney," also starring Lucille Ball and Gale Gordon.

The Jean Arthur Show. CBS, September 12, 1966

Episode: "Lament of a Horseplayer" (series premiere), produced and directed by Richard Quine, also starring Jean Arthur and Ron Harper.

Return of the Original Yellow Tornado. Unsold 1967 pilot from Universal Pictures for NBC

MR and Eddie Mayehoff are two once-famous superheroes, long retired. They are menaced by their archenemy whom they'd put in prison two decades before and who now is free to wreak havoc on the world.

The Name of the Game. NBC, October 2, 1970

Episode: "Cynthia Is Alive and Well and Living in Avalon," produced and directed by Gene Levitt, also starring Robert Culp, Barbara Feldon, Tom Skerritt, Gene Barry and Susan Saint James.

Santa Claus Is Coming to Town. ABC, December 13, 1970

Animated Rankin/Bass special with MR as the voice of Santa and Fred Astaire as the narrator; also featuring the voices of Keenan Wynn and Paul Frees.

Dan August. ABC, March 11, 1971

Episode: "The Manufactured Man," with MR as a political candidate's campaign manager. Also starring Burt Reynolds, Peter Brown, Richard Anderson, Norman Fell, Ned Romero, David Soul, Keith Andes, Harrison Ford, Billy Dee Williams and Barney Phillips.

Fol-De-Rol. ABC, February 27, 1972

Hour-long musical special set in a medieval fair, with entertainers, witches and the Marty Krofft puppets, and hosted by Ann Sothern (who also stars as an evil queen). MR, Cyd Charisse, Rick Nelson, Yma Sumac, Howard Cosell, Totie Fields, Guy Marks and Milt Kamen also appear.

Night Gallery. NBC, October 22, 1972

Episode: Rod Serling's "Rare Objects," directed by Jeannot Szwarc, with MR as vicious crime kingpin Augie Kolodney. Also starring Raymond Massey and Fay Spain.

Evil Roy Slade. NBC, February 18, 1972

TV movie (see filmography)

Mickey Rooney's Small World. Syndicated daily half-hour series, September 1974

The Year Without Santa Claus. ABC, December 10, 1974

Animated Rankin/Bass special with MR again as the voice of Santa; also featuring the voices of Shirley Booth (as Mrs. Claus), Dick Shawn, George S. Irving and Paul Frees.

A Year at the Top. CBS, August 5, 1977
Pilot to the short-lived series.

The Wonderful World of Disney. NBC, January 14 and 21, 1979
TV movie "Donovan's Kid," shown in two one-hour parts (see filmography).

Rudolph and Frosty. ABC, November 25, 1979
Animated Rankin/Bass special (later called "Rudolph and Frosty's Christmas in July"), with MR as the voice of Santa once more. Also featuring the voices of Red Buttons, Ethel Merman, Shelley Winters, Jackie Vernon (voice of Frosty), Alan Sues, Don Messick, Shelby Flint and Paul Frees.

My Kidnapper, My Love. NBC, December 8, 1980
TV movie (see filmography).

CBS Library: Misunderstood Monsters. CBS Children's Afternoon special April 7, 1981
Episode: "Creole" by Stephen Cosgrove, with MR narrating, and featuring the voices of Georgia Engel and Arte Johnson.

Leave 'Em Laughing. CBS April 29, 1981
TV movie (see filmography).

Bill. CBS, December 22, 1981
TV movie, for which MR won an Emmy as Best Actor (see filmography).

Senior Trip. CBS, December 30, 1981
TV movie in which MR had a cameo as himself, backstage at *Sugar Babies.*

One of the Boys. NBC, January 23–June 19, 1982. Weekly series

The Love Boat. ABC, December 18, 1982
Episode: "The Christmas Presence," with MR once more playing Santa Claus. Also starring Gavin MacLeod, Fred Grandy, Ted Lange, Bernie Kopell, Donny Osmond, Keenan Wynn, Henry Gibson and Maureen McCormick.

O'Malley. NBC, January 8, 1983
Pilot for prospective weekly series (filmed in 1980), directed by Michael O'Herlihy, and written by George Schenk and Frank Cardea; also starring Anne Francis, Peter Coffield, Sarah Abrell, Tom Waits, Paula Trueman Jeffrey DeMunn, Mark Linn-Baker and Richard Clarke.

Bill: On His Own. CBS, November 9, 1983
TV movie sequel to *Bill* (see filmography).

It Came Upon a Midnight Clear. Syndicated, December 15, 1984

TV movie (see filmography).

The Return of Mickey Spillane's Mike Hammer. CBS, April 18, 1986

TV movie (see filmography).

There Must Be a Pony. CBS, October 5, 1986

TV movie in which MR plays himself in a cameo, opposite Elizabeth Taylor and Robert Wagner.

Little Spies. ABC, October 5, 1986

TV movie (see filmography).

The Golden Girls. NBC, February 27, 1988

Episode: "Larceny and Old Lace," directed by Terry Hughes, with MR guest starring as Rocco, latest boyfriend of Sophia (Estelle Getty).

Bluegrass. CBS, February 28–29, 1988

Two-part TV movie (see filmography).

Murder, She Wrote. CBS, November 7, 1993

Episode "Bloodlines," directed by Don Mischer, with lead guest star MR — as racetrack owner Matt Cleveland — bumped off as the show's weekly victim. Also starring Angela Lansbury (Rooney's costar in *National Velvet*), Don Murray, Tippi Hedren, Ami Dolenz, Stephen Macht, Sean O'Bryan, Blake Gibbons and Shawnee Smith. This was the venerable mystery show's two hundredth episode.

Full House. ABC, December 13, 1994

Episode: "Arrest Ye Merry Gentlemen," with MR as a grouchy novelty store owner; also starring Candace Cameron, Dave Coulier, Lori Loughlin, John Stamos, Bob Saget and Ashley & Mary-Kate Olsen.

The Simpsons. Fox, September 24, 1995

Episode: "Radioactive Man," with MR voicing himself, with Bart and Milhouse becoming involved in a movie version of their favorite comic book.

Conan. Syndicated, September 22, 1997

Episode: "The Heart of an Elephant (Part 1)," series premiere guest starring MR Grobe. Also featuring Ralf Moeller (as Conan), Andrew Craig, Jeremy Kemp, Aly Dunne, Andrew Divoff, Kim Kelley, Steve Matilla, Edward Albert, James Garrett, Arthur Burghardt and Cindy Margolis.

Mikhail Baryshnikov's "Stories from My Childhood." Syndicated, 1998

In this Russian-made animated series by Baryshnikov, he relates classic Russian and English fairy tales. MR provides the voice of Ole Lukoje in a version of "The Snow Queen," along with the voices of Kathleen Turner, Laura San Giacomo,

Kirsten Dunst and others. This episode and others have been made available on a series of DVDs.

ER. NBC, February 26, 1998

Episode: "Exodus," guest starring MR as a retired science teacher, called in when a hazardous waste spill contaminates the ER.

Mike Hammer, Private Eye. WB, May 3, 1998

Episode: "Lucky in Love," also starring Stacy Keach as Mike Hammer, Sharon Whirrey as Velda and Kent Williams as Barrington.

Remember Wenn. AMC, July 31, 1998

Episode: "The Follies of WENN," guest starring MR as Mr. Hardy, a baggy pants comedian.

Safe Harbor. WB, October 1, 1999

Episode: "Life Insurance," also starring Orlando Brown, Gregory Harrison, Rue McClanahan, Jamie Williams, Tom Nowicki and Liz Torres.

Chicken Soup for the Soul. PAX, October 26, 1999

Episode: "Goodbye My Friend." TV anthology series hosted by Michael Tucker. MR plays an old man who reluctantly is forced to find a new home for a dog that he no longer can care for.

Norm. ABC, March 18, 2000

Episode: "Retribution," guest starring MR as himself, and featuring Norm Mac-Donald, Harrison Young, Kate Walsh, Randall Carver and Nikki Cox.

Radio Work

Maxwell House Coffee Show: "Judge Hardy's Children" (CBS, March 1938) with Lewis Stone

National Redemption Movement Program (December 14, 1938) with Judy Garland, Lewis Stone and Jean Parker in a Hardy Family sketch

Screen Guild Players: "Variety Review #5" (CBS, April 9, 1939) with Joan Bennett, George Murphy and Rudy Vallee

Screen Guild Players: "Variety Review #8" (CBS, September 24, 1939) with Judy Garland, Ann Sothern and Cary Grant

Lux Radio Theatre: "Strike Up the Band" (CBS, October 28, 1940) with Judy Garland

Lux Radio Theatre: "Young Tom Edison" (CBS, December 23, 1940) with Beulah Bondi and Virginia Weidler

Bundles for Britain (NBC, January 1, 1941) with Judy Garland, Jack Benny, Claudette Colbert, James Cagney, Ronald Colman and others

Lux Radio Theatre: "Stablemates" (CBS, March 31, 1941) with Wallace Beery

The Treasury Hour: "Millions for Defense" (CBS, July 2, 1941) with Judy Garland, Grace Moore and Charles Laughton

Screen Guild Players: "Babes in Arms" (CBS, November 9, 1941) with Judy Garland

Lux Radio Theatre: "Merton of the Movies" (CBS, November 17, 1941) with Judy Garland

Silver Theatre: "Christmas in July," adapted from Preston Sturges' 1940 screen comedy (CBS, March 4, 1942), hosted by Conrad Nagel

Screen Guild Players: "The Human Comedy" (CBS, July 12, 1943) with Frank Morgan

Bing Crosby Philco Radio Time (ABC, January 8, 1947) with Crosby and Peggy Lee

Lux Radio Theatre: "National Velvet" (CBS, February 3, 1947) with Elizabeth Taylor

Shorty Bell, weekly CBS series December 18, 1947, through June 27, 1948

The Hardy Family, syndicated series (1948-49); later on Mutual (1951-52) with Lewis Stone, Fay Holden and Sara Haden

Suspense: "The Lie" (CBS, April 28, 1949)

Lux Radio Theatre: "Merton of the Movies" (CBS, June 20, 1949) with Arlene Dahl

Suspense: "For Love or Murder" (CBS, December 8, 1949)

Theater Guild on the Air: "National Velvet" (NBC, April 23, 1950) with Peggy Ann Garner

Suspense: "Alibi Me" (CBS, January 4, 1951)

Stage Performances

(Aside from personal appearances for his films and on the RKO and MGM circuits in presentation shows)

A Midsummer Night's Dream
Hollywood Bowl, September 17, 1934, for 27 nights, followed by brief tour including San Francisco Opera House, Chicago (Blackstone Theatre), Kansas City, Detroit and New York.

The famed Max Reinhardt production that included MR as Puck and Olivia de Havilland as Hermia (both later re-creating their roles in the Warner Bros. screen adaptation). Erich Wolfgang Korngold adapted the 1842 Mendelssohn score, and Bronislava Nijinska and Nina Theilade staged the ballet.

Walter Connolly (*Bottom*), Sterling Hayden (*Flute*), Philip Arnold (*Oberon*), Evelyn Venable (*Helena*), MR (*Puck*); Olivia de Havilland (*Hermia*)

Murray Schumach in *The New York Times* (reporting from Los Angeles): "[Mickey Rooney] moved with an elfin, quicksilver grace ... [and] revealed a greater comprehension of his role than almost anyone in the cast."

Sailor, Beware! (1951) Sombrero Playhouse, Phoenix, Arizona

Tunnel of Love
Regional tour, summer 1963. Book directed by Mickey Rooney; staged by William Chambers; the 1957 play by Joseph Field and Peter DeVries.

MR (*Augie Poole*), Bobby Van (*Dick Pepper*), Nina Shipman (*Isolde Poole*), Cindy Robbins (*Alice Pepper*), Evadne Baker (*Estelle Novick*), Gerry Johnson (*Miss McCracken*)

A Funny Thing Happened on the Way to the Forum
Summer 1965. Opened Valley Music Theatre in Woodland Hills, September 1, 1965. Director: Jack Collins; the 1962 musical with book by Larry Gelbart and music and lyrics by Stephen Sondheim; choreographer: Howard Parker. This was the first of two tours of the Sondheim show for MR, two decades apart.

MR (*Prologus/Pseudolus*), Jack Collins (*Hysterium*), Norma Larkin (*Domina*), Jerry Lanning (*Hero*), Cliff Norton (*Senex*), Willard Waterman (*Lycus*), Tanya Lemani (*Tintinnabula*), Ginny Gam (*Panacea*), Virginia Lee (*Vibrata*), Jan Davis

(*Gymnasia*), Mary Griver (*Philia*), Roy Johnson (*Erronius*), Rhodes Reason (*Miles Gloriosus*).

Charles Champlin, in *Los Angeles Times* wrote, under the headline "A Roman Romp for Rooney": "Rooney leers, chortles, giggles, struts, runs, dances, sings like a laryngical foghorn, and ad-libs all manner of regional and topical asides. The evening remains a largely personal triumph for Rooney."

Los Angeles Herald Examiner said: "Marvelous Mickey pulls out all the stops to give a simply mad, mad, mad, mad performance."

The Odd Couple

1967, Caesars Palace in Las Vegas. The Neil Simon play, directed by Harvey Medlinsky.

MR (*Oscar Madison*), Tony Randall (*Felix Unger*)

George M!

1969 and 1970 summer tours. Produced by Lee Guber and Shelly Gross; directed and choreographed by Wakefield Poole; a musical with book by Michael Stewart and John and Fran Pascal; music and lyrics by George M. Cohan.

MR (*George M. Cohan*), William McDonald (*Jerry Cohan*), Mary Ann Niles (*Nellie Cohan*), Kathy Conry (*Josie Cohan*), Carol Fox (*Agnes Nolan*), Kathie Savage (*Ethel Levey*), Marian Henderson (*Fay Templeton*), Roger Braun (*Sam Harris*), Wallis Clark (*Theodore Roosevelt*); Georgia Carroll (*Betsy Ross*); Joan Winfield (Sally)

Hide and Seek 1971 Dinner theatre and regional tour

Three Goats and a Blanket

Written by Woody Kling and Robert J. Hilliard. Premiere at Eddie Bracken's Coconut Grove Playhouse, Miami, April 4, 1971. Staged by Jeremiah Morris; settings and lighting by James Riley.

MR (*Howard Travis*) (TV game show host with alimony woes), Barbara Andres (*Elinor Travis*), Dan Frazer (*Teddy*), James Cahill (*Raymond*), Gaye Edmund (*Delores*), Robert Jackson (*Kenneth*), Bill Lazarus, Julian Gallo, Clifford A. Pellow (*Cops*)

Variety wrote: "Putting Mickey Rooney into a farce about a man with alimony troubles must have seemed a likely gimmick. However, it's doubtful whether [the show] will get much farther without lots of help.... The acting is worthy of the vehicle. Rooney enters all over the place."

(Later production in 1971, directed by Annabelle Weenick, with MR along Carlene Watkins, Gary Wilbanks, John Galt, Rob Babbit and Gene Ross.)

W.C.

A musical produced by David Black and directed by Richard Altman. Book, Milton Sperling and Sam Locke; music and lyrics by Al Carmines; based on the book *W.C. Fields: His Follies and Fortunes* by Robert Lewis Taylor; dances and musical numbers staged by Bob Herget. Pre-Broadway tour beginning in Baltimore in late May 1971 and closing in Detroit in October 1971.

MR (*W.C. Fields*), Bernadette Peters (*Carlotta Monti*), Virginia Martin (*Blondie*), Gary Oakes (*Ben Ross*), Rudy Tronto (*Paddy O'Mara*), Jack Bittner (*K.G.*), David Vaughan (*Rodney, the Butler*), Sam Stoneburner (*Ron Kirkland*), Martin J. Cassidy (*Smitty*), Pip Sarser (*Benjy*), Diana Barone, Essie Borden, Linda Jorgens, Bernice Martell, Cindy Roberts, Jaclyn Villamil, Fred Benjamin, Dennis Britten, Barry Preston, Marie Anderson, Charlotte Povia, Cornel Richie, Louis Garcia, Clark James, Allan Sobek, Sid Marshall, David McCorkle

New York Newsday wrote, during its pre–Broadway run at Westbury Music Fair: "With Mickey Rooney playing W.C. Fields, the musical has a measure of charm, some bright tunes and solid lyrics by Al Carmines, a fairly interesting book by Milton Sperling and Sam Locke, and an engaging Fields impersonation by Rooney."

A Midsummer Night's Dream

William Shakespeare. Regional tour (including Paper Mill Playhouse, Milburn, New Jersey, November 13–December 9, 1973), directed by Frank Carrington.

MR (*Bottom the Weaver*), Katherine McGrath (*Hermia*), Ken Kliban (*Demetrius*), Caroline Thomas (*Helena*), Gregory Abels (*Lysander*), Steven D. Newman (*Oberon*), Angela Thornton (*Titania*), Sheldon Epps (*Puck*), Lionel Wilson (*Flute the Bellows-Mender*), Jeffrey DeMunn (*Starveling the Tailor*), Robert Frink (*Snout*), Ackie Byrd (*Snug*), Robert Gaus (*Peter Quince*), Harvey Solin (*Theseus*), Diane Burak (Hippolyta), Lucien Zabielski (*Philostrate*), John Straub (*Egeus*), Ron Paul Little (*Cobweb*), Daniel Cass (*Peasebottom*), Jody Locker (*Moth*), Danny Ruvolo (*Mustardseed*), and Gale McNeely, David Parker, Michael Tolaydo, Bruce Gandy (*Soldiers*).

The Bergen Record (New Jersey) reported: "It stars Mickey Rooney as Bottom the Weaver. When he was 18 [ed. note: he was 14 at the time], Rooney was a brilliant Puck in the 1930s version of the play, and last night [November 14] he was equally brilliant as an eye-rolling, tongue-lolling peasant. He played the role broadly enough as Pyramus when the play within the play slipped into marvelous burlesque."

See How They Run

Written by Philip King (1951), a play in three acts, set in a Hall at the Vicarage, Merton-Cum-Middlewick, a small English village in 1949. Summer tours with MR (1972, 1973, 1974), under the direction of Christopher Hewitt.

MR (*Sgt. Clyde Vinton*), Joan Bassie (*Penelope Toop*), Paddy Croft (*Miss Skillon*), George Pentacost (*Rev. Arthur Humphrey*), Geoff Garland (*Rev. Lionel Toop*), Benjamin H. Stack (*Bishop of Lax*), Ariel Sebastian (*Ida, a Maid*), Steve Parris (*The Intruder*), Jon Barry Wilder (*Sgt. Towers*)

The Bergen Record (New Jersey) wrote of the production that played regionally at the Mall In Paramus in August 1972: "Indescribably daffy. Mickey Rooney and the farce *See How They Run* establish a new peak in outlandishness on the local stage. Farce? This was no farce, it was a riot!... Don't ask any first-nighter to describe what he saw. He'd probably tell he never laughed so hard in all his life — and that's no exaggeration."

Show Boat

Bicentennial revival, staged at the Arle Crown in Chicago in April 1974 and then the Opera House at the Kennedy Center in Washington, May 7–19, 1974. Staged by Herb Rogers; music: Jerome Kern; book and lyrics: Oscar Hammerstein II;

based on the novel by Edna Ferber; choreography by Sandra West; conducted by Karen Gustafson.

MR (*Cap'n Andy Hawks*), Harve Presnell (*Gaylord Ravenal*) (in Chicago), Jerry Lanning (*Gaylord Ravenal*) (in Washington), Linda Michele (*Magnolia*), Gloria Hodes (*Julie*), Leonard Hayward (*Joe*), Fran Stevens (*Parthy Ann*), Harvey Evans (*Frank*), Peggy Gohl (*Ellie*)

Goodnight Ladies

1975 dinner theatre tour. Based on Avery Hopwood's 1945 farce, *Ladies' Night.*

MR stars in this sex romp as a shy(!) professor who is terrified of women, but is coaxed by his male friends to a pagan revel party where they plan on breaking down his phobia. The whole thing winds up in a Turkish bath with a bevy of beauties.

Alimony (formerly called Three Goats and a Blanket)

Written by Woody Kling and Robert J. Hilliard. 1976-77 dinner theatre tour, including Tropicana, Las Vegas, January 28, 1977. Directed by Gene Ross for Mickey Rooney/Dick Davis Productions.

MR (*Howard Travis*), Janet Adams (*Elinor Travis*), David Cooper (*Teddy*), Hank Roberts (*Raymond*), Julie Corda (*Delores*), Tim Rooney and Gene Ross (*Cops*)

Variety wrote: "It's nothing more or less than a personal high energy vehicle for the indefatigable Rooney, who takes the plot and curves it around his diminutive frame until it is completely bound and gagged."

Show Boat

The Kenley Players, Akron, Ohio. June 27–July 2, 1978, then brief tour. Director, Leslie Cutler; choreographer, Mario Melodia.

MR (*Cap'n Andy Hawks*), Terence Monk (*Gaylord Ravenal*), Christine Andreas (*Magnolia*), Leigh Beery (*Julie*), Dan Tullis, Jr. (*Joe*), Hamp Dickens (*Frank*), Jill Choder (*Ellie*), Carol Trigg (*Parthy Ann*), Terri White (*Queenie*), Les Freed (*Steve*), Jean Blair (*Landlady*)

Sugar Babies

World premiere, San Francisco, May 13–June 9, 1979; then Los Angeles, Chicago, Detroit, Philadelphia, and finally Broadway (opened at the Mark Hellinger Theatre, October 8, 1979–August 28, 1982), then national tour over the next five years. In San Francisco, under the direction of Norman Abbott, then Rudy Tronto, finally Ernest Flatt.

Supervised, staged and choreographed by Ernest Flatt; sketches directed by Rudy Tronto; conceived by Ralph G. Allen and Harry Rigby with sketches by Allen; music by Jimmy McHugh; lyrics by Dorothy Fields and Al Dubin; "Sugar Baby Bounce" by Jay Livingston and Ray Evans.

Starring (at Broadway opening) MR, Ann Miller, Sid Stone, Ann Jillian, Jack Fletcher, Bob Williams, Peter Leeds, Jimmy Mathews, Scot Stewart, Tom Boyd

Los Angeles Times (in June 1979): "Rooney's mugging goes in for grotesque contortions of the tongue, which he sticks out of his mouth in every conceivable direction — while Miller, of the frozen hair and famous legs (still famous, by the way), contributes anemic tap-dancing, mediocre acting, and acceptable singing.... *Sugar*

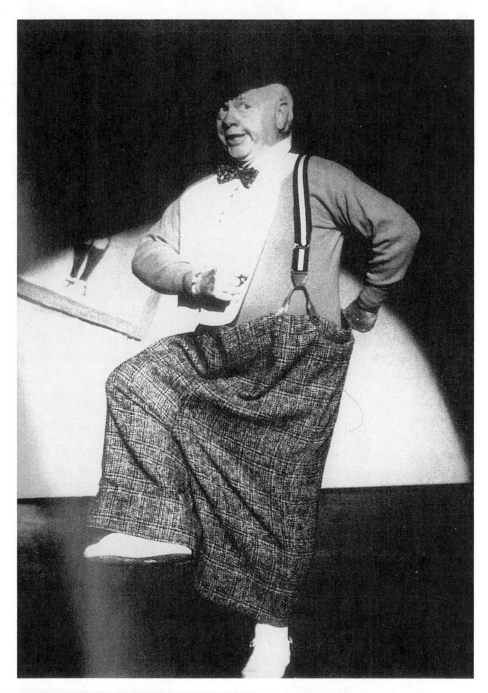

Clowning on the stage in *Sugar Babies* (1979) (Mickey Rooney collection).

Babies is basically a cheat that may find an audience, not among theatergoers but the Magic Mountain crowd." [Author's note: The show, of course, did find an audience — for the next eight years, and then in London sometime later.]

When the show returned to Los Angeles five years later *Variety* wrote: "It has become a very refined tuner that's full of yocks, terrific scenery, lovely ladies in tawdry glitter gowns, baggy-pants comics, top banana Mickey Rooney, and costar hoofer Ann Miller.... If *Sugar Babies* is not the perfect family entertainment, it's close to it. If it had the time, it could run forever."

Go Ahead and Laff

Summer 1986 at the Kenley Playhouse, Akron, Ohio; starring MR and Jane Kean, in a revised version of *Three Goats and a Blanket.*

A Funny Thing Happened on the Way to the Forum

15-week national tour, opened Shubert Theatre, New Haven, March 2, 1987. Director: George Martin; the 1962 musical with book by Larry Gelbart and music and lyrics by Stephen Sondheim; choreography, Ethel Martin.

MR (*Prologus/Pseudolus*), Lenny Wolpe (*Hysterium*), Marsha Bagwell (*Domina*), Bob Walton (*Hero*), Robert Nichols (*Senex*), Mitchell Greenberg (*Lycus*), Zoie Lam (*Tintinnabula*), Karen Byers (*Panacea*), Victoria Dillard (*Vibrata*), Lesley Durnin (*Gymnasia*), Jennifer Lee Andrews (*Philia*), Frank Nastasi (*Erronius*), Michael Dantuono (*Miles Gloriosus*)

Mickey told the press: "Playwright Larry Gelbart hadn't been happy with the liberties Rooney has taken with his script. [but] we've thrown caution to the winds, without degrading anything."

Mickey Rooney in Mickey Rooney

1988, then in 1994 in Australia and New Zealand.

"If we need any proof of his astonishing versatility," Gerald Nachman wrote in the *San Francisco Chronicle* in June 1988 (in an otherwise negative review), "Rooney gladly supplies it at the top of the show in 30 minutes of film clips from a career that includes every kind of role, from his kid-star days as scrappy waif Mickey McGuire to his Emmy-winning role as *Bill*, an amazing stretch for a performer of seemingly unending gifts as song-and-dance man, teen idol, serious actor, comic, mimic, everyone from Andy Hardy to Puck. The little guy has done it all, usually with an instinctive charm that defies him in his meandering show ... a 200-mile hike up memory lane."

Sugar Babies

Savoy Theatre, London, September 20, 1988–January 7, 1989. Supervised, staged and choreographed by Ernest Flatt; décor by Raoul Pene du Bois.

Starring MR, Ann Miller, Rhonda Burchmore, Chris Emmett, Peter Reeves, Len Howe, Bryan Burdon, Michael Davies.

Two for the Show

1989 20-city tour with Donald O'Connor. MR described this in *Life Is Too Short*: "Two old farts singing and telling jokes."

Howard Reich wrote in the *Chicago Tribune* (9/25/89): "The top-hatted song-

and-dance man may be a vanishing breed, but you'd never know it watching the two hoofers who stormed the stage of the Rialto Theatre in Joliet over the weekend. Both O'Connor and Rooney have been singing, dancing and clowning for audiences for half a century ... yet both still have enough energy, grace and wit to charm the most skeptical audiences.... Vaudeville doesn't come much better."

The Sunshine Boys

14-city tour with Donald O'Connor. Opened Orlando, Florida, January 30, 1990; closed Houston, Texas, June 30, 1990. Produced by Jerry Kravat Entertainment in association with Pace Theatricals; a comedy by Neil Simon; directed by Jeffrey B. Moss.

MR (*Willie Clark*), Donald O'Connor (*Al Lewis*), Lewis J. Stadlen (*Ben Silverman*), Allan Mark Byrns (*Patient in Sketch*), Robert Isaac Russell (*Assistant TV Director*), Ann Connors (*Nurse in Sketch*), Claudia Robinson (*Registered Nurse*)

[Rooney was to have starred in Toronto in a production of Murray Schisgal's *Luv* with Sue Ane Langdon, in February 1991, but the producer went belly-up during previews.]

Lend Me a Tenor

Apollo Theatre, Chicago, April–June 1993 (the show had been playing since 1991). The 1989 play by Ken Ludwig. Produced and directed by Michael Leavitt for Fox Theatricals.

MR (*Henry Saunders*), David Bonanno (*Max*), Jamie Baron (*Bellboy*), Mary Seibel (*Julia*), Dale Morgan (*Tito Morelli*), Jeanne Dwan (*Maggie*), Mary Easterling (*Maria*), Cynthia Judge (*Diana*)

"Rooney can't help but bring some of his inimitable personality to the show," *Chicago Tribune* critic Richard Christiansen wrote. "Inevitably he works in funny lines about his size (short) and his wives (many).... And whenever the action threatens to sag, there's always Mickey Rooney, spitting out fruit or snoozing off during a long stretch of plot explanation. He's one of the last, and the greatest, of all-time buffoons."

The Will Rogers Follies

The original show, directed by Tommy Tune from a book by Peter Stone and with a score by Cy Coleman, Betty Comden and Adolph Green, opened at the Palace Theatre, New York, in 1991, with Keith Carradine in the lead. He was succeeded by Mac Davis and then Larry Gatlin. MR joined the show on July 6, 1993, playing Will Rogers' father, and stayed with it until it closed in following September.

Larry Gatlin (*Will Rogers*), MR (*Clem Rogers*), Nancy Ringham (*Betty Blake Rogers*), Lisa Niemi (*Ziegfeld's Favorite*), Vince Bruce (*The Roper*), Tom Flagg (*Wiley Post*), Gregory Peck (*The Voice of Mr. Ziegfeld*), Lynne Michele, Kelly Woodruff, Jeanne Jones, Troy Britton Johnson, Bonnie Brackney, Tom Brackney, Robert Mann Kayser, Gina Rizzo Bishop, Brandon Espinoza, Jeffrey Stern, Jason Opsahl, Tara T. Murphy, Wendy Waring, Kimberly Hester, Ganine Giorgione, Luann Leonard, Kristi Cooke, Colleen Dunn, Sally Mae Dunn

Sugar Babies
Desert Inn, Las Vegas, June 27–September 3, 1995.
  With MR and Juliet Prowse

Crazy for You
Royal Alexandra, Toronto, September 29–December 31, 1995. The musical play by Ken Ludwig, with a score by George and Ira Gershwin.
  With MR as Everett (taking the show's long run in Toronto to its ultimate closing on New Year's Eve); Ruthie Henshall, who starred in the original London company, repeating her role as his daughter, Polly; and Jim Walton as Bobby Child, the part he played in assorted productions of the musical.
  The *Toronto Star*'s critic found the show to be "Glitzy, polished, funnier than ever. Mickey Rooney adds his unmistakable stamp to *Crazy for You.*"

A Celebration of the MGM Musical
Carnegie Hall, New York, June 17, 1997.
  With June Allyson, Cyd Charisse, Arlene Dahl, Gloria De Haven, Betty Garrett, Kathryn Grayson, Celeste Holm, Van Johnson, Tony Martin, Skitch Henderson's Orchestra. ["Where, for instance, were Jane Powell — who lived just blocks away, Esther Williams, Debbie Reynolds, and Dolores Gray?" one reviewer wondered.]
  Critic Stephen Holden observed in *The New York Times*: "Van Johnson recalled his struggles with the MGM studio chief, Louis B. Mayer, whom Mickey Rooney, in a rambling reminiscence, defended from the slings and arrows of his biographers. Mr. Rooney went on to introduced a haunting montage of images of Judy Garland, whom he saluted for having 'the greatest talent.'"

The Wizard of Oz
The Theatre at Madison Square Garden, May 6–31, 1998, then a North American tour, and a second stand at Madison Square Garden, May 1–30, 1999, followed by another national tour — first with Eartha Kitt and then with Lilliane Montevecchi and finally with Jo Anne Worley as the Wicked Witch.
  Produced by Tim Hawkins (for Madison Square Garden Productions — later Radio City Entertainment); Adapted and directed by Robert Johanson; A musical in one act, adapted by John Kane for the Royal Shakespeare Company from the MGM motion picture and the book by L. Frank Baum; Music, Harold Arlen; Lyrics, E.Y. Harburg; Background music, Herbert Stothart; Choreography, James Rocco, Sets, Michael Ananaia; Lighting, Tim Hunter; Costumes Gregg Barnes
  MR (*Prof. Marvel/The Wizard of Oz*), Eartha Kitt [succeeded by Lilliane Montevecchi and then Jo Anne Worley] (*Almira Gulch/Wicked Witch of the West*), Jessica Grové (*Dorothy*), Ken Page [succeeded by Francis Ruvivar] (*Zeke/The Cowardly Lion*), Bob Dorian [succeeded by Tom Urich] (*Uncle Henry*), Lara Teeter [succeeded by Casey Colgan] (*Hunk/The Scarecrow*), Dirk Lumbard (*Hickory/The Tin Man*); Judith McCauley (*Aunt Em/Glinda*)

The One Man One Wife Show
2003-4 tour with Mickey and Jan Rooney.

Mickey Rooney's Christmas Memories

Tropicana, Atlantic City, December 6–22, 2003, featuring Mickey and Jan Rooney.

The (young) critic for *The Press of Atlantic City* wrote niggardly of "the legendary and beloved Mickey Rooney": "Some will say that I don't understand how great Mickey Rooney is because I'm too young. Untrue. I admire Rooney and even own a few of his movies…. But it is disheartening to see Rooney still at it on the Tropicana stage when he clearly doesn't have the energy or the singing ability to anchor a Christmas show at 83 years old."

Let's Put on a Show!

Irish Repertory Theatre, New York, August 12–September 12, 2004, featuring Jan and Mickey Rooney. Produced by Ciaran O'Reilly; original music by Mickey Rooney; musical direction, Sam Kriger.

Anita Gates (chief television critic!) wrote in *The New York Times*: "[The show] is bringing out Mr. Rooney's devoted fans. His jokes are old [and] his singing is mostly a shout, trying not to be drowned out by his excellent three-piece band. But Mr. Rooney still has star power, or stage presence, or whatever you call the eager desire to entertain and be liked. When that quality is uncensored and pure (sometimes expertly so), it makes up for a lot…. The show is wisely organized, giving us Mr. Rooney, the star attraction, for the entire first act, then opening Act II with Jan Rooney coming onstage…. And compared with her husband in terms of singing ability, Ms. Rooney is Maria Callas."

Discography

Mickey and Judy: A four-disc CD set, compiled by Rhino Records and released in 1995, with the complete song scores from the four MGM musicals that Judy Garland and MR did together (*Babes in Arms, Strike Up the Band, Babes on Broadway* and *Girl Crazy*)

Girl Crazy (Selections): Mickey and Judy Garland sing from the pre-movie soundtrack 1943 MGM film. Originally released as a 78 rpm set and a decade later reissued on LP (Decca DL 5413). Some of these selections also appear in the British compilation "Hollywood Sings, Vol. 3: The Boys and the Girls" (Ace of Hearts 69) as well as in "Hollywood Soundstage" (HS-5008)

Words and Music: The original cast soundtrack from the 1948 MGM film allegedly about Rodgers and Hart, with MR singing "Manhattan" and, with Judy Garland, "I Wish I Were in Love Again" (MGM Records E-505)

Mickey Rooney Sings George M. Cohan: An album released in conjunction with his TV portrayal of Cohan in "Mr. Broadway" in 1957. (RCA Victor LPM 1529)

Pinocchio: Television soundtrack of the 1957 musical written by Alec Wilder and William Engvick, with MR in the title role (Columbia CL-1055)

Sugar Babies: Original Broadway Cast recording from the 1979 show; belatedly released in 1993 by Varese Records (IBR-9012)

The Wizard of Oz: The 1998 Madison Square Garden theatrical production of the Harold Arlen-E.Y. Harburg film musical, with MR in the title role (TVT Soundtrax 1020)

Go Ahead and Laff: Songs and anecdotes by MR, released in 2000 by Prestige Records

Summer Holiday: (Original Cast Soundtrack) The Harry Warren–Ralph Blane score, originally cut in half for the film's release in 1948, was painstakingly reassembled in its reported entirety and belatedly issued on CD for the first time in 2004 by Turner Classic Movies Music/Rhino Handmade

One Man, One Wife: Songs and anecdotes by Mickey and Jan Rooney, on a CD from Redsail Productions, sold online or at their touring revue

There also is a recording of "Bronco Busters," which MR, Judy Garland and Nancy Walker performed initially in *Girl Crazy* but which ended up on the cutting room floor. It appears in the album "Cut! Outtakes from Hollywood's Greatest Musicals" (DRG SBL-12587).

Index

*References to photographs are in **bold italics***

Abbott, Dorothy 119
Ace of Hearts 142
Adams, Edie 133, 139
Adams, Stanley 123, 124, 130, 133
Adamson, Harold 88
The Addams Family 51
The Adventures of Black Stallion 147
The Adventures of Huckleberry Finn 24, 101
The Adventures of the Black Stallion 69, 166
Ah, Wilderness! 15, 20, 38, 90, 118
Aiello, Danny 139, 158
Akins, Claude 155
Albert, Eddie 161
Albertson, Frank 90, 97
Albertson, Jack 108, 148, 169
Alda, Alan 136
Alexander, Katherine 92, 113, 114
Alexander, Ross 90
All Ashore 122
Allen, Elizabeth 94
Allen, Steve 137
Allyson, June 114, 115, 117, 119, 157, 169, 184
Altman, Robert 170
Ambush Bay 134
Anders, Luana 138, 139
Anderson, Maxwell 46, 166
Andrews, Anthony 154
Andy Hardy Comes Home 45, 126
Andy Hardy Gets Spring Fever 103
Andy Hardy Meets Debutante 107
Andy Hardy's Blonde Trouble 115
Andy Hardy's Dilemma 163

Andy Hardy's Double Life 112, 163
Andy Hardy's Private Secretary 108
Animals 158
Anka, Paul 129
Ankles Aweigh 45
Anthony, Ray 128
Antrim, Harry 119
Arabian Adventure 147
Archer, John 122
Arlen, Harold 103, 184, 186
Armstrong, Louis 45, **46**, 121
Armstrong, R.G. 137
Arnold, Edward 85
Arnold, Philip 177
Asher, William 135
Astaire, Fred 14, 115, 169, 171
Astin, John 139
Astor, Mary 82, 84, 115
Atherton, William 160
The Atomic Kid 42, 123
Austin, Pam 139
Autry, Gene 163
Avalon, Frankie 135, 136
Axton, Hoyt 146
Ayers, Ann 113

B.J. Lang Presents 138
Babe: Pig in the City 159
Babes in Arms 25, 30, 32, 103, 175, 186
Babes on Broadway 25, 32, 111, 186
Baby Face Nelson 49, 125
Backus, Jim 128, 133, 137, 144, 164
Bagnold, Enid 116, 117
Bailey, Pearl 148
Bainter, Fay 105, 111, 112, 119

Baker, Reginald 88
Ball, Lucille 115, 171
Ballard, Carroll 146
Ballis, Socrates *141*
Balsam, Martin 130
Bancroft, George 105
Barbier, George 97
Barker, Lex 134
Barnes, Clive 65, 68
Barnett, Vince 80, 91, 162
Barry, Don "Red" 124, 126, 128, 137, 147
Barry, Gene 155, 169, 170, 171
Barrymore, Dolores Costello 92
Barrymore, Ethel 24
Barrymore, John 13
Barrymore, Lionel 16, *24*, 32, 90, 93, 114, 115
Bartholomew, Freddie 15, *17*, 20, *21*, 50, 51, 92, 93, 95, 97, 112
Barty, Billy 9, 90, 139, *141*, 142, 158
Bat-Adam, Michal 143
Bates, Barbara 119, 120, 122
Bavier, Frances 125
Baxter, Alan 113
Baxter, Warner 94
The Beast of the City 12, 78, 118
Beatty, Clyde 13, 79, 80, 84
Beatty, Ned 158
Beery, Noah, Jr. 137
Beery, Wallace 13, 90, 94, 100, *100*, 175
Bellamy, Ralph 88, *89*
Beloved 82
Belson, Jerry 139
Benchley, Robert 95
Bennett, Joan 175
Benny, Jack *31*, 133, 163, 175
Bergen, Candice 144
Bergen, Edgar 163, 169
Berkeley, Busby 25, 103, 108, 111, 115
Berle, Milton 133, 139, 142
Berlin, Irving 24
Berlinger, Warren 129
Bezencenet, Peter 134
The Big Cage 13, 79
The Big Chance 81
The Big Operator 128
The Big Sleep 42
The Big Wheel 20, 119
Bigard, Barney *46*
Bill 49, 149
Bill: On His Own 150, 172
Bissell, Whit 123, 167
The Black Stallion 69, 71, 146
Blaine, Vivian 139

Blair, George 124
Blake, Blake 95, 96, 98
Blake, Bobby 112
Blake, Marie 104
Blane, Ralph 118, 186
Blane, Sally 83
Blechman, Corey 149
Blind Date 87
Blocker, Dan 137
Blondell, Joan 7
Blue, Ben 115
Bluegrass 152, 154, 173
Blystone, John 87
Blyth, Ann 118
Bob Hope Chrysler Theater 170
Boehm, Sydney 125, 126
Bogart, Humphrey 42
The Bold and the Brave 45, 124
Boles, John 82, 115
Bolton, Guy 114, 118
Bon Baisers de Hong Kong 142
Bond, Ward 78, 86, 87, 168
Booth, Shirley 172
Borgnine, Ernest 158
Bottoms, Timothy 161
Bouchey, Willis 123, 125
Boxleitner, Bruce 152
Boys Town 24, 34, 98
Boys Will Be Boys 159
Brabin, Charles 78
Bracken, Eddie 62, 65, 122, 164, 178
Brackett, Charles 95
Brady, Alice 81
Brand, Max 120
Brando, Jocelyn 168
Breakfast at Tiffany's 46, 129
Breakston, George 98, 103, 104, 107, 108, 109, 111
Brecher, Irving 118
Breen, Bobby 37
Brennan, Walter 83, 87
Breslin, Howard 129
Breslin, Patricia 126
The Bridges at Toko-Ri 45, 123
Briskin, Mort 37
Brissac, Virginia 93, 108, 118
Broadbent, Jim 154
Broadway to Hollywood 27, 81
Brodie, Steve 119
Brothers' Destiny 158
Brown, Clarence 76, 86, 90, 112, 116, 117
Brown, James *121*
Brown, Joe E. 15, 88, 133, 163, 164
Brown, Nacio Herb 86, 92, 95, 103, 107

Brown, Tom 79, *80*, 101
Bruce, Virginia 162
Bryant, Nana 101
Buffington, Adele 78
Bunce, Alan 128
Burnett, Frances Hodgson 92
Burnett, W.R. 78
Burns, Bob 84, 162, 163
Burns, George 2
Burrows, Abe 168
Burton, Richard 164
Busey, Gary 155
Bushman, Francis X. 95
Butler, Hugo 101, 105
Butler, Jimmy 82, 84, *85*, 99
Buttons, Red 37, 144, 148, 172
Buttram, Pat 139, 148
Buzzi, Ruth 159
Byington, Spring 19, 20, 90, *90*, 93, 114, 119, 167

Caan, James 170
Caesar, Arthur 82, 84
Caesar, Sid 133
Cagney, James 15, 88, 175
Cagney, Jeanne 119, 120
Cahn, Sammy 142
Caine, Michael 139
Callas, Charlie 144
Calleia, Joseph 91
Candy, John 144
Capshaw, Kate 155
Captains Courageous 15, 93
The Care Bears Movie 150
Carney, Art 133
Carradine, David 155
Carradine, John 93, 139
Carrera, Barbara 161
Carrillo, Leo 84, 162
Carroll, Leo G. 93
Carson, Jack 124, 130, 164, 169
Carter, Arthur 125
Carter, Jack 136
Carter, Nell 5, 7, 43, *104*
Caruso, Anthony 125, *126*
Carver, Lynne 101, 113
Carvey, Dana 66, 165
Cassell, Wally 113, 115, 117, 118, 119, 122
Cassidy, Jack 138
Castle, Don 98, 101, 108
Chaffey, Don 144
Chained 86
Chamberlin, Jan *see* Rooney, Jan
Champion, Marge 137

Chaney, Lon, Jr. 94
Channing, Carol 65, 136
Chaplin, Charles, Jr. 128
Chaplin, Charlie 13, 58, 164
Charisse, Cyd 119, 157, 171, 184
Les Charlots 143
Chenoweth, Kristen 161
The Chief 82
Chiffre, Yves 142
Chodorov, Edward 82
Christmas in July 175
A Christmas Too Many 162
Churchill, Berton 79, 83, 87
Cinema Circus 162
Clark, Wallace *81*
Clarke, Betty Ross 97, 98
Clay, Cassius 133
Clemens, William 93
Clements, Stanley 122, 125
Clive, E.E. 92, 95
Cobb, Lee J. 108
Coburn, Charles 97
Cochran, Steve 128
The Cockeyed Cowboy of Calico County 137
Cohan, George M. 49, 167, 170, 178
Colbert, Claudette 175
Coleman, Gary 162
Collier, Constance 92
Collins, Ray 112
Collyer, June 162, 163
Colman, Ronald 164, 175
Colonna, Jerry 126, 167
Comden, Betty 183
The Comedian 46, 167
The Comic 71, 137
Como, Perry 119
Conan 173
Connelly, Marc 93
Connolly, Walter 101, 177
Connor, Kevin 147
Connors, Chuck 155, 170
Conroy, Frank 84, 128
Conte, John 115
Coogan, Jackie 50, 51, 128
Cook, Donald 82
Cook, Elisha, Jr. 95, 125, 129, 148, 150
Cook, Jimmy 37
Cooper, Gary 13, 164
Cooper, Jackie 3, 11, *16*, *17*, 27, 60, 66, 81, 92, 131, 148, *149*, 163, 164, 168
Coppola, Francis Ford 146
Corbett, Glenn 120, *121*
Corey, Wendell 124

Corman, Roger 134, 157
The County Chairman 68, 87
The Courtship of Andy Hardy 111
Cox, Wally 137
Craig, James 112, 121
Craven, Frank 95
Craven, John 113
Crawford, Joan 13, 15, 86
Crazy for You 2, 70, 115, 184
Crehan, Joseph 93, 103, 108, 110, 111, 118
Crisp, Donald 116
Cromwell, James 159
Cromwell, John 92
Cromwell, Richard 76
The Crowd Roars 38, 118
Crowley, Mart 152
Cukor, George 84
Curtis, Tony 139
Cushing, Peter 147

Dahl, Arlene 176, 184
Dale, Jim 144
Damita, Lili 162
Damone, Vic 121
Dane, Lawrence 144
Dane, Patricia 109, 163
Daniels, Billy 128
Danton, Ray 128, 152
Dark, Christopher 125, 129
Darmour, Larry 9, 75
Darnell, Linda 170
Darren, James 125, 164
Darro, Frankie 95
Darwell, Jane 87, 94
Davies, Marion 162
Davis, Elaine 42, 123
Davis, Sammy, Jr. 66, 72, 125
Davis, Valentine 123
Deacon, Richard 124, 125, 131
Deal, Borden 152
Dean, James 58
Death on the Diamond 87
December Bride 20
De Corsia, Ted 125
DeFore, Don 113
De Haven, Gloria 3, 11, 38, 115, 118, 158, 167, 168, 184
de Havilland, Olivia 14, **89**, 90, 177
Delépine, Benoit 160
Dell, Gabe 45, 165
Dell, Myrna 121
Delon, Alain 43
Del Rio, Dolores 76, 162
Del Ruth, Roy 84

DeLuise, Dom 139, 159
DeLuise, Michael 159
Demarest, William 120, 121, 130
Dempsey, Jack 119, 122, 133
Dern, Bruce 170
Deutsch, Helen 116
The Devil in Love 134
The Devil Is a Sissy 27, 92
Devine, Andy 79, 80, 84, 133
De Young, Cliff 157
The Dick Powell Show 168, 169
The Dick Van Dyke Show 49
Dieterle, Willam 14, 88
The Difference Between Night and Day 61
Diller, Phyllis 164
Dillinger, John 85, 125
DiMaggio, Joe 160
Dix, Tommy 115
Dixon, Richard M. 139, **140**
Dobkin, Lawrence 128
The Domino Principle 144
Donat, Robert 26
Donen, Stanley 118
Donlevy, Brian 118, 135
Donnell, Jeff 124, 137
Donovan's Kid 147, 172
Dorff, Red 52
D'Orsay, Fifi 80
Dorsey, Tommy 114, **114**, 115
Douglas, Melvyn 93
Down the Stretch 15, 93
Dozier, Bill 45
Drake, Tom 38, 119
Dressler, Marie 12, 76, 82
Drive a Crooked Road 123
Drury, James 155
Ducich, Dan 42
Dumke, Ralph 120, 124
Dunaway, Faye 135, 136
Duncan, Sandy 148
Dunn, James 118, 167
Durante, Jimmy 82, 133
Durbin, Deanna 11, 163
Duryea, Dan 129

Early, Margaret 104, 108
Eastwood, Clint 170
Ebert, Roger 154, 155
Ebsen, Buddy 130
Eddie 47, 167, 168
Eddy, Nelson 24, 82
Edens, Roger 98, 103, 108
Edwards, Blake 45, 122, 123, 125, 129
Edwards, Cliff 163

Edwards, Vince 152
80 Steps to Jonah 137
Elam, Jack 119, 125, 137
Elias, Louis 148
Ellis, Patricia 82, 93
Emma 12, 76
L'Empereur du Pérou 149
Erdman, Richard 164
Erik the Viking 71, 154
Errol, Leon 162
Erskine, Marilyn 122
Erwin, Stuart 86, 163
Estabrook, Howard 112
Evans, Gene 144
Evans, Linda 155
Evans, Madge 82, 87
Evans, Muriel 82, 84, 85
Everson, William K. 76
Everything's Ducky 27, 130, 132
Evil Roy Slade 139, 171
Ewell, Tom 125
Ewing, Diana 137
The Extraordinary Seaman 135

Fabares, Shelley 147
Fabray, Nanette 137
The Face on the Barroom Floor 159
Fairbanks, Douglas 76, 162
Fairbanks, Douglas, Jr. 80, 164
Falk, Peter 133
A Family Affair 16, 18, 93
Farrell, Glenda 7
Fast Companions 12, 79
Faulkner, William 94
Faye, Alice 144, 146, 163
Fenton, Leslie 98
Ferguson, Frank 110, 120, 126
Field, Virginia 92
Fields, W.C. 13, 62, 178
Find the Lady 143
Finklehoffe, Fred 45, 108, 111, 114, 118
The Fireball 120
The First of May 160
Fitzmaurice, George 95
Fleming, Eric 170
Fleming, Victor 88, 93
Flynn, Errol 162
Fol-De-Rol 171
Fontaine, Frank **141**
Ford, Constance 167
Ford, Dorothy 117
Ford, Harrison 171
Ford, Paul 139, 142
Ford, Wallace 78, 80

Forman, Joey 43, 123, 124, 126, 128, 165, 167, 168
Forrest, Sally 121
Forsythe, John 169
Foster, Dianne 123, 130, 168
Foster, Lewis R. 124
Foster, Preston 87, 128
Fowler, Eddie, Jr. 167, 170
The Fox and the Hound 148
Francis, Anne 118, 166, 172
Francis, Connie 115
Francis in the Haunted House 124
Frankenheimer, John 135, 136
Frawley, William 101
Frazier, George 5, 23
Freed, Arthur 86, 92, 95, 103, 107, 108, 111
Freedman, Benedict 123, 130
Funicello, Annette 135
A Funny Thing Happened on the Way to the Forum 2, 61, 66, 177, 182

Gable, Clark 13, 15, **24**, 26, **36**, 84, 86, 92, 94, **110**, 128, 163
Gabor, Zsa Zsa 164
Gage, Ben 128
Gallico, Paul 128
The Gambler Returns: The Luck of the Draw 155
Garbo, Greta 13
Gardner, Ava 12, 22, 32, 34, **52**, 111, 120, 164
Garfield, John 81, 163, 164
Garland, Judy 2, 11, 19, 21, **23**, 25, **25**, **26**, **27**, **28**, 34, 38, 39, 58, 59, 60, 61, 66, 70, 71, 95, 98, 101, 103, 107, 108, 109, **109**, **110**, 111, 114, **114**, 115, 117, 119, 142, 157, 164, 175, 184, 186, 187
Garnett, Tay 94, 120
Garr, Teri 146
Garrett, Betty 119, 184
Garrett, Oliver H.P. 84
Gassman, Vittorio 134, **135**
Gates, Nancy 124
Gateson, Marjorie 82, 86, 100, 107
Gatlin, Larry 68, 158, 183
Gazzara, Ben 170
George, Gladys 26, 96
George, Susan 152
George M! 49, 61, 178
Gershwin, Ira 108, 114, 184
Gibney, Sheridan 82
Gilbert, Billy 93, 95
Girl Crazy 25, 32, 68, 70, 114, 186, 187
Glamorous Hollywood 164

Gleason, Jackie 49, 133, 136
Gleason, James 79, 111, 163
Glenn, Scott 155
Go Ahead and Laff 182, 186
Goddard, Paulette 164
Godfrey, Peter 120
The Godmothers 9, 139
Gold, Sid 5
Goldbeck, Willis 117
Gone with the Wind 22, 72
Goodnight Ladies 62, 180
Goodrich, Frances 85, 90, 118
Goodwin, Bill 123
Gorcey, Leo 133
Gordon, Leo 125, 128
Gordon, Mack 98
Gorshin, Frank 136, 156
Gould, Elliott 160
Graff, Wilton *44*
Grant, Cary 162, 175
Grant, Kathryn 125
Granville, Bonita 11, 90, *90*, 115, 117, 144, *145*
Grapewin, Charley 90, 93
Gray, Coleen 124
Grayson, Kathryn 20, 63, 108, 115, 184
The Great Movie Series 19, 20
The Great Movie Shorts 9
Green, Adolph 183
Green, Alfred E. 95
Grefe, William 139, *141*
Grey, Virginia 101
Grieco, Richard 160
Griffin, Eleanore 95, 98
Grimes, Scott 150
Grové, Jessica 70, 184
Gruning, Ilka 119
Gwenn, Edmund 112

Haas, Charles 128, 129
Hackett, Albert 85, 90, 118
Hackett, Buddy 131, 132, *132*, 133
Hackett, Hal 117, 118
Hackman, Gene 144
Haden, Sara 19, 45, 90, 93, 95, *96*, 101, 103, 104, 107, 108, 109, 111, 112, 115, 117, 126, 128, 176
Haggerty, Julie 159
Haley, Jack, Jr. 142
Half a Sinner 83
Hamill, Pete 70, 71
Hamilton, Margaret 100, 103, 142
Hamilton, Murray 147
Hamilton, Neil 87

Hammerstein, Oscar, II 88, 121, 179
Harburg, E.Y. 103, 184, 186
Hardwicke, Sir Cedric 125
The Hardy Family 19, 41, 176
The Hardys Ride High 101
Harlow, Jean 15, 78, 85, 88, 91, *91*, 92
Harmon, Tom 122
Harper, Tess 155
Harris, Julie 133, 160
Hart, Lorenz 38, 39, 49, 103, 119
Hart, William S. 162
Hatcher, Mary 119
Hatton, Raymond 80, 98, 124
Havoc, June 167
Hayden, Sterling 177
Haydon, Julie 78, 93
Hayes, Grace 103
Haymes, Dick 122
Hayworth, Rita 163
Hazlitt, Frederick 118
The Healer 88
Healey, Myron 125
Healy, Ted 87, 88, 96
Hecht, Ben 84
Hedren, Tippi 162, 173
Hendrix, Wanda 120
Henry, Louise 85, 88
Henshall, Ruthie 70, 184
Hepburn, Audrey 46, 129
Herman, Albert 75, 81
Hernandez, Juano 136
Hersholt, Jean 76, 78, 84
Hervey, Irene 162
He's a Cockeyed Wonder 120
Hey Mulligan 49, 165
Hickman, Darryl 108, 113
Hickman, Dwayne 135
Hide and Seek 62, 178
Hide-Out 85
High Speed 12, 78
Hill, Robert 129
Hiller, Arthur 169
Hines, Mimi 65
Hitzig, Rupert 158
Hockett, Carolyn 59, *59*
Hodges, Mike 139
Hold That Kiss 97
Holden, Fay 19, 41, 45, 93, 95, 96, *96*, 97, 98, 101, 103, 107, 108, 109, *109*, 111, 112, 115, 117, 126, 128, 176
Holden, Gloria 118
Holden, William 123
Holliman, Earl 123
Holloway, Jean 118, 144

Hollywood Blue 138
Hollywood Handicap 163
Holm, Celeste 184
Holmes, Taylor 119
Home for Christmas 154
Hoosier Schoolboy 94
Hope, Bob 2, 45, 49, 73, 122, 170
Hopper, Hedda 20, 76
Horne, Lena 115, 119, 157
Horton, Edward Everett 133
How to Stuff a Wild Bikini 135
Howard, Mary 98
Hoyt, John 125
Hugh, Herbert 15, 88
Hull, Henry 98, 103, 104
The Human Comedy 34, 112, 175
Hume, Cyril 95
Hunt, Helen 150
Hunt, Marsha 101, 112, 115
Hunter, Ian 88, 92, 108, 112
Hunter, Kim 167
Hurst, Paul 79, 91, 94
Hussey, Ruth 97
Huston, Walter *10, 11*, 12, 13, 78, 118
Hutton, Lauren 152

I Like It That Way 83
i.e.: An Autobiography 58
Inescort, Frieda 111
The Information Kid 12, 79
Ingram, Rex 101
It Came Upon a Midnight Clear 150, 173
It's a Mad, Mad, Mad, Mad World 133
Iturbi, Jose 115

Jackson, Anne 148
Jaeckel, Richard 129, 169
Jaffe, Sam 164
Jaguar 162
James, Anne 122
Jamison, Bud 7, 75
Janssen, David 124, 130, 170
Jarrico, Paul 115
Jenkins, Allen 119
Jenkins, Jackie "Butch" 113, 116, 118
Jenks, Frank 96, 113, 115
Jillian, Ann 72, 180
Johnson, Ben 155, 158
Johnson, Van 34, 113, 163, 184
Johnston, Agnes Christine 101, 109, 111, 112, 115
Jolson, Al 163
Jones, Allan 88, 163

Jones, Buck 78, 162
Jones, Carolyn 122, 125, *126*, 169
Jones, Gordon 101, 122, 131
Jones, Henry 137
Jones, Spike 164
Jones, Terry 154
Jordan, Mearene 34
Jory, Victor 90
Journey Back to Oz 142
Judels, Charles 95, 96, 97
Judge Hardy and Son 103
Judge Hardy's Children 97, 175

Kahn, Gus 94
Kahn, Roger 58
Kalmar, Bert 121
Kanter, Hal 122
Kardos, Leslie 121
Karloff, Boris 162, 164
Karns, Todd 108, 111
Kaye, Danny 43, 164
Kaye, Stubby 137, 167
Keach, Stacy 152, 174
Keane, Robert Emmett 93, 95, 99, 101, 103, 109, 123
Keaton, Buster 133, 135, 163
Keel, Howard 157
Keeler, Ruby 163
Keith, Brian 155
Kellaway, Cecil 129
Kelly, Gene 114, 115, 119, 157
Kelly, Grace 123
Kelly, Jack 123, 155
Kelly, Paul 86, 87
Kelsey, Fred 76, 83, 94
Kendall, Cy 107
Kennedy, Madge 125
Kern, Jerome 88, 179
Kerwin, Brian 154
Keyes, Evelyn 22
Kibbee, Guy 80, 82, 92, 103, 114
Kilburn, Terry 97, 98, 103, 112, 117
Kilian, Victor 91, 99, 101, 105
Killer McCoy 38, 118
Killing Midnight 159
King of the Roaring '20s 130
Kipling, Rudyard 93
Kissel, Howard 68
Kitt, Eartha 70, 154, 184
Knotts, Don 133
Koch, Howard W. 126, 128
Kovacs, Ernie 125
Kramer, Stanley 133, 144
Kristofferson, Kris 158

Kruger, Otto 86
Kyser, Kay 115, 164

Ladd, Cheryl 154
Ladd, Diane 154
Lady and the Tramp II: Scamp's Adventure
    161
Lahr, Bert 25
Lamarr, Hedy 163
Lamont, Charles 124
Lancaster, Burt 164
Lane, Burton 88, 111
Lane, Margie *57*, 59
Lane, Nathan 66, 165
Lansbury, Angela 116, 117, 173
LaRue, Jack 93
Lassie 117, 144
The Last Mile 128
The Last Night of a Jockey 48, 169
Lawford, Peter 97, 98, 112, 114, 136, 164
Leader, Tony 137
Leave 'Em Laughing 27, 148, 172
Lederman, D. Ross 78
Lee, Christopher 147
Lee, Michelle 137
The Legend of O.B. Taggart 9, 71, 158
The Legend of Wolf Mountain 156, 157
Lehman, Ernest 167
Lehman, Gladys 87, 94
Leigh, Janet 119
Lembeck, Harvey 135
Lemmon, Jack 125, 139
Lend Me a Tenor 2, 68, 70, 183
LeRoy, Mervyn 76, 82, 117
Leslie, William 125, 126
Lessey, George 107, 108, 109
Lester, Jerry 139, *141*
Let's Put on a Show! 185
Levene, Sam 118
Levey, William A. 152
Levin, Henry 125
Lewis, Diana 107
Lewis, Jerry 133
Life Begins for Andy Hardy 109
Life Is Too Short 13, 19, 22, 26, 40, 64,
    123, 182
The Life of Jimmy Dolan 80
Lightning — The White Stallion 152
Linden, Eric 90, 93
Linden, Marta 112, 115
Lindsay, Margaret 82
Little Lord Fauntleroy 15, 21, 92
Little Nemo: Adventures in Slumberland
    156

Little Spies 152, 173
Live, Love and Learn 95
Lockhart, Gene 92
Lockhart, Kathleen 92
Logan, Joshua 37
Loos, Anita 91
Lord Jeff 97, 112
Lorre, Peter 94, 119
The Lost Jungle 84
Louise, Anita 15, 90
Love Birds 83
Love Finds Andy Hardy 98
Love Is a Headache 26, 96, 97
Love Laughs at Andy Hardy 38, 117
Lowry, Dick 155
Loy, Myrna 13, 76, 84
Ludwig, Edward 119
Ludwig, Ken 2, 68, 70, 183, 184
Ludwig, William 98, 101, 115, 117
Lukas, Paul 164
Lumet, Sidney 49
Lundigan, William 111, 112

MacDonald, J. Farrell 88, 91, 94
MacDougall, Ranald 137
Mack, Willard 81
Mackaill, Dorothy 82
MacMahon, Aline 80, 82, 90
MacMurray, Fred 163
Macnee, Patrick 155
The Magic of Lassie 144
Magnificent Roughnecks 124
Maguire, Toby 157
Mahin, John Lee 78, 86, 92, 93
Mahnken, Elaine 35, 42, 43, 53, *55*
Maibaum, Richard 95, 100
Majors, Lee 162
Making Waves 157
Maltin, Leonard 9
Mamoulian, Rouben 118
Manhattan Melodrama 84
Mankiewicz, Joseph L. 84
The Many Sides of Mickey Rooney 168
March, Alex 170
March, Fredric 123
March, Hal 123
Marin, Edwin L. 97
Marion, Frances 76, 91
Marquis, Margaret *18*
Marshall, Garry 139
Marshall, George 122
Marshall, Herbert 115
Marshall, Penny 139
Martin, Ross 147, 169

Martin, Tony 184
Martinson, Leslie H. 123
Marx, Arthur 32, 35, 50, 170
Marx, Groucho 137, 164
Massey, Raymond 171
Mathison, Melissa 146
Maurey, Nicole 124
Maximum Force 156
Maxwell, Marilyn 115, 118, 122
Mayehoff, Eddie 122, 171
Mayer, Louis B. 15, 18, 22, *24*, 38, 51, 78, 92, 184
Mayo, Archie 80
Mazurki, Mike 120, 144
McAllister, Lon 103
McArdle, Andrea 61
McCarthy, Kevin 123, 139
McClure, Doug 155
McCoy, Horace 120
McCrea, Joel 83
McDaniel, Hattie 119
McDonald, Ray 109, 111, 122
McEntire, Reba 155
McEveety, Bernard 147
McGavin, Darren 147, 164
McGowan, Jack 103
McGraw, Charles 123
McGuinness, James Kevin 97, 108
McHugh, Frank 90
McIntire, John 148
Meehan, John 98
Meek, Donald 111
Men of Boys Town 100, 108
Meredith, Burgess 136
Merkel, Una 82, 91
Merman, Ethel 133, 142, 172
Merrill, Dina 125
Merton of the Movies 175, 176
Meyer, Emile 125
Michael Kael Contre La World News Company 160
Michener, James 123
Mickey 165
Mickey Rooney in Mickey Rooney 66, 70, 182
Mickey Rooney Macaroni 58
The Mickey Rooney Show 49, 165, 167, 168
Mickey Rooney, Then and Now 164
Mickey Rooney's Christmas Memories 185
Mickey Rooney's Delicious Inc. 58
Mickey Rooney's Small World 171
A Midsummer Night's Dream 2, 9, 13, 15, 88, 177, 179
Miljan, John 76, 78

Miller, Ann 65, 68, 157, 180, 182
Miller, George 159
Miller, Marilyn 71
Miller, Robert Ellis 168, 170
Miller, Seton I. 128, 144
Miller, Sidney 29, 30, 99, 103, 108, 110, 111, 156
Millhauser, Bertram 80
Milner, Martin 129
Milosevic, Milos 43
Mimieux, Yvette 129
Mineo, Sal 137
Minnelli, Liza 61, 142
Minnelli, Vincente 108, 117
Mr. Broadway 49, 167, 186
Mitchell, Carolyn 43; *see also* Thomason, Barbara Ann
Mitchell, Grant 90, 92
Mitchell, Thomas 119
Mitchum, James 134
Mitchum, Robert 113, 114
Mix, Tom 13, 79, *81*
Monks, John, Jr. 108
Monroe, Marilyn 58, 71, 120, *121*
Montgomery, Elizabeth 135, 170
Montgomery, Robert *24*, 85, 95
Mooch Goes to Hollywood 164
Moore, Colleen 9, 11, 76, *77*
Moore, Dickie 84
Moore, Terry 120, 129
Moorehead, Agnes 61, 118
Morehouse, Ward, III 63
Morgan, Frank 34, 81, 112, *113*, 114, 115, 118, 175
Morgan, Ralph 96, 101
Morley, Karen 88
Morley, Sheridan 69
Morris, Dorothy 111, 113
Morse, Robert 65
Morton, Danny 43
Mowbray, Alan 82, 112
Muir, Jean 82, 88
Muni, Paul 82
Murder, She Wrote 173
Murphy, George 175
Murphy, Mary 122, 169
Murray, John Fenton 123, 130
Murtin, Jane 108
Muse, Clarence 146
My Heroes Have Always Been Cowboys 154
My Kidnapper, My Love 148, 172
My Outlaw Brother 120
My Pal, the King 13, 79
My True Story 41, 162

Nagel, Anne 94
Naish, J. Carrol 78, 81, 84
Naked City 169
Nash, Mary 108, 113
National Velvet 34, 116, 152, 173, 175, 176
Neal, Patricia 129
Neill, Roy William 87
Nelson, Barry 113
Nelson, Ralph 133
Nelson, Rick 171
Neumann, Kurt 79, 93
Newman, Joseph 130, 169
Newman, Laraine 157
Newman, Paul 58
Newton, Wayne 137
A Nice Little Bank That Should Be Robbed 125
Nigh, William 94
Night Gallery 171
Nilsson, Harry 137
The Nine Lives of Mickey Rooney 32, 50, 170
Niven, David 135, 136, 164
Nolan, Jeanette 119, 148
Nolan, Lloyd 150, 169
North, Jay 128
Northwest Rangers 85
Not to Be Trusted 7, 75
Nugent, Elliott 120
Nugent, Frank S. 94, 98, 106

O'Brian, Hugh 124, 134, 155
O'Brien, Edmond 167
O'Brien, Margaret 111, 115
O'Brien, Pat 120
O'Brien, Virginia 115
O'Connell, Arthur 125
O'Connor, Donald 30, 67, 122, 124, 182, 183
O'Connor, Glynnis 148
O'Connor, Una 86, 92
The Odd Couple 2, 61, 178
O'Driscoll, Martha 104
Off Limits 45, 122
Officer Thirteen 12, 79
O'Herlihy, Dan 130
O'Keefe, Dennis 97
Oliver, Edna May 95
Olivier, Laurence 26, 69
Olsen and Johnson 162
O'Malley 166, 172
The One Man, One Wife Show 71, 184
One of the Boys 66, 165, 172
O'Neill, Eugene 15, 90, 118

O'Neill, Henry 82, 84, 108, 113, 114, 115
Operation Mad Ball 125
Oppenheimer, George 112, 118
Orchids and Ermine 9, 76
O'Shea, Michael 119
O'Shea, Milo 147
O'Shea, Oscar 93, 96, 97, 100
O'Sullivan, Maureen 79, 85, **86**, 97
Oswald, Gerd 137
Ouspenskaya, Maria 104
Out of This World Series 163
Out West with the Hardys 101
Overton, Frank 128
Owen, Reginald 100, 117
Oxenberg, Catherine 159

Page, Anita 80
Page, Anthony 149, 150
Pal of My Cradle Days 5, 7, 11
Pallette, Eugene 105
Pankey, Fred 7
Pankey, Nell **104**; see also Carter, Nell
Paradise 161
Paris, Jerry 123, 139
Parish, James Robert 19
Parker, Cecilia 19, 45, 84, 90, 93, 95, **96**, 97, 98, 101, 103, 107, 111, 112, 126, 128
Parker, Jean 175
Parker, Lew 45
Parks, Bert 170
Parnell, Emory 105, 113, 115, 118, 119
Parsonnet, Marion 95, 96
Parsons, Louella 20
Pendleton, Nat 78, 82, 84, 87, 88
Penn, Leo 152
Peters, Bernadette 63, 179
Peters, Susan 112, 163
Peterson, Dorothy 78, 82, 92
Peterson, Les 22, 32
Pete's Dragon 144
Phantom of the Megaplex 161
Phillips, William "Bill" 119, 120, 122
Pichel, Irving 119
Pickens, Slim 137
Pickford, Mary 14, 76, 92, 162
Pinocchio 49, 167, 186
Pirate Party on Catalina Isle 162
Pitts, ZaSu 83
Platinum High School 129
Playhouse 90 46, 133
Playtime in Hollywood 164
Porter, Cole 98
Porter, Jean 111, 115

Potts, Annie 150
Powell, Dick 15, 48, 88
Powell, Eleanor 115
Powell, William 15, 84, 88
Powers, Tom 121
Praskins, Leonard 100
Pratt, Purnell B. 76, 82, 109
Preisser, June 103, 104, 108
Preminger, Otto 136
Preston, Robert 120
Prevost, Marie 76, 162
Price, Vincent 164
Principal, Victoria 160
The Private Lives of Adam and Eve 129
Prowse, Juliet 65, 184
Pryor, Roger 83
Pulp 139

Quaid, Dennis 149, 150, *151*
Quicksand 119
Quigley, Juanita 91, 112, 116
Quillan, Eddie 82
Quine, Richard 11, 45, 50, 111, 119, 120, 122, 123, 125, 171
Quinn, Anthony 133

Rachel's Man 71, 143
Rafferty, Frances 114, 115, 163
Raft, George 137
Rainbow 60, 66
Ralph, Jessie 92, 96, 97
Randall, Tony 61, 178
Rapf, Harry 81
Rase, Betty Jane 34, 35, 42, 52, *53*
Rawhide 170
Raye, Martha 163
Reckless 88
Reddy, Helen 144
Reed, Donna 20, 111 113, 115, 163
Reeves, Theodore 116
Reilly, Charles Nelson 159, 160
Reiner, Carl 71, 133, 137
Reinhardt, Max 13, 88, 177
Reno, Kelly 146, *146*
Requiem for a Heavyweight 133
Rettig, Tommy 121
Return of Mickey Spillane's Mike Hammer 152, 173
Return of the Original Yellow Tornado 171
Revel, Harry 98
Revenge of the Red Baron 157
Revere, Anne 108, 116, 117
Revier, Dorothy 78
Reynolds, Burt 171

Reynolds, Debbie 157, 184
Reynolds, Gene 94, 98, 108, 124
Richard 139
Richards, Addison 98, 103, 107, 108, 112, 117
Ridgely, John 122
Riesner, Charles F. 82
Riffraff 91, 92
Risdon, Elizabeth 101
Ritter, John 139
The Ritz Brothers 162, 163
Rivkin, Allen 121, 128
Robbins, Tim 71, 154
Robertson, Willard 82, 84, 87
Robinson, Chris 142
Robinson, Edward G. 125, 164
Robson, Mark 123
Robson, May 82, 88
Rodann, Ziva 128, 129
Rodeo Dough 163
Rodgers, Richard 38, 103, 119
Rogers, Charles "Buddy" 162
Rogers, Ginger 84
Rogers, Kenny 155
Rogers, Roy 163
Rogers, Wayne 154
Rogers, Will 15, 87, 88, 183
Romance of Celluloid 18, 163
Romay, Lina 117, 119
Romero, Cesar 137, 164
Rooney, Jan Chamberlin *60*, 63, *64*, *72*, 162, 184, 185, 187
Rooney, Jimmy 59
Rooney, Jonell 59
Rooney, Kelly Ann 43
Rooney, Kerry Yule 43
Rooney, Kimmy Sue 43
Rooney, Michael Joseph Kyle 43
Rooney, Mickey, Jr. 34, *39*, *40*
Rooney, Teddy 42, 45, 52, 126, *127*, 168
Rooney, Tim 35, *48*, 130, 165, 180
Rose, Sherman A. 124
Rosenberg, Stuart 154
Ross, Joe E. *141*
Ross, Shirley 84, 85
Roth, Tim 158
Rouverol, Aurania 93, 95, 97, 98, 101, 103, 107, 108, 109, 111, 112, 115
Rowland, Roy 118, 162
Royle, Selena *11*
Rubin, J. Walter 91, 95
Ruby, Harry 121
Rudolph and Frosty 172
Ruskin, Harry 96, 108, 115, 117

Russell, Jane 164
Russell, Kurt 148
Russell, Rosalind *24*, 88, 95
Rutherford, Ann 3, 19, 21, 22, *23*, 45, 93, 95, 97, 98, 101, 103, 104, 107, 108, 109, *109*, 111, 112
Ryan, Meg 66, 165
Ryan, Peggy 122

Sailor, Beware 44
St. John, Jill 164
Saldana, Theresa 161
Samms, Emma 147
Sande, Walter 118
Sanders, George 94
Santa Claus Is Coming to Town 171
Saroyan, William 112
Saturday's Children 46, 166
Savalas, Telly 170
Scala, Ettore 134
Schary, Dore 45, 98, 105
Schertzinger, Victor 82
Schildkraut, Joseph 94, 130
Scott, Lizabeth 139
Scott, Randolph 162
The Search for Sonny Skies 71
Secret Invasion 134
Sedgwick, Edward 87
See How They Run 62, 179
Sciter, William A. 83
Seitz, George B. 18, 78, 93, 95, 97, 98, 101, 103, 107, 108, 109, 111, 112, 115, 163
Seligsohn, Leo 63
Selwyn, Edgar 86
Selznick, David O. 15, 21, 85, 88
Senior Trip! 162
Serling, Rod 46, 133, 167, 169, 171
The Seven Little Foys 49, 170
Shaughnessy, Mickey 125, 130
Shaw, Artie 12, 22, 34, *35*
Shawn, Dick 133, 139, 168, 172
Shearer, Norma *24*
Sher, Jack 122
Shields, Frank 94
Shoemaker, Ann 103, 108
Shorty Bell 41, 176
Show Boat 2, 63, 179, 180
Show Business at War 163
Shulman, Irving 125
Sidney, George 115
Siegel, Don 125
Silent Night, Deadly Night 5: The Toy Maker 155
Silvers, Phil 30, 108, 133

Simmons, Dick 115, 117
Simon, Neil 2, 68, 178, 183
Sinatra, Frank 34, 164, 169
Sinbad: The Battle of the Dark Knights 160
Sinclair, Ronald 95
Sin's Pay Day 12, 78
Skelton, Red 72, 115
Skidding 16, 93
Skidoo 136
Skolsky, Sidney 20, 29
Slave Ship 94
Slezak, Walter 134, 167
A Slight Case of Larceny 122
Smith, C. Aubrey 92, 95
Smith, Robert 119, 128, 129
Smith, Roger 125
Somebody's Waiting 48
Sommers, Joanie 131
Sondergaard, Gale 97
Sondheim, Stephen 177, 182
Sothern, Ann 87, 115, 119, 171, 175
Sound Off 122
Spain, Fay 129, 171
Spaulding, Harry 147
Spike Jones in Hollywood 164
Spillane, Mickey 152
Stablemates 100, 175
Stack, Robert 120
Stacy, James 148
Stander, Lionel 139
Stanwyck, Barbara 169
Staub, Ralph 163, 164
Steiger, Rod 158
Stephenson, Henry 88, 92
Sterling, Jan 148
Stewart, Elaine 122
Stewart, James 26, 144, 146
Stiefel, Sam 37, 39
Stockwell, Dean 160
Stone, Lewis 19, 41, 93, 95, *96*, 97, 98, 101, 103, 107, *107*, 108, 109, 111, 112, 115, 117, 175, 176
Stone, Milburn 118, 120
Storm, Gale 170
Stratton, Gil 114
Strauss, Robert 123
Strickling, Howard 22
Strike the Tent 162
Strike Up the Band 25, 32, 108, 175, 186
The Strip 45, 121
Stuart, Gloria 82, 83
Sturges, Preston 175
Subotosky, Milton 128

Sugar Babies 1, 2, 32, 64, 65, 68, 69, 72, 162, 165, 172, 180, 182, 184, 186
Sullivan, Ed 20, 68
Summer Holiday 38, 91, 118, 186
Summerville, Slim 83
Sundberg, Clinton 117, 119
The Sunshine Boys 2, 68, 183
Susskind, David 167
Swanson, Gloria 92
Sweet Justice 156
Swerling, Jo 130

Tabas, Daniel 56
Talbot, Lyle 80
Talenttown U.S.A., Inc. 57
Tamiroff, Akim 86
Taurog, Norman 98, 105, 108, 112, 114, 118
Taylor, Don 113, 114, 115, 124, 130, 169
Taylor, Elizabeth 34, 116, *116*, 118, 162, 173, 175
Taylor, Joan 122
Taylor, Kent 87
Taylor, Rip 65
Taylor, Robert *24*
Teagarden, Jack *46*, 121
Teal, Ray 115, 118, 119
Teasdale, Verree 90
Temple, Shirley 21, *110*, 111
Templeton, Fay 82, 178
Terry, Phillip 96, 97, 99
That's Entertainment 71, 142
That's Entertainment III 157
There Must Be a Pony 173
Thomas, Danny 142, 164
Thomas, Frankie 17, 98
Thomason, Barbara Ann 43, *56*
Thompson, Marshall 119
Thoroughbreds Don't Cry 19, 95, 98
Thorpe, Richard 93, 96, 101
Thousands Cheer 115
Three Goats and a Blanket 62, 178, 180, 182
The Three Stooges 133
Thunder County 142
Toler, Sidney 82, 84
Tone, Franchot 87, 88, 96
Toomey, Regis 130, 165
Topa Topa Bluffs 161
Torme, Mel 119, 128, 129, 167
Tracy, Lee 162
Tracy, Spencer 15, 24, 91, 93, 98, *99*, 106, 108, 117, 128, 133
Tracy, William 108

Travis, Randy 158, 159
Treacher, Arthur 15, 90, 116
Trotti, Lamar 94
Tucker, Sophie 95
Tully, Tom 118
Tunnel of Love 61, 177
Tunnell, Dee 119
Turan, Kenneth 33
Turner, Lana 11, 20, 22, 30, 34, 98
Turner, Ted 58
Turturro, John 158
Tushingham, Rita 143
Twain, Mark 101
Twenty-Four Hours to Kill 134
The Twilight Zone 48, 169
The Twinkle in God's Eye 45, 124
Twitty, Conway 129
Two for the Show 67, 68, 182
Tyler, Beverly 120

Upper World 84

Vallee, Rudy 164, 175
Van Doren, Mamie 128, 129, *130*
Van Dyke, Dick 71, 137
Van Dyke, W.S. 84, 85, 92, 103
Van Every, Dale 79, 83, 93
Van Fleet, Jo 137
Van Heusen, James 142
Van Riper, Kay 93, 95, 97, 101, 103
Van, Bobby 58, 61, 177
Venable, Evelyn 87, 177
Vera-Ellen 119
Vickers, Martha 42, 52, *54*
La Vida Lactea 71, 157
Vinson, Helen 95
Viola, Michael *141*
Vogan, Emmett 83, 84, 93, 107, 115
Voight, Jon 159

W.C. 63, 178
Wagner, Robert 173
Wagon Train 168
Walker, Clint 155
Walker, Helen 41, *44*, 162
Walker, Nancy 114, 115, 187
Wallace-Stone, Dee 158, 161
Wallach, Eli 144
Walpole, Hugh 92
Walters, Charles 114
Wanamaker, Sam 148
Warren, Harry 118, 186
Warwick, Dionne 152
Watkin, Pierre 95, 109, 115

Watson, Bobs 98, 108, 124
Watson, Minor 98, 100, 101
Waxman, Franz 94, 130
Wayne, David 164
Wayne, John 81
Weaver, Dennis 124
Webb, Ruth 63, 69
Weidler, Virginia 86, 96, 101, 105, 111, 175
Weis, Don 122
Weissmuller, Johnny 163
Welbeck, Peter 134, 152
Weld, Tuesday 129
Welles, Orson *31*
Welles, Virginia 124
Wells, Robert 122
Wexley, John 128
When the Boys Meet the Girls 115
White, Alice 162
Whiteman, Paul 108
Whorf, Richard 170
Widmark, Richard 144
Wilde, Cornel 137
Wilder, Alec 167, 186
Wilkinson, June 129, 138
The Will Rogers Follies 68, 88, 183
William, Warren 84
Williams, Billy Dee 171
Williams, Esther 20, 112, 157, 163, 184
Wilson, Carey 76, 103, 107, 163
Wilson, Earl 20
Wincer, Simon 152
Windom, William 148
Winninger, Charles 103
Winslow, Dick 43, 123, 124, 131, 147
Winston, Ron 134, 170

Winters, Jonathan 61, 133
Winters, Roland 131, 170
Winters, Shelley 118, 144, 172
The Wizard of Oz 2, 25, 70, 98, 103, 184, 186
Wolfson, P.J. 124
Wood, Sam 97, 100
Woolf, Edgar Allan 81
Woollcott, Alexander 111
Woolley, Monty 95, 98
Words and Music 38, 39, 118, 186
The World Changes 82
Worley, Jo Anne 70, 184
Wrather, Bonita Granville *145*; *see also* Granville, Bonita
Wright, Teresa 150
Wynn, Ed 82, 133
Wynn, Keenan 114, 130, 137, 138, 164, 171, 172

Yablonsky, Yabo 138
A Yank at Eton 112
A Year at the Top 165, 172
The Year Without Santa Claus 171
York, Dick 125
Young, Loretta 80, 86, 163
Young, Robert 87, 129, 163
Young Tom Edison 24, 105, 175
You're Only Young Once 19, 95
Yule, Joe, Sr. 5, 41, 73, *105*, 111, 164

Ziegfeld Follies of 1946 117
Zucco, George 97
Zugsmith, Albert 125, 128, 129